As one of the
and
Thomas Coo

For
guidebooks
of dest
sha
experience and a passion for travel.

**Rely on Thomas Cook as your
travelling companion on your next trip
and benefit from our unique heritage.**

Thomas Cook **traveller** guides

BUDAPEST
Louis James

Your travelling companion since 1873

Thomas
Cook

Written by Louis James, updated by Wendy Wrangham

Published by Thomas Cook Publishing
A division of Thomas Cook Tour Operations Limited
Company registration no. 3772199 England
The Thomas Cook Business Park, Unit 9, Coningsby Road,
Peterborough PE3 8SB, United Kingdom
Email: books@thomascook.com, Tel: + 44 (0) 1733 416477
www.thomascookpublishing.com

Produced by Cambridge Publishing Management Limited
Burr Elm Court, Main Street, Caldecote CB23 7NU
www.cambridgepm.co.uk

ISBN: 978-1-84848-341-5

© 2003, 2006, 2008 Thomas Cook Publishing
This fourth edition © 2011
Text © Thomas Cook Publishing
Maps © Thomas Cook Publishing/PCGraphics (UK) Limited
Transport map © Communicarta Limited

Series Editor: Karen Beaulah
Production/DTP: Steven Collins

Printed and bound in Spain by GraphyCems

Cover photography: © MIVA/SuperStock

Contents

Background   4–19
Introduction   4
The city   6
History   8
Politics   12
People and culture   14

First steps   20–31
Impressions   20

Destination guide   32–117
Buda   32
Pest   72

Getting away from it all   118–37

Directory   138–89
Shopping   138
Entertainment   144
Children   152
Sport and leisure   154
Food and drink   158
Accommodation   170
Practical guide   177

Index   190–91

Maps
Budapest and environs   21
Buda   33
Várhegy walk   37
Rózsadomb and Víziváros walk   49
Tabán and Gellért hegy walk   51
Margit sziget walk   59
Óbuda walk   64
Pest   73
Szabadság híd to Ferenciek
   tere walk   77
Erzsébet híd to Deák Ferenc
   tér walk   84
Andrássy útca walk   95
Oktogon to Gundel Étterem walk   101
Deák Ferenc tér to
   Fehér ház walk   111
Hungary   119
Budapest transport map   184

Features
The 1956 revolution   10
Hungarian national style   18
Bridges   42
Spa city   54
A city and its river   68
Széchenyi Chain Bridge   70
Operetta   88
Jugendstil architecture   92
Hungarian lifestyle   116
Where are they now?   136
Hungarian folk arts   142
The Roma and their music   148
Dog days in Budapest   156
Wines of Hungary   168

Walks
Várhegy   36
Rózsadomb and Víziváros   48
Tabán and Gellért hegy   50
Margit sziget   58
Óbuda   64
Szabadság híd to Ferenciek tere   76
Erzsébet híd to Deák Ferenc tér   84
Andrássy útca   94
Oktogon to Gundel Étterem   100
Deák Ferenc tér to Fehér ház   110

Introduction

At the end of the 19th century, a traveller to Budapest neatly described the enigmatic quality of the city: 'If one is travelling from the east in the direction of Western Europe, it is in Budapest that one experiences the breath of Western civilisation. However, if one is travelling in the opposite direction, it is here that one first gets a taste of the East . . .'

When the seven Magyar (Hungarian) tribes came over the Carpathians more than 1,000 years ago, one group pitched their tents at this strategic point on the mighty River Danube. Although they were always to retain a proud memory of their Asian origins, they now began a new and settled existence in Europe.

In the Middle Ages, the Royal Castle of Buda and its ancillary town grew wealthy under Magyar, Anjou (Angevin) and Luxembourg rulers.

The subsequent 150-year-long Turkish occupation, and the Habsburg rule that followed, then reduced Buda to provincial status. In the mid-19th century, the hitherto insignificant town of Pest rapidly expanded into a great industrial metropolis. Until around 1860, half its inhabitants were German-speaking and there was also a large influx of Jews; most of the latter rapidly assimilated and became leading figures in the arts and in business.

By 1900, Buda and Pest (united since 1873) had acquired the patina of mixed culture from the technological advancement of industrialisation and

WHAT IT MEANS TO BE A MAGYAR

'Anyone who wants to understand Hungary,' writes the poet and journalist István Eörsi, 'needs to find the answer to one great secret: how is it that this country has survived at all? ... No nation is so experienced in defeat as the Hungarians.' This feeling of being the victims of history is recurrent in the Magyar psyche.

On two occasions in the past – when the Tartars invaded in the 13th century and during the Turkish occupation – there was a real danger of national extinction. In the 18th century, the German philosopher Johann Herder predicted that the Magyar nation and culture would soon disappear, absorbed by their Slav and German neighbours.

It is language that most isolates Hungarians. Arthur Koestler summed up the fears and contradictions in the Magyars' image of themselves: 'To be Hungarian is a collective neurosis.'

urbanisation. Between the two world wars, in both of which Hungary reluctantly sided with Germany, the Hungarian Democratic Republic was created but was almost immediately curtailed by the Trianon Treaty of 1920, through which Hungary lost about two-thirds of its lands.

Today, an era of buoyant capitalism has resurfaced after 40 years of suspended animation under Communism.

Back to the future

As in other cities of the former Eastern Bloc, the gap between the haves and have-nots remains wide.

Renovation, restoration, redevelopment and development are popping up all over the city, but the homeless, the beggars and the hard-pressed pensioners remain.

On the plus side, Hungarians are natural entrepreneurs and despite the worldwide economic gloom, much is being done to make the city buzz again. Budapest retains a unique and independent streak that acknowledges the double-edged sword of landmark buildings being earmarked for redevelopment. Without commercial funding, these wonderful edifices would crumble but with funding comes a slow transformation into a city flooded with international brands. The new (elected in May 2010) government's continuing austerity programmes have cut the budget deficit and won economic plaudits so there are grounds for optimism.

But don't expect Hungarians to admit that things have improved. As the local saying goes: 'A pessimist is only a well-informed optimist'.

On the banks of the River Danube

The city

Budapest lies 47 degrees 23 minutes north and 19 degrees 9 minutes east, on either side of the River Danube (Duna). Within the river's 28km (17-mile) passage through the city, the width of the channel varies between 1km (²/₃ mile) and 230m (755ft). The mighty waterway has shaped the character of the city. For the Romans it was a defensive barrier – they built their garrison and administrative capital at Aquincum on the western bank.

The Magyar kings shifted the focus to the natural citadel of *Buda Hill*, while Pest was the gateway to the East, a town of travellers and traders, later a dynamic centre of business and industry. In the landscape, too, the characteristics of the two cities reflect the aspects of Hungary: from the flattish terrain of Pest, the Alföld (Great Hungarian Plain) stretches to the east and south; on the west bank the gentle hills of Buda (the highest is the 529m/1,735ft János hegy) point the way to the rolling landscapes of Transdanubia.

Economy

The new centre-right government elected in May 2010 has promised to cut bureaucracy and taxes while pledging to boost the economy and jobs. Despite being the fifth-largest economy in Central and Eastern Europe, in 2008 Hungary reached an agreement with the International Monetary Fund and the European Union for a rescue package worth US$25 billion. Inflation has

almost halved to 5.9 per cent but public debt remains at about 80 per cent of GDP, which is expanding at about 3.7 per cent per annum. Foreign investment and the travel and tourism sector are expected to keep growing and help revitalise the economy.

Environment

Like other former Eastern Bloc cities, Budapest still suffers from decaying infrastructure and serious pollution, although the environmental nihilism inherent in Communism has diminished in the face of stricter EU policies. An initiative has greatly reduced the smoke-belching Trabants on the roads and power stations have been made cleaner and more efficient, although a new nuclear station is being touted to limit Hungary's dependence on Russian gas (80 per cent of consumption annually). The new government promises renewable energy but all possibilities need foreign investment as public spending is being seriously hampered by the recession.

Budapest's water supply remains endangered by the Slovak government's decision to persist with the Gabăíkovo hydroelectric dam on the Danube, a project from which Hungary withdrew in 1992. The International Court of Justice has determined that the treaty is still valid, but Hungary has ignored the

GOODBYE TRABI!

An elegiac piece in the press in 1991 lamented the passing of East German imports – the Trabant, which provided an experience 'like riding a four-wheel moped in a raincoat'; the Practica 35mm SLR, 'a good workhorse camera designed for planets without gravity'; and 'nifty kitchen wares made of slag-iron'. The 'Trabi' will soon be consigned to history so snap a souvenir photo when you spot one.

The city

ruling. The fertile agricultural area of Szigetköz in western Hungary is badly affected.

The reduction of fuel emissions and the cleaning of public buildings have given Budapest a new face. The M0 ring-road motorway has surmounted delays and debts and is now open.

Pollution has taken a heavy toll on many of Pest's façades

History

AD 106 — The Roman garrison of Aquincum (in Óbuda) becomes the capital of Lower Pannonia.

5th century — According to legend, Attila the Hun ruled from the abandoned Roman amphitheatre in Aquincum. His brother, Bleda, is supposed to have given his name to a new city – 'Buda'.

896 — Seven Magyar tribes under Árpád cross the Carpathians and settle on the Danubian plains.

Late 10th century — The Magyar Prince Géza converts to Christianity; his son Vajk is baptised as István (Stephen).

1000 — Stephen is crowned King of Hungary on Christmas Day, with a crown sent by the Pope. Between 997 and 1038, King (later Saint) Stephen turns Hungary into a Christian feudal state.

1241 — Tartar (Mongol) invaders virtually destroy Hungary. To rebuild it, King Béla IV invites Germans and other foreigners to settle. The Castle of Buda is built (1247–65).

1301 — The Hungarian Árpád line dies out. The House of Anjou succeeds, followed by Sigismund of Luxembourg in 1387.

1458–90 — Under Matthias I (Corvinus), Buda achieves its golden age.

1526–41 — Buda falls to the Turks.

1686 — Charles of Lorraine and Eugene of Savoy reconquer Buda. Hungary falls under Habsburg rule.

1710–11 — Buda and Pest are blockaded during the War of Independence waged by Ferenc Rákóczi II.

1795 — A Jacobin revolt is crushed. Archduke Joseph becomes Palatine of Hungary.

1848 — Hungary, under Lajos Kossuth, briefly achieves independence from Habsburg rule.

1867 — Franz Joseph and Ferenc Deák negotiate the

Ausgleich (Compromise) to create the Austro-Hungarian Empire.

1872–73	The towns of Buda, Óbuda and Pest are united to form Budapest.
1896	The Millennial celebrations mark 1,000 years of Hungary's existence.
1918–19	The Austro-Hungarian Empire collapses; the Hungarian Republic is proclaimed. The Communist Republic of Councils is formed.
1920	By the Treaty of Trianon, Hungary loses two-thirds of its territory. Three million Hungarians are marooned in the empire's successor states.
1945–48	Soviet armies 'liberate' an almost totally flattened Budapest; Communists seize power.
1956	Soviet armies invade Hungary to suppress a popular anti-Commuist revolt. János Kádár forms a puppet regime.
1988	Kádár is ousted; an interim government of reform

Communists works for free elections.

1990	Right-of-centre Hungarian Democratic Forum led by József Antall wins the country's first multi-party elections.
1994	Socialists and Free Democrats win elections.
1998	The right-of-centre Hungarian Civic Party under Viktor Orbán forms a government with the Smallholders' Party.
2002	Socialists and Free Democrats regain power.
2004	Hungary becomes a member of the EU.
2006	October sees violent anti-government protests during the 50th anniversary commemorations of the 1956 revolution.
2008	US$25 billion bailout secured from the IMF and the EU.
2010	Elections oust the Socialist government and install a centre-right mandate, Hungary's first non-coalition government.

The 1956 revolution

The year 1956 saw a spontaneous and nationwide revolt against Soviet-imposed policies and the domestic government that upheld them. Moscow reacted with false reassurances and a massive military intervention, while no Western government answered Nagy's appeal for aid. The West had no appetite to fight the USSR while the Suez Crisis was in full swing in the Middle East.

The heroism of the Hungarian revolution of 1956 has passed into history – a brave battle against appalling odds. For a few brief days of euphoria, it looked as if it might succeed, and the Stalinist tyranny seemed on the brink of extinction.

Heroes' Square: the site of Imre Nagy's reburial

Pressure for change came from the 'Petőfi Circle', named after Hungary's national poet and freedom fighter of the 1848 revolution. Then student demonstrations attracted thousands of supporters. Finally, factory workers became the driving force of the revolution. Much of the Hungarian army, led by Pál Maléter, also fought for freedom.

Timetable of a revolution

6 October 1956 Some 200,000 people attend the reburial of László Rajk, the interior minister executed after a show-trial by the Rákosi regime.

23 October In solidarity with ongoing political opposition in Poland, students lead a march to the statue of the Polish general and Hungarian freedom fighter József Bem. The Communist emblem is cut out of Hungarian flags and a statue of Stalin is toppled, leaving only his boots (now in Szoborpark, *see pp67 & 137*). At 6pm, Imre Nagy, previously prime minister in 1953 and expelled from the Party for his espousal of a more humane government, speaks to vast crowds before the Parliament. At 11pm, students besiege the radio station and the ÁVH (Security Service) open fire on them.

24 October Imre Nagy becomes prime minister and calls for calm. Soviet tanks take strategic positions in Budapest while *Pravda* publishes a report promising greater equality in relations between the USSR and its Eastern European satellites.

31 October A truce is arranged and the Soviets agree to withdraw tanks. Meanwhile, Soviet troops begin amassing at Hungary's borders.

1 November Nagy announces that Hungary is to leave the Warsaw Pact and appeals to the UN for national neutrality.

3 November Pál Maléter, negotiating with the Soviet Army under guarantee of safe conduct, is arrested and transported to an unknown destination.

4 November The Soviet Army reinvades. Nagy, in a 35-second broadcast on national radio, announces: 'Our troops are fighting. The Government is in place.' But with no foreign intervention, János Kádár announces the formation of his puppet government and Nagy flees to the Yugoslav Embassy (now the Serbian Embassy).

22 November Nagy leaves the Yugoslav Embassy with a promise of safe conduct, but is arrested and flown to Romania.

16 June 1958 Nagy and Maléter are returned to Budapest, executed, then buried in unmarked graves.

Aftermath of the revolution
While the borders remained open, 200,000 people fled the country. There were an estimated 2,000 revenge executions; thousands more were imprisoned. To mention Nagy's name was a punishable offence until 1989.

16 June 1989 A ceremony is held on Heroes' Square to honour Nagy and Maléter, whose remains are reburied.

6 July 1989 The Supreme Court declares Nagy innocent of the charges on which he was convicted and executed. János Kádár dies.

2006 The i-ypszilon group completes a new monument to the 1956 revolution. The triangular rusted-metal construction marks the spot where Stalin's boots remained (*see* 23 October 1956).

'If my life is necessary to prove that not all Communists are enemies of the people, then I willingly give it up.'
IMRE NAGY, reportedly his last words in 1958.

Politics

In 1989, the Soviet Union's satellite regimes buckled one by one under the combined pressure of failing economies and Mikhail Gorbachev's policy of glasnost *(openness). The smooth transition from totalitarianism to democracy was possible in Hungary chiefly because the last Communist government accepted the inevitable gracefully.*

The end of Communism

During János Kádár's long rule (1956–88), the oppressive paraphernalia of Stalinism had been softened and a small private sector allowed to develop. This had led to Hungary being regarded as 'the happiest barracks in the Socialist camp'. But in the 1980s, the country suffered from rising inflation and an alarming increase in foreign debt. The ageing Kádár compounded his economic mismanagement by the decision to go ahead with the construction of an ecologically catastrophic dam at Nagymaros on the Danube, part of a joint energy project with the Slovaks.

At the May 1988 Party Congress, reformers and technocrats joined forces to oust Kádár from the leadership. By July 1989 four of them, under the impressive leadership of the youthful Miklós Németh, were in control of the government. By October the Communists had reconstituted themselves as the Socialist Party, the 'iron curtain' on the Austrian border had been dismantled, and free elections were announced for the following year. In November, on the 33rd anniversary of the 1956 revolution (*see pp10–11*), the Republic of Hungary was proclaimed.

The elections of 1990

Two parties dominated the second round of voting (25 March): the populist and conservative Hungarian Democratic Forum and the intellectual metropolitan Alliance of Free Democrats, with the Democratic Forum emerging a clear winner. A worrying sign was the low turnout, which seemed to indicate that much of the electorate expected very little to be achieved by any political grouping. The government subsequently formed by József Antall was a coalition that included the revived Smallholders' Party (winners of the last free elections in 1945, but now a sentimental relic) and the Christian Democrats. A distinguished Free

Democrat and former Communist victim, Árpád Göncz, was elected president by Parliament.

The Antall government

In facing the severe economic and political problems inherited from Communism, the Antall government looked increasingly beleaguered. Its image was also tarnished by the right wing of the Democratic Forum, led by the writer István Csurka, indulging in anti-Semitic rhetoric and demanding witch-hunts against former Communists.

Until his death in December 1993, Antall ploughed on with his strategy of gradual adjustment to the free market economy. But while fiscal retrenchment and conscientious debt servicing preserved Hungary's credit rating on the financial markets, inflation at over 20 per cent, high unemployment and social hardship produced a Socialist victory in the 1994 elections.

Hungary at the crossroads

In the 21st century, there are many negative factors in Hungarian life. The economy has been buffeted by the world recession and society has been hamstrung by the contrast between the poverty of many and the wealth of a few. The public frequently turns in disgust from politicians seemingly more interested in the spoils of power than in the enlightened use of it. Yet there are also auspicious signs for the future. Hungarians are entrepreneurial and resourceful as a nation: if the opportunities arise, they will be quick to seize them.

Elections in 2010 saw the centre-right Fidesz Party win a historic mandate. Fidesz promises to rebuild Hungary, a challenging proposition considering the nation's near financial collapse, but the party is working from a strong position, being the first non-coalition government in Hungary's 20-year post-Communist history.

A strong government and continuing spending cuts should stabilise the economy and inspire continuing investor confidence.

Freedom Monument on Gellért hegy

Politics

People and culture

The numerous warm, healing springs of the Budapest area attracted settlers from earliest times, the first of them occupying the limestone caves formed by spa waters on the Danube's west bank. Eventually, these spas (see pp54–5) were to become a significant source of wealth for the inhabitants. The Danube itself was crucial to the development of Hungary, bringing trade and valuable immigrants, as well as less welcome invaders and floods.

The historic name of the Hungarian people is 'Magyars', 'Hungary' being 'Magyarország'. Now much diluted, the Magyars are descended from the Ugrian branch of the Finno-Ugric people who once populated the land between the Urals and the River Ob. While their northern cousins, the Finns and Estonians, are descendants of the group that migrated north and west around 2000 BC, the Magyars were influenced by Turkic and other cultures around the Caucasus before crossing into the Carpathian Basin in AD 896.

City population

Buda and Pest have had a mixed population since early times, including foreign craftsmen and merchants. Large numbers of Germans were settled by the Austrian Empress Maria Theresa in order to rebuild the country after 150 years of Turkish devastation; then in the 19th century thousands of Jews migrated to Hungary from Moravia and Galicia, the majority settling in Pest.

Today, the population of Budapest is nearly two million, one in five of the Hungarians living within Hungary. Some five million live beyond the borders, most of them as minorities in neighbouring countries (lands lost under the Trianon Treaty of 1920). Movement out of Budapest to the wider conurbation is increasing.

Religion

Hungary has been Christian since the 11th century, when King Stephen forcibly converted the population. Although Orthodoxy had a toehold of influence through royal marriages, the country was firmly Catholic until the Reformation, but 90 per cent of Hungarians had become Protestant by the late 16th century. Habsburg rule and its attendant Counter-Reformation sought to reverse this situation, but Protestantism hung on in the east and on the Great Plain. Today, Hungary is 57 per cent Catholic and 30 per cent Protestant.

People and culture

Statue of Franz Liszt by László Martou on the square named after him

A European culture

Hungary's artistic legacy reflects the country's attachment to the traditions of Western European culture, and the further back we look, the more apparent this becomes. From the establishment of the feudal state under King Stephen (997–1038) until the Turkish invasions in the 16th century, Hungary was part of the supranational European Christian culture. Artists and craftsmen came from the Low Countries, Germany and Italy to work for the Hungarian kings of the late Árpád, Anjou and Luxembourg dynasties. The Cistercian, Benedictine and Premonstratensian orders built churches in the pan-European Romanesque and Gothic styles: fine examples have survived at Ják in western Hungary and Bélapátfalva in the east.

The palaces of Buda and Visegrád (*see pp44–7 & 128*) reached the summit of splendour under King Matthias Corvinus (1458–90), who invited the best Italian craftsmen to work there. His Renaissance court was a glittering centre of the arts and humanist scholarship. Half a century later, Hungary was dismembered in the Turkish wars; Transylvania retained its political and cultural autonomy under the leadership of Protestant princes, but the rest of the territory was carved up between the Turks and the Habsburgs.

The rise of national culture

The expulsion of the Turks at the end of the 17th century brought with it the Counter-Reformation and Habsburg dominance. The Baroque town of Buda and Baroque churches in Pest date from this period. National resistance to the Austrian oppressors was conducted through warfare in the 18th century, but increasingly found expression through culture after Emperor Joseph II (1780–90) tried to Germanise his Hungarian subjects. The epics of Mihály Vörösmarty (1800–55) revived consciousness of Magyar history and the poet Sándor Petőfi became a hero of the 1848 War of Independence against the Habsburgs. The early 19th-century architecture of Pest, while reflecting the Central European taste for neoclassicism, was created by Hungarian masters such as Mihály Pollack and József Hild. Later in the 19th century, Miklós Ybl (*see p90*) built many of the great neo-Renaissance palaces on the graceful boulevards of the expanding city.

Back to the roots

In the late 19th century, we encounter a different kind of Hungarian self-perception, one that reconciles semi-mythical Eastern roots with Western civilisation. The national revival in literature began with the proclamation by Ferenc Kölcsey (author of the Hungarian national anthem) that poetry must be sought 'in the songs of the common people', while in the late 19th century architects and artists began to cultivate a consciously Hungarian manner. Ödön Lechner (*see pp18–19*) was one such architect, and

Károly Kós (*see p123*), in the early years of the 20th century, drew inspiration from Transylvanian vernacular forms and the English Arts and Crafts Movement. The latter also influenced the members of the Gödöllő artists' colony, founded in 1902 near Budapest, whose work exploited Hungarian folk motifs. In the fine arts the *plein-air* school of Nagybánya produced distinctively Hungarian landscape paintings, while the idiosyncratic work of Tivadar Csontváry Kosztka embodied a mystical sense of Hungarian identity.

In music, Franz Liszt was the first to popularise Hungarian themes. He also founded the Budapest Music Academy, which was to nurture innumerable great talents. In 1905, Béla Bartók and Zoltán Kodály began their great work of systematically collecting Hungarian folk music from all over the country and this was to influence their own music.

People and culture

The Royal Palace of Buda

Hungarian national style

'Hungarian form did not exist – but it will now!' With these auspicious words Ödön Lechner (1845–1914) began his idiosyncratic quest for a national style. His remark echoes and complements a similar declaration by Count István Széchenyi in 1830: 'Many people think "Hungary once was": I want to believe "she will be".'

Lechner spent some years abroad, and English and French influences are present in his early work. When Jugendstil/Art Nouveau arrived in Hungary, he embraced it enthusiastically. In a whimsical interpretation of ethnic roots he happily incorporated Indian, Persian and Moorish motifs, together with ornamentation derived from Hungarian folk art.

Magisterially indifferent to mere technical details of weight or stress, which he left to his long-suffering partners (notably Gyula Pártos), Lechner was equally cavalier about expense – or so his enemies on the city council claimed. (In the end they managed to prevent him getting any more commissions.) For his part, Lechner pointed out that he used brick, which was cheaper than the stone used by his main rival, and majolica (the colourful Zsolnay ceramic tiles from Pécs (*see pp133–5*), the style of which originated in Renaissance Italy), which was easier to clean. When asked why he ornamented the backs of roofs, which could not be seen, he replied: 'Why shouldn't the birds have something to enjoy?'

LECHNER BUILDINGS
Iparművészeti Múzeum
(Museum of Applied Arts)

The restored Moorish-style stucco of the interior is superb. The stairwell's tiers of undulating carved banisters are topped by an attractive stained-glass cupola. (*See p77.*)

Detail from Ödön Lechner's fine Post Office Savings Bank

The Institute for Geology

IX, Üllői útca 33–37. Tel: (36 1) 456 5100; www.imm.hu. Open: 10am–6pm. Closed: Mon. Metro: M3 to Ferenc körút; Tram: 4, 6 to Üllői útca.

Magyar Állami Földtani Intézet (Institute for Geology)

Pale yellow walls, strips of brown brickwork and a light blue ceramic roof topped by a huge globe make this one of Lechner's most eye-catching buildings.

XIV, Stefánia útca 14. National Geological Museum. Tel: (36 1) 251 0999; www.mafi.hu. Metro: M2 to Stadionok, then Trolleybus: 75 to Egressy útca.

Postatakarékpénztár (Post Office Savings Bank)

The walls rise to crenellations of yellow majolica; beyond these is a roof with coloured hexagonal tiles, richly ornamented with floral motifs, angels' wings, dragons' tails and other exotica. The recurrent representations of bee and honeycomb (originally also reflected in the fittings of the interior) symbolise the bank's activity (*see p111*). Tours can be arranged over the European Heritage Day weekend in September.

V, Hold útca 4. Metro: Arany János útca.

Impressions

The outskirts of Budapest are little different from those of other cities of the former Eastern Bloc: decaying factories ring the Pest side and blocks of prefabricated 'panel housing' disfigure the skyline. Budapest is still a modest-sized city by contemporary European standards and the centre is quickly reached from the airport. Good public transport and lovely walks make the city inviting to explore.

The historic cores of Pest and Buda hug opposite banks of the Danube. You can gain an overall impression of them by taking one of the trams that run along either side of the river (*Tram: 2 from Jászai Mari tér; Tram: 19 from Batthyány tér*); or you could climb to the Halászbástya (Fishermen's Bastion) on Castle Hill for a bird's-eye view of Pest.

Pest is a bustling, lively town with towering 19th-century blocks and great boulevards. At first, it is easy to get lost in the urban density of the Belváros (District V, the Inner City), but a few minutes' walk in any direction brings you to a major landmark, square or avenue. By contrast, residential Buda is on a smaller scale and more private, while Castle Hill is a historical tableau.

In his *Budapest Walks* of 1916, city chronicler Gyula Krúdy wrote: 'This city smells of violets in the spring, as do the ladies along the promenade above the river on the Pest side. In the autumn, it is Buda that suggests the tone: the odd thud of chestnuts dropping on the castle walk, fragments of the music of a military band wafting over the forlorn silence: autumn and Buda were born of the same mother.' Today, though a Transylvanian fiddler may have replaced the military band and ladies on the promenade are redolent of high fashion names like Louis Vuitton or Hilfiger rather than the scent of violets, nostalgia is in: Budapest is selling old style to a new clientele.

Orientation

Budapest is divided by the Danube, with the hilly Buda to the west and flat Pest to the east. Pest is neatly subdivided by the Kiskörút (Small Boulevard), a ring road made up of Károly Körút, Múzeum Körút and Vámház Körút following the medieval walls of Pest and containing the Belváros (V) district. The second ring road, the Nagykörút (Great Boulevard), runs from the southern tip of Margit sziget and marks the boundary of the XIII, VI, VII, VIII and IX districts.

Budepest and environs

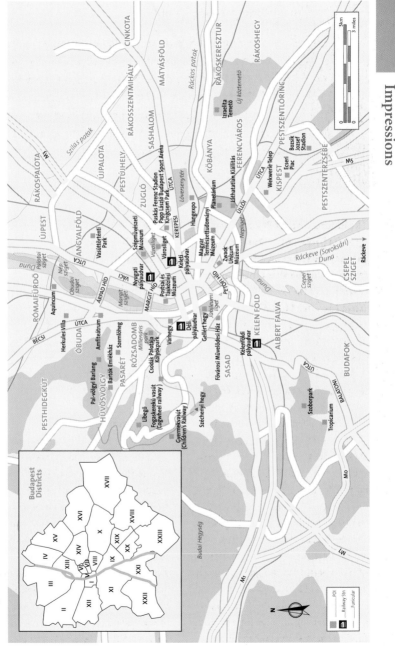

Budapest Districts

II, III, IV, XIII, XV, XVI, XVII, VI, VII, XIV, V, X, I, IX, XIX, XVIII, VIII, XX, XXIII, XI, XXI, XII, XXII

0 5km
0 3 miles

Legend:
- POI
- Railway Stn
- Funicular

Map labels:
CINKOTA, RÁKOSKERESZTÚR, RÁKOSHEGY, MÁTYÁSFÖLD, RÁKOSSZENTMIHÁLY, SASHALOM, Rákos patak, Izraelita Temető, Új köztemető, PESTSZENTLŐRINC, Bozsik József Stadion, KŐBÁNYA, FERENCVÁROS, Ecseri Piac, Wekerle Telep, KISPEST, PESTSZENTERZSÉBE, M5, RÁKOSPALOTA, ÚJPALOTA, PESTÚJHELY, ZUGLÓ, Szilas patak, Puskás Ferenc Stadion, Papp László Budapest Sport Aréna, Kincsem Park, Hungexpo, Láthatatlan Kiállítás, ÚLLŐI ÚTCA, Planetárium, Magyar Természettudományi Múzeum, Zwack Unicum Múzeum, Népliget, Ráckeve (Soroksári) Duna, Ráckeve, ÚJPEST, ANGYALFÖLD, VÁCI ÚTCA, Vasúttörténeti Park, Szépművészeti Múzeum, Városliget, KEREPESI ÚTCA, Lóversenytér, Keleti pályaudvar, Palotai sziget, Duna, Nép sziget, Óbudai sziget, ÁRPÁD HÍD, Margit sziget, MARGIT HÍD, Nyugati pályaudvar, Postai és Távközlési Múzeum, Jubileumi liget, PETŐFI HÍD, CSEPEL SZIGET, Csepel sziget, Duna, RÓMAIFÜRDŐ, Aquincum, BÉCSI ÚTCA, Herkules Villa, ÓBUDA, Amfiteátrum, Szemlőhegy, Millenáris park, ROZSADOMB, Csodák Palotája Kölyökpark, Várhegy, Déli pályaudvar, Gellért hegy, Fővárosi Művelődési Ház, KELEN FÖLD, Kelenföldi pályaudvar, ALBERT FALVA, PESTHIDEGKÚT, Pál-völgyi Barlang, Bartók Emlékház, PASARÉT, HŰVÖSVÖLGY, Libegő, Fogaskerekű vasút (Cogwheel railway), Gyermekvasút (Children's Railway), Széchenyi hegy, SASAD, BUDAFOK, BALATONI ÚTCA, Szoborpark, Tropicarium, Budai Hegység, M1, M7, M0, XI, XII, N

Radial avenues include Andrássy útca (between VI and VII) and Rákóczi útca (between VII and VIII) and Üllői útca (between VIII and IX). For more information on districts, see pp25–6. It is remarkable to remember that almost all of Budapest was flattened in World War II and all the bridges were blown up as the Nazis retreated, meaning everything we see today is a faithful re-creation.

When to go

Central Europe's continental climate is extremely hot in summer, raw and cold in winter. The nicest times to visit are between April and the end of June and, especially, between September and the end of October. The long Indian summer provides ideal weather for excursions (see pp118–35). If you must visit in high summer, you can keep cool by heading for the spas (see pp54–5) during the heat of the day and lodging in the Buda Hills rather than down in the stifling city. August sees the spectacular fireworks display above the Danube which usually marks the beginning of the end of the canicula – as Hungarians call the broiling midsummer season.

The Budapest Arts Weeks kick off on the anniversary of Béla Bartók's birth (25 September). Annual events include a wine festival, an international dog show in May, the Budapest Spring Festival in the second half of March and the enormous Sziget Festival in August.

Arriving

Flights arrive at Ferihegy, Budapest's international airport, 24km (15 miles)

The Danube sweeps through the city, dividing Buda from Pest

to the southeast of the city centre. Budapest has several daily international rail connections, with most arriving at and leaving from the Keleti pályaudvar (Eastern Railway Station). Budapest has three major railway stations and a new bus station, all of which are served by one of Budapest's three metro lines. A fourth metro has some stations under construction, but planning the route is not yet completed! From April to October, a hydrofoil runs once daily on the Danube between Vienna and Budapest, taking five and a half hours. For more information, *see pp177–8*.

Fiakers can be used for painless sightseeing on Castle Hill

Getting around

Getting around in Budapest is no great problem for the visitor, although unpronounceable names may cause difficulties at first. The areas of interest to visitors are relatively small and compact, and are well served by metro, trams, trolleybuses and buses. It is worth buying the modestly priced three-day tourist ticket (*túristajegy 3 napra*) or seven-day ticket (*hetijegy*) valid on all forms of city transport and on sale at larger metro stations. The Budapest Card (*see p185*), valid for 48 or 72 hours, includes free public transport, two tours, admission to 60 museums and other sights, as well as eligibility for discounts at various shops and restaurants.

The metro has three lines, colour coded and numbered: M1 = yellow, M2 = red, M3 = blue. All meet at the central junction on Deák Ferenc tér.

M3 runs the length of Pest and M2 crosses the Danube to south Buda. M1 follows the radial Andrássy útca through the centre of Pest and, as the second underground system in the world after London, is UNESCO World Heritage listed. Trolleybuses run only on the Pest side. Yellow trams run along either side of the Danube, along the Pest boulevards and on main arteries elsewhere. There is also an excellent bus service. (*More transport details are given on pp177–8*.) Be aware that you need to press the button whether you want to get on or off if the doors do not open automatically. The HÉV suburban railway (green trains) is useful for excursions to Szentendre from Batthyány tér, Ráckeve from Kőzvágóhíd or Gödöllő from Őrs vezér tere (*see pp122–3, 125 & 129–30*), although rides beyond the Budapest city boundary need a supplementary ticket.

Other means of transport in Budapest are principally for sightseeing. The boats criss-crossing the Danube afford views of the Országház (Parliament) and Buda Castle from the river; a cable car (*sikló*) runs up to Castle Hill from Clark Ádám tér; a chairlift takes you from Zugliget to János hegy in the Buda Hills; a cogwheel railway (*Fogaskerekű vasút*) runs from Városmajor on the Buda side up to Széchenyi hegy (Széchenyi Hill); and the Children's Railway (*see p152*) runs through the Buda woods.

Taxis are cheap by Western standards. There are rather too many rogues – stick to the well-established companies, including City Taxi and Fő taxi – *see p188*).

Manners and mores

Hungarians do not expect foreigners to master their language, but it is best to learn greetings, which are always offered on entering or leaving a shop or when addressing strangers. These are: *jó reggelt* (good morning), *jó napot* (good day – from about 10am), *jó estét* (good evening) and *jó éjszakát* (good night). *Viszontlátásra* is 'goodbye' (*see pp186–7*). Silence or a nod could be taken as rudeness.

When you introduce yourself or are introduced, always shake hands and say your complete name. Your interlocutor will do likewise, but remember that Hungarian names are in reverse order, whether written or spoken. Thus, Englishman John

Walk or take a cable car up to Castle Hill

Smith meets Hungarian Kovács János (Smith John).

Punctuality is not a Hungarian obsession. If a business partner arrives 15 minutes late, no insult is intended. Business meetings invariably begin with ritual coffee drinking. The decision-making process is slow and the inbred instinct of functionaries to check everything with higher layers of authority is still common.

Hungarians are extremely hospitable, and proud housewives will probably press on you more food than you want. Trying to foot the bill in a restaurant is usually a struggle – accept *force majeure* with good grace unless there are compelling reasons for not doing so. If you are invited to somebody's home, flowers and wine are usual. You may be asked to remove your shoes and put on house slippers – simply to protect the invariably spotless home. When it comes to the meal, never drink before your host has raised his glass and wished everyone good health.

Feminists will note that male chauvinism is alive and well, often masquerading as old-style gallantry. Yet battle-hardened women have been known to melt just a little when greeted with *kezét csókolom* (I kiss your hand).

Areas of Budapest
Administration

For administrative purposes Budapest is divided into 23 districts, of which about 14 will be of interest to the visitor. The others are primarily residential or industrial.

Hop on the waterbus for a spot of sightseeing

Districts of Budapest

I – Várhegy & Viziváros. Várhegy, literally meaning 'Castle Hill', dominates the Buda side of the city with Viziváros (Water Town) lying between it and the Danube as well as running behind to Moszkva tér at Várhegy's north.

II – Rózsadomb (Hill of Roses) & Hűvösvölgy contains some of the most expensive real estate in Budapest such as the villas nestled in the wooded Buda Hills behind Várhegy. Hűvösvölgy is home to the Children's Railway (*see p152*).

III – Óbuda & Aquincum. Also in Buda, the location of Budapest's extensive Roman remains.

IV – Újpest, New Pest, in Pest's north.

V – Belváros & Lipótváros. Belváros is the inner city, the central historic old town of Pest. Lipótváros lies to the north of the historic zone and comprises the economic and political area of Budapest. The V district has much for the traveller to explore and is easily traversed on foot.

VI – Terézváros lies between the Kiskörút (Small Boulevard) and the Nagykörút (Great Boulevard) and is home to Budapest's Opera House on Andrássy útca. Pest's grand boulevards, highly influenced by Hausmann's redevelopment of Paris, are most obvious in the VI district.

VII – Erzsébetváros is the bullet-scarred, Jewish quarter of Pest, home to the city's highest concentration of people and bars. It is currently undergoing extensive regeneration.

VIII – Józsefváros. The beautiful, mostly residential area home to the Hungarian National Museum, Erkel Theatre, Keleti railway station, one of Budapest's biggest parks, Orczy-kert, and Kerepesi cemetery (*see pp72–5 & 113–15*).

IX – Ferencváros is the large, mostly working-class district of Pest south along the Danube. It is home to the Great Market Hall, the Zwack Unicum Museum, new Palace of Arts and Lechner's stunning Museum of Applied Arts.

X – Kőbánya. One of Pest's largest districts, home to Népliget park and bus station.

XI – Újbuda. New Buda, the area south and east of Gellért hegy including the hotel and spa.

XII – Also Buda, the area from Várhegy west into the Buda Hills, similarly expensive and dotted with glorious villas.

The church of Krisztínaváros from Castle Hill

XIV – Városliget. Literally translated as the 'City Park', Városliget lies in the east of Pest. Its western entrance is marked by Heroes' Square.

Buda

Gellért Hill and the small plateau of the Buda Castle with its adjacent town rise on the west bank of the Danube. Between the plateau and the river is a narrow strip of land settled since the Middle Ages and known as Víziváros (Water Town). To the north is Óbuda (Old Buda, *see pp30–31*).

Gellért hegy (Gellért Hill)

This dolomite rock (235m/771ft high) was the earliest inhabited part of Budapest. In prehistoric times, cave-dwellers took advantage of the hot springs bursting through a geological fault – springs that still supply the Gellért spa today. In Roman times, the surviving Celts lived in this area, some 2km (1¼ miles) from the military and civil settlements of Aquincum to the north. Nowadays, the hill is an agreeable park (*see p67*) with footpaths winding up to the Freedom Monument and Citadella on the summit. The grotto chapel (just above the Gellért Hotel) has been reconsecrated, after being walled up by the Communists (who, incidentally, located their command bunker, for use in the event of Armageddon, in the bowels of the Gellért rock).

Várhegy (Castle Hill)

The town and fortress of Buda only achieved real significance in the second half of the 10th century. Of the four ancient royal and religious centres in Hungary – Székesfehérvár, Esztergom (*see p129*), Veszprém and Buda – the last to develop was Buda. An economic boom in the 11th and 12th centuries led to the expansion of Buda, Óbuda and Pest, and an increase in religious foundations. The Tartar invasion of 1241 devastated the whole region, but thereafter King Béla IV, known as the refounder of the nation, encouraged settlers from abroad and built the first fortress on Castle Hill.

The rise of Buda

The basic layout of the town of Buda, which has endured until today, dates from the last third of the 13th century, when the two-storeyed Gothic houses for wealthy burghers were built. Buda had

two communities: the Germans, whose Church of Our Lady (later the Matthias Church) stood to the south; and the Hungarians, whose Church of Mary Magdalene was at the northern end.

The first Anjou king, Charles Robert (1308–42), chose to build his great palace upstream of Buda at Visegrád (*see p128*), and it was not until 1347 that Louis I ('the Great') moved his court to Buda and major expansion of the Royal Palace began. Sigismund of Luxembourg (1387–1437) built a lavish new palace in the 15th century and invited masters from Paris, Stuttgart and Augsburg to decorate it. The apotheosis was reached under Matthias Corvinus (1458–90), whose Italian masons and craftsmen created the most glittering royal court in contemporary Europe.

Decline and restoration

After the Turkish conquest of 1541, churches were vandalised and turned into mosques; Buda slowly decayed until its liberation by Habsburg troops in 1686, though the reconquest itself left most of the town in ruins. Subsequently, a small Baroque Buda grew up, together with a very plain and functional Baroque palace, erected under Maria Theresa.

In the late 18th and early 19th centuries, high-ranking officials lived in Buda and the Diet (parliament) met there (for the last time in 1807). While Pest expanded rapidly, Buda stagnated, although areas bordering on Castle Hill, such as Krisztinaváros and Rózsadomb, became desirable residential areas. The last rebuilding of the Royal Palace took place after the 1867 Ausgleich (Compromise) with the Habsburgs that created the Austro-Hungarian Empire. Subsequently, Buda was destroyed by the Russian siege at the end of World War II and rebuilt in the 1950s and 1960s as a showcase of historic restoration.

Pest

The origins of Pest lie in the Roman period, when a small fortress to protect the ferry crossing at the narrows was built at what is now the Pest end of the Erzsébet híd (Elizabeth Bridge). In the late 10th century, traders settled near the ferry to exploit the Danubian ship traffic.

In the 11th century, a burial chapel for St Gellért was erected, the first sanctuary on the site of the Belvárosi plébániatemplom (Inner City Parish Church, *see p82*). The unfortunate missionary had in fact been about to cross from the Buda side when he was intercepted and drowned in the river by supporters of the pagan faction (1046).

Shortly afterwards (1061), the first documentary mention of the town of Pest appears.

Medieval and Baroque Pest

In the 11th and 12th centuries, Pest expanded to become a substantial and wealthy trading town, with a royal residence, a Dominican cloister and a parish church. After the Tartar invasion of 1241, King Béla IV renewed its privileges as a Royal Free Town, but many of its mainly German inhabitants

Poet Attila József sculpted in a brooding pose

moved to the comparative safety of Buda. In the 14th century, it boomed again under the Anjou dynasty, when the parish church was enlarged and altered to the form of a *hallenkirche* (hall church).

After the Turkish occupation (1541–1686), building began again in Pest; a hospital for war veterans was built by Italian architects in 1716, together with several Baroque convents and churches (for example, those of the Servites, the Franciscans and the Hungarian order of Paulites). Of the Baroque palaces built by aristocrats, few traces remain; Andreas Mayerhoffer's Péterffy Palace (1755) in Pesti Barnabás útca (now the Százéves restaurant) is a rare example.

Expansion

Pest came into its own in the 19th century. In 1805, János Hild presented his plans to improve the city to the Embellishment Commission supported by the palatine. The proposed parks and public buildings were to be financed by selling building plots and by the revenues of customs and local taxes. The inner city (Belváros) thereafter became a largely residential area with churches and schools. Neighbouring Lipótváros (Leopold's Town) was the business centre, increasingly also the domain of wealthy assimilated Jews. Neoclassical buildings – the Magyar Nemzeti Múzeum (Hungarian National Museum), the Calvinist and Lutheran churches – gave the city its monumental character up to the unsuccessful revolution against the Habsburgs of 1848, when many neoclassical dwellings were destroyed.

In the second half of the 19th century, Pest became the hub of a rapidly expanding and industrialising capital. Whereas in 1850 the populations of Buda and Pest were roughly equal, by 1900 only one in six Budapestians lived in Buda. The great boulevards crossed by the radial of Andrássy útca were now built, as were three new bridges. Miklós Ybl located magnificent neo-Renaissance palaces along the streets and designed a graceful opera house (1884). Theatres, museums and hotels, many on a grand scale, enriched the cityscape of Pest. The monumental Szent István bazilika (St Stephen's Basilica) was begun in 1851 and the even more grandiose Országház (Parliament) was completed just after the turn of the century. The Millennial Celebrations of 1896 put the seal on all this dynamism and self-confidence, while the idiosyncratic

The Parliament (Országház) as seen from Buda

buildings of Ödön Lechner (*see pp18–19*) and his school gave expression to the Magyar soul in architecture.

From the 20th century onwards, Pest has begun to sprawl into suburbia, but at its heart is still the bustle and business of that dynamic 19th-century city, now reawakening to capitalistic enterprise, artistic creativity and gourmet refinement.

The Ancient Town of Óbuda

The Roman province of Pannonia was created in the 1st century BC and divided by Trajan into Upper and Lower Pannonia around AD 106. Aquincum (*see pp61–3*) was the civil capital of Lower Pannonia. Close to it was the military *castrum* (camp), at the Óbuda end of Árpád híd (Árpád Bridge), and its associated domestic buildings known as *canabae*.

Two of the chiefs of the seven Magyar tribes (Kende and Kurszán) took up residence in Óbuda, and the first church – a burial chapel built over the grave of the paramount chief, Árpád – was raised in Óbuda at the end of the 10th or the beginning of the 11th century.

In the Middle Ages, the town increased in wealth and importance, particularly under Béla III, who entertained Frederick Barbarossa here in 1189. A Cistercian cloister was built, and other religious orders followed in the 14th century, when the widowed queen of King Charles Robert of Anjou moved her palace to the town. Under Sigismund of Luxembourg, Óbuda even boasted a university (founded in 1389, the first in Hungary).

Like Buda and Pest, the town suffered under the Turkish occupation, but in the 18th century the Habsburgs bestowed the Óbuda lands on the Zichy family. They built their great mansion close to Fő tér (*see p65*), and encouraged Jews to settle, thus boosting the area's economy. Crafts and trade received further stimulus in the 19th century when Count István Széchenyi founded the shipyard on Óbuda Island and the Goldberger textile factory began operations (both now closed).

Fő tér in Óbuda

Sadly, Óbuda has suffered from the ravages of time and Communism. The once picturesque provincial town is now a concrete jungle with a few isolated pockets of Roman and Baroque charm and elegance. A visit to these relics (and the delightful local museum at Kiscelli) will give a hint of past glories.

The Royal Palace as viewed from the Gellért Monument

Buda

The Buda side of the Danube is dominated by Várhegy (Castle Hill), below which is Víziváros (Water Town) stretching as far as Moszkva tér behind the hill's northern tip. To the northwest is Rózsadomb (the Hill of Roses), where the most sought-after villas are to be found. Further north is Óbuda, and to the south and beyond Gellért hegy (Gellért Hill) is the rather bleak suburb of Kelenföld.

Buda was the capital of Hungary from 1361 until its capture by the Ottoman Empire in 1541. In 1868, after devastating wars against Austria, Germans were brought into Buda to resettle the town and they quickly became the majority. Rural migration during the 19th century meant that Hungarians became the dominant nationality in Buda again. Unification in 1873 brought together the towns of Buda, Pest and Óbuda to form today's capital of Hungary, Budapest.

In 1987, UNESCO granted Buda Castle, both banks of the Danube and Andrássy útca (on the Pest side) World Heritage List status.

VÁRHEGY (CASTLE HILL)

The wedge-shaped limestone plateau rising 160m (525ft) on the west side of the Danube consists of the Royal Palace complex (*see pp44–7*) at the southern end and the ancient town of Buda (the Várhegyed or Castle Quarter)

encompassing the middle and northern parts of the plateau.

From the time of Béla IV in the 13th century, old Buda was a residential area ancillary to the court, where retainers, officials, craftsmen and merchants lived (*see pp30–31*). Each component of its mixed population of Germans and Hungarians (also Walloons, Italians and Jews) has left traces here; even the last Turkish pasha has his monument, although there is very little else left to recall the 145-year-long Turkish rule. After the Diet ceased to meet in Buda at the beginning of the 19th century, Pest increasingly eclipsed Buda, until it gradually became the quiet, historical backwater of today.

Access to Várhegy

Whether you want to visit the Royal Palace, the town or both, the following access routes will apply: from the south the approach is on foot from Szarvas tér (reached by bus 86 on the Buda side, buses 5 and 78 from Pest) and

0 250 metres
0 250 yards

Bartók Emlékház

FELHÉVÍZ

Hajós-Alfréd
Sport Uszoda

Lukács Gyógyfürdő

Malom-
tó

VERHALOM UTCA
BÓLYAI UTCA
RÓMER FLÓRIS UTCA
TÖRÖK UTCA
GÜL BABA UTCA
FRANKEL LEÓ ÚT
ÁRPÁD FEJEDELEM ÚTJA
LIPTHAY

Margit
sziget

Centenáriumi
emlékmű

RÓZSADOMB

Gül Baba
türbéje

ÚJLIPÓTVÁROS

MARGIT HÍD

ÚPESTI
POZSONYI

RAKPART

Mechwart
Liget

Csodák
Palotája

Millenáris
Park

BEM JÓZSEF ÚTCA

Bem szobor

BEM

Duna

Vígszínház

JÁSZAI
MARI TER

RAKPART

Mammut
II

LÓNYAI UTCA
MARGIT KÖRÚT

Flórián
kapolna

Öntödei
Múzeum

Király
Gyógyfürdő

FŐ

RAKPART

BALASSI
FALK MIKSA UTCA
HONVÉD UTCA
MÁRKÓ

HEGEDŰS GYULA UTCA

Mammut
Shopping
Mall

NAGY
IMRE
TÉR

SZALAY UTCA

Néprajzi
Múzeum

Raoul
Wallenberg
emlékmű

Moszkva
tér

OSTROM UTCA

BATTHYÁNY
ÚTCA

Szent
Erzsébet
templom

Országház

Mezogazdasági és
Élelmezésügyi
Minisztérium

VÁRFOK UTCA

ÚTCA
DON
VÁM

Batthyány
tér

Szent
Anna templom

Cipők a
Duna-parton

Nagy Imre
Emlékmű

BÁTHORY UTCA
NÁDOR UTCA

Szovjet
Emlékmű

Postatakarékpénztár

Hadtörténeti
Múzeum

KRISZTINA KÖRÚT

Léveltár
Koller
Gallery

Kodály Zoltán
szobor

Erdődy
Palota

Szilágyi Dezső
téri templom

Kossuth
Lajos tér

LIPÓTVÁROS

Szabadság
tér

TV Székház

Nemzeti
Bank

BECSI
KAPU
TÉR
TÁNCSICS
MIHÁLY U.
FORTUNA UTCA
SZILÁGYI
DEZSŐ
TÉR

SZÉCHENYI

Szökőkút

Europa
Liget

Vörös
Sün ház

Hilton

Magdolna
templom

Mátyás templom
Halászbástya

Alsóvizivaros
templom

Magyar
Tudományos
Akadémia

ARANY JÁNOS UTCA

VÁRHEGY

KAPISZTRÁN
TÉR
HESS
ANDRÁS
TÉR
SZENTHÁROMSÁG

CORVIN
TÉR

Café Kör

Vérmező

ATTILA
ÚTCA

Ruszwurm
Labrintus

Régi budai
városháza

Hagyományok
Háza

PONTY UTCA

Szent István
bazilika

Déli
pályaudvar

KRISTINAVÁROS

Francia
Kultúra Intézete

Gresham
Palota

Bajcsy-
Zsilinszky útca

Déli
pályaudvar

TÓTH ÁRPÁD SÉTÁNY
DÍSZ TÉR

Nemzeti
Táncszínház

SZÉCHENYI LÁNCHÍD

ROOSEVELT
TÉR

JÓZSEF ATTILA UTCA

Danubius
kút

MIKÓ
KÖRÚT

CLARK
ÁDÁM
TÉR

József Nádor szobor

PESTI

SZENT
GYÖRGY
TÉR

Sándor
palota

Gerbeaud

Erzsébet
tér

N

ALKOTÁS ÚTCA
MÁRVÁNY ÚTCA
GYÖZÖ ÚTCA
MÉSZÁROS ÚTCA
TÁBOR ÚTCA
ALAGÚT ÚTCA
PÁLOTA
LÁNCHÍD
GRÓZA PÉTER RAKPART

Vörösmarty
tér

Vigadó

Krisztinavárosi
templom

Ludwig
Múzeum

Magyar
Nemzeti
Galéria

VIGADÓ TÉR

APÁCAI CSERE JÁNOS UTCA
DOROTTYA UTCA
BELGRÁD RAKPART ALSÓ

ATTILA
KRISZTINA
KÖRÚT

Budavári
palota

Budapesti
Történeti
Múzeum

Várbazár

Ybl Kiosk

Görög Orthodox templom

Petőfi emlékmű

NAPHEGY

Török
sírok

Semmelweis
Orvostörténeti
Múzeum

Contra
Aquincum

Aranyszarvas
Étterem

TABÁN

Tabáni
plébániatemplom

Erzsébet
Királynő
szobra

DOBRENTEI
TÉR

Belvárosi
plébánia-
templom

ÚTCA

HEGUALJA

GELLÉRT HEGY

Gellért
emlékmű

Rudas
Gyógyfürdő és
Uszoda & Romkert

SZT GELLÉRT RAK
ERZSÉBET HÍD

Budapest Ferihegy
International

Jubileumi liget

......POI
Ⓜ ......Metro Stop
✝ ......Cathedral
ℹ ......Information
Ⓒ ......Police Station
✈ ......Airport
Ⓡ ......Railway Stn
✚ ......Hospital
......Funicular

brings you through the southern fortifications of the old castle. (Trams 18, 19, 41 stop at nearby Döbrentei tér.) There are also various flights of steps up from Fő útca in Víziváros (Water Town). The bus to the Castle Quarter is the No 16 that runs between Erzsébet tér on the Pest side (Deák Ferenc tér metro is served by all three lines) and Moszkva tér (metro M2) on the Buda side. The *siklò* (funicular) climbs from Clark Ádám tér at the west end of the Chain Bridge (*daily 7.30am–10pm*) and arrives at Szent György tér (there is a special fare for this). The *várbusz* (minibus) is now bus 16A; it runs between Dísz tér and Moszkva tér (*until 11pm*).

Bécsi kapu tér
(Vienna Gate Square)

To the left of the gate are the sombre State Archives and opposite is the Lutheran Church containing Bertalan Székely's picture *Christ Blessing the Bread*. There are attractive Baroque houses at Nos 5 and 6, and the façade of No 7 is adorned with medallions of Virgil, Socrates, Quintillian, Cicero, Livy and Seneca.

Hess András tér
(András Hess Square)

The square is named after the printer of the first Hungarian book, *Budai krónika* (*The Chronicle of Buda*, 1473) – his printing shop was at No 4. The Hilton Hotel (Nos 1–3) is a modern adaptation of a former Dominican monastery and church. On the St Nicholas Tower of the former church is a copy of a 15th-century Saxon relief showing a triumphant King Matthias. Also on the square is the monument to Pope Innocent XI, initiator of the Holy Alliance formed to reconquer Buda from the Turks.

Gates to the former Royal Palace

Táncsics Mihály útca (Mihály Táncsics Street)

At No 5 is the contemporary Koller Gallery and No 7 is the Baroque Erdődy Palace (1769) housing the Museum of the History of Music. No 9 may once have been the royal mint; it certainly became the Magna Curia (Royal Court) and was latterly a prison. The writer and agitator Mihály Táncsics was imprisoned here before the War of Independence. The Jewish ghetto was around Nos 21 and 23. No 26, formerly a medieval synagogue, is now a museum. A wall plan shows the location of Buda's Jewish community at various periods. Dependent on the goodwill of the ruler, they suffered periodic persecution or expulsion. The Christian armies that reconquered Buda in 1686 massacred the Jewish inhabitants, who had established a *modus vivendi* with the Turks.
Medieval Synagogue Museum, Táncsics Mihály útca 26. Tel: (36 1) 225 7816. www.btm.hu. Open: 10am–6pm. Closed: Nov–Apr. Admission charge.

Tárnok útca (Treasurers' Street)

The name refers to the administrators of the royal monopolies (salt, minerals, etc) who resided in the area. The street was also the site of a market in the Middle Ages. No 18 is a 15th-century alchemist's lab, which was used as an apothecary's shop from the 18th century. It is now the lovely, though somewhat sinister, Golden Eagle Pharmacy Museum.

Arany Sas Patikamúzeum, Tárnok útca 18. Tel: (36 1) 375 9772. Open: Tue–Sun 10am–6pm, to 4pm Nov–Feb. Free admission.

Úri útca (The Street of the Lords)

At No 9 is the entrance to the cave labyrinth under Castle Hill (*see p67*), while at the junction with Szentháromság útca is an equestrian statue of Maria Theresa's successful Hungarian general, András Hadik, who was also commandant of Buda for a while. His horse is a portrait of a famous stallion from the stud at Bábolna.

Fortuna útca (Fortuna Street)

French and Walloon craftsmen lived in the street in the Middle Ages. Gothic elements can be seen in several houses, notably the so-called *sedilia* (sitting niches) in the doorways (for example, at Nos 5 and 30), a unique feature of Buda. They may have been used by traders for their wares or by servants waiting for their masters.

Országház útca (The Street of the Diet)

The Italian craftsmen working on the Royal Palace once lived in this street (it was then called Olasz útca – Italian Street). From the 1780s to 1807, the Hungarian Diet met at No 28, formerly a convent. Of the many attractive survivals, Nos 18–22 retain Gothic and Baroque features, while No 2 was a place of some splendour at the time of Sigismund of Luxembourg (note the sitting niches).

Walk: Várhegy

This walk round Castle Hill gives a flavour of the old town of Buda, painstakingly restored after terrible destruction in World War II.

Allow 1½ hours.

Start from the top of the funicular railway (sikló) that climbs to Castle Hill from Clark Ádám tér.

1 Sándor palota (Sándor Palace)

On your right is the beautifully restored neoclassical former prime minister's residence (*see pp40–41*). A plaque on the east wall honours Count Teleki, head of the government in 1941, who committed suicide here when the decision was taken to allow German troops through Hungary to attack Yugoslavia. It is now the home of the president of the Republic and is nicknamed the White House. Next door is the **Várszínház** (*see p40*), a monastery converted into a dance theatre, and opposite is a wide expanse of **medieval excavations**.

Walk through Dísz tér and along Tárnok útca, past the pharmacy museum (see p35), to Szentháromság tér.

2 Régi Budai Városháza (Former Town Hall of Buda)

The early 18th-century town hall on the west side of the square has a pretty bay window; below it is a statue of Pallas Athene, protectress of Buda.

3 Mátyás templom, Halászbástya (Matthias Church, Fishermen's Bastion)

The striking neo-Gothic reconstruction of the Matthias Church (*see pp38–9*) dominates the square's east side, with the Fishermen's Bastion beyond it (by the same architect, *see p38*).

4 Hilton Hotel

The Hilton Hotel (1976) at Hess András tér 1–3 was designed by Béla Pintér, incorporating parts of a medieval tower, a Gothic church and a Baroque seminary. A detour down Táncsics Mihály útca brings you past the Erdődy Palota (No 7) containing the Museum of the History of Music; next door (No 9), leading dissidents were imprisoned before the 1848 revolution. The other side (No 5) is the Koller Gallery for contemporary art.

5 Hess András tér/Fortuna útca

At No 3 on the square is the ancient Vörös Sün-ház (House of the Red

Hedgehog – look above the door). It is worth a detour on to the Anjou bastion to see the monument to the last Turkish pasha (*see p41*). Walk back across Kapisztrán tér, passing the Magdolna templom (Church of St Mary Magdalene, *see p41*) on your right, and then turn right onto Országház úcta. On the opposite corner (with Petermann bíró utca), note the plaque of 'The Flying Nun'. It recalls the convent of the Poor Clares at Országház útca 28.

Cut through Dárda útca and head south along Úri útca, where there are unusual Gothic sitting niches in the entrance to Nos 31, 32 & 34. After catching the view from the west rampart (Tóth Árpád sétány), turn left by the statue to András Hadik into Szentháromság útca.

MUËMLEK

You will notice the word 'Muëmlek' etched on to most buildings in the Castle District and on many across Budapest. Muëmlek means the building is 'Listed' and cannot be structurally changed. Many here are private residences but to see inside one, head to the Koller Gallery (*Táncsics Mihály útca 5. Tel: (36 1) 356 9208. www.kollergallery.com. Open: 10am–6pm*).

6 Ruszwurm

At No 7 is the famous confectioner's (*see p167*). In the late 19th century, Vilmos Ruszwurm's pastries were in such demand that well-to-do Viennese ordered them to be sent by post-chaise.

Turn south out of the street for Dísz tér for bus 16 to Pest or Moszkva tér.

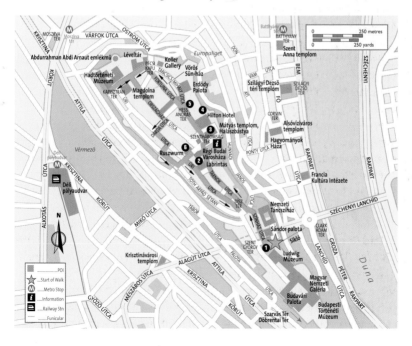

Walk: Várhegy

Stained glass at the Matthias Church ∘

HISTORY OF THE MATTHIAS CHURCH

The earliest church on this site dates back to the reign of Béla IV (1235–70). It was enlarged in the late 14th century and subsequently added to by Matthias Corvinus, who built the oratory and replaced the south tower that had collapsed in 1384.

During the Turkish occupation, it was used as a mosque. Then, between 1874 and 1896, Frigyes Schulek entirely rebuilt it in neo-Gothic style, though he stuck to the original ground plan.

In the Middle Ages, the Church of Our Lady was where the German burghers of Buda held their services. The kings of Hungary had to be formally accepted by the community in the church following their coronation in Székesfehérvár.

After the Compromise of 1867, Franz Joseph and Elizabeth were crowned in this church, as were the last Habsburgs, Karl IV and Zita, in 1916.

The year 2010 saw a superbly extensive restoration completed.

Stróbl's equestrian statue of St Stephen (1903) holding the (doubled) apostolic cross that symbolises his role as Christianiser of the Hungarians.

Halászbástya (Fishermen's Bastion)

Frigyes Schulek designed this neo-Romanesque viewing terrace to the east and south of the Mátyás templom (Matthias Church); completed in 1905, it was named after the Danube fishermen who defended this bastion in the Middle Ages. The conical turrets are supposedly a romantic allusion to the tents of the original seven Magyar tribes. In front of the bastion is Alajos

Mátyás templom (Matthias Church)

The Church of Our Lady is known as the Matthias Church after King Matthias Corvinus (1458–90), who considerably enlarged and enriched it. The interior was painted with polychrome geometric patterns and frescoes in the 19th century by Károly Lotz and Bertalan Székely; the stained-glass windows show scenes from Hungarian history.

Against the north wall of the choir stalls is the St Ladislas Chapel with a copy of the 14th-century silver bust of the 11th-century saint and king, Ladislas I, and frescoes by Lotz illustrating legends about him. In the crypt are grave slabs of the Árpád dynasty. From there, you begin a tour which includes St Stephen's Chapel, painted with scenes from the life of the saint-king, the Royal Oratory (containing Habsburg coronation robes) and the exhibition of ecclesiastical treasures in the north gallery. Below it, in the Trinity Chapel, is the tomb of Béla III and his consort, Anne of Châtillon.
Szentháromság tér 2. Tel: (36 1) 355 5657. Open: Mon–Fri 9am–5pm, Sat 9am– 1pm, Sun 1–5pm). Admission charge (also for gift shop).

Szentháromság tér (Trinity Square)

Trinity Square is the focus of the old town: to the east is the Matthias Church (*see opposite*), to the north the neo-Gothic Central Archive (formerly the Finance Ministry) and to the west the Régi budai városháza (Old Town Hall). This Baroque fusion of five Gothic houses was the seat of the council from 1710 to 1873. Szentháromság utca leads off to the west; at No 7 is the Biedermeier café Ruszwurm (*see pp37 & 167*). In the middle of the square is the Trinity Column (1713) commemorating the

Athena guards the Old Town Hall, Trinity Square

abatement of a plague epidemic. This is largely a post-war replica and marks the spot where Masses were held when plague closed the churches.

Dísz tér (Parade Square)

The square is flanked by the Water Gate to the east and the Fehérvári or Jewish Gate to the west; to the south are the ruins of the War Ministry. Jews were settled close to the castle by Béla IV and held a Friday market here, until driven out by Louis of Anjou in 1360. Executions (a popular spectacle) were held on the square. In the middle is György Zala's Honvéd Monument (1893), honouring Hungarians who died for freedom in 1848–49.

Nemzeti Táncszínház (National Dance Theatre)

Also known as the Várszínház, it was originally a 13th-century Franciscan monastery. Later, between 1541 and 1686, the building was occupied by the Turkish pashas. It was turned into a German theatre in 1787 and saw the first ever Hungarian stage performance in the city on 25 October 1790. Beethoven performed here in 1800.
Színház útca 5–9. Tel: (36 1) 457 0848. www.dancetheatre.hu

Sándor palota (Sándor Palace)

Mihály Pollack and the Viennese Johann Aman designed this imposing neoclassical palace (1805–21). It was

Trinity Column and the neo-Gothic Central Archive, Trinity Square

the official lodging of the prime minister between 1867 and 1944 (*see p36*) and is now home to the president of the Republic. Note Anton Kirchmayer's frieze on the façade, a mixture of patriotic themes and scenes from antiquity.
Szent György tér 1–2.

Kapisztrán tér
(Giovanni Capistrano Square)

Capistrano was a fiery Franciscan preacher who gathered an army against the Turks and took part in the successful siege of Belgrade in 1456.

Appropriately, the Museum of Military History is on the square (*Nos 2–4; see p61*). On the Anjou Bastion beyond it is the monument to the last pasha of Buda, Abdurrahman Abdi Arnaut (actually an Albanian), who died at his post in 1686.

Magdolna templom
(Church of St Mary Magdalene)

The tower and a solitary Gothic window are all that was reconstructed after the Communists demolished the church, which had managed to survive wartime bombardment. It belonged to the Hungarians in the Middle Ages; after prolonged dispute a borderline between the German and Hungarian parishes had been drawn at the Dominican Monastery (now the Hilton) in 1390. Under the Turkish occupation the church was for a while shared between Protestants (worshipping in the nave) and Catholics (using the choir).
Kapisztrán tér.

Church of St Mary Magdalene

Bridges

In 1870, when Gusztáv Zsigmondy was carrying out a survey of the Danube, he discovered, just north of today's Árpád Bridge, the sunken piles of a wooden Roman bridge. This was the first and only bridge in the vicinity of Budapest until the 19th century when Széchenyi lánchíd was constructed (*see pp70–71*).

Although Sigismund of Luxembourg and Matthias Corvinus seem to have planned stone bridges in the 15th century, nothing came of their projects. A pontoon was in operation by the beginning of the 16th century; Turkish engineers subsequently built a more sophisticated 70-drum version, roughly where the Elizabeth Bridge is now.

After the reconquest, an ingenious so-called 'flying bridge' was put into operation by the enterprising Viennese. It consisted of a catamaran that was attached to the banks by long ropes resting on barges. By manipulating the rudder, the boat could be made to swing from shore to shore, using the force of the current. It was in use until 1790, by which time an elegant 'swaying promenade' with 43 pontoons had been built. Opened at dawn and midday, it had to be dismantled in winter because of ice-floes. The municipal authorities would bed safe paths across the ice with straw, charging users double the pontoon toll (nobles, soldiers and students went free). During a big freeze, fairs and balls would be held on the river. The last ball (in 1883) ended in tragedy when the ice suddenly gave way, tipping the dance floor into the glacial waters and drowning 40 people.

Overview of Széchenyi Chain Bridge

Building and naming bridges

Since the first of Budapest's bridges in modern times was completed in 1848, nine more have been built within the city boundaries to relieve traffic congestion in the centre. The vicissitudes of history are reflected in the various name changes: today's 'Liberty Bridge' was planned as 'Customs House Square Bridge' but was inaugurated by the emperor himself as 'Franz Joseph Bridge'. The 'Chain Bridge' later became 'Széchenyi Chain Bridge' in honour of its originator, while 'Petőfi Bridge', to the south, bore the name of the interwar regent Miklós Horthy for a while.

The Árpád Bridge to the north was officially 'Stalin Bridge' in the 1950s, and reverted to its original name after the 1956 revolution. All Budapest's bridges had to be rebuilt after World War II, as they were blown up by the retreating Germans.

The government's decision to allow the public to choose the name for Budapest's newest bridge – the northern Megyeri híd built in 2008 to complete the M0 ring road – backfired spectacularly. With only a month of voting left, newswires reported that Chuck Norris was topping the polls. Stephen Colbert, the American TV satirist, then used his millions of viewers to hijack the vote. Colbert only rescinded his claim when the government informed him he had to speak fluent Hungarian and be dead in order for the bridge to be named after him.

Erzsébet híd (Elizabeth Bridge)

The 290m (951ft) suspension bridge was built between 1897 and 1903 and reconstructed to a modern design after World War II. Its structure weighs just over 1,000 tonnes, but carries 29 90-tonne components of carriageway. Building it entailed wholesale destruction of the medieval core of Pest – the Old Town Hall was demolished and the Inner City Parish Church only escaped thanks to vociferous popular protest.

Margit híd (Margaret Bridge)

A French engineer, Ernest Gouin, designed the second bridge to be built (1876) after the Chain Bridge (*see pp70–71*). To keep its two sections vertical to the current (divided here by Margaret Island) there is a 30-degree angle at the apex. A supplementary ramp (1900) leads down to the island.

Szabadság híd (Freedom Bridge)

An all-Hungarian effort in design and construction, this iron console bridge was inaugurated by Emperor Franz Joseph in 1896. The silver spike he ceremonially struck into the Pest abutment was stolen during the 1956 revolution. The Hungarian coat of arms is displayed on the central arches, topped by the mythical turul bird, supposed begetter of the Árpád dynasty.

BUDAVÁRI PALOTA (ROYAL PALACE)

Following the devastating Tartar invasions of 1240–41, King Béla IV decided to fortify the southern part of the Buda plateau, since the 11th century a defenceless agrarian settlement and part of Minor Pesth (Lesser Pest).

The castle remained modest until Louis the Great of Anjou moved his court here from Visegrád, probably in 1347. His successor, Sigismund of Luxembourg (1387–1437), built a new palace known as the Friss Palota (New Palace). Sigismund, son of Charles IV of Bohemia, scoured Europe for first-rate craftsmen whom he could lure to Buda. Various engineering projects were undertaken under Sigismund, including the building of a horse-driven pump to supply the palace with Danube water. He was also responsible for placing the vast chain across the river so as to ensure that before merchants went elsewhere they gave the people of the city a chance to buy their goods and thus earn an income for the city.

The golden age

The golden age of the court at Buda was that of King Matthias Corvinus (1458–90): his chapel was equipped with a water organ and his marvellous Bibliotheca Corviniana had 2,000 illuminated codices fastened to lecterns with golden chains. An army of craftsmen made beautiful ceramic stoves for the winter quarters, carved marble fireplaces and doorways, and gilded the coffered ceilings of sleeping chambers. Foreigners were duly impressed. An Italian wrote: 'In all Europe the three most beautiful cities are Venice on the sea, Buda on the hill and Florence on the plain.' Matthias's chief architect was in fact a Florentine, Chimenti Camicia; another great contemporary architect, Giovanni Dalmata (builder of the magnificent cathedral of Sibenik in Dalmatia), also worked for Matthias.

Decay and revival

During the 145-year-long Turkish occupation (1541–1686) the palace fell into decay. In 1678, lightning struck the gunpowder store, causing an explosion that destroyed most of the palace. After the reconquest of Hungary by the Habsburgs and their allies, Charles VI's and Maria Theresa's architects razed much of the Gothic and Renaissance remnants and built a small Baroque palace. No longer used as a royal

PALACE APPROACH

The Royal Palace can be approached from Szarvas tér in the south, which is reached by buses 86 (Buda side) and 5 or 78 (from Pest). Trams 18, 19, 41 stop at nearby Döbrentei tér. Leaving the Southern Rondella on your right, you pass through the Ferdinand Gate, close to the menacing Mace Tower. Access to the entrance to the Budapest History Museum is via walled gardens.

From the north, the palace may be reached using the *sikló* (funicular railway) from Clark Ádám tér, by bus 16 or bus 16A.

residence – at different times it housed a convent and a university – it was eventually turned over to the Austrian palatine (viceroy) in 1790.

After being damaged in the 1848 War of Independence, the palace enjoyed its last flowering after the Compromise with Austria of 1867. Miklós Ybl altered and enlarged the Baroque structure between 1869 and 1905. During the interwar period, the so-called Regent of Hungary, Admiral Horthy, installed himself here. In the closing days of World War II, the whole place was reduced to rubble by the Russian bombardment. Though it has since been rebuilt incorporating some relics of the earlier palaces, it lacks the grace and splendour of its predecessors.

Budapesti Történeti Múzeum (Historical Museum of the City of Budapest) Wing E
Remnants of the Old Palace

Descend the stairway from the ticket office for a tour through the layers of the Gothic and Renaissance castle. At the entrance are the coats of arms of the Árpáds, the Anjous, Matthias Corvinus and the Jagiellon dynasties.

Highlights include the Renaissance Hall, with a fragment of ceiling by Giovanni Dalmata, an imposing marble fireplace and reliefs of King Matthias and Queen Beatrice. You will also pass an ice-pit connected to the garden above by a chute, and the location of the cistern.

Further on are the former Queen's Quarters and the Royal Chapel of 1380

(the chapel's lower part was rededicated on 18 August 1990 as St Stephen's Chapel). From here, you will come to the large, partly Renaissance hall, where concerts are held.

Tel: (36 1) 487 8854. www.btm.hu. Open: Mar–Oct 10am–6pm; Nov–Feb 10am–4pm. Closed Mon. Admission charge but free on the 1st Sat of each month. For the topographical and 19th-century part of the museum, see Kiscelli Múzeum (p61).

Gothic statues from the Royal Palace

A special display has been created for the beautiful Gothic statues unearthed in 1974. They were made during the reign of Sigismund and appear to have been thrown into a builder's trench as rubble.

The rear courtyard of the Royal Palace complex, rebuilt after total devastation in World War II

The statues date to the third decade of the 15th century and fall into two categories, profane and sacred. Of the profane, some have lean, elegant features, and could be members of the Anjou dynasty with their ladies, and contemporary knights and bishops. Others in this category are foreshortened, suggesting that they were placed high up; they have rounder, more typically Magyar features. Figures in the sacred series have been identified as apostles or prophets.

The striking quality of these works is eloquent testimony to the wealth of Buda in the late Middle Ages, which could afford to employ the best European masters.

History of Budapest

The rest of the museum is a rather old-fashioned exhibition concerning the history and development of Buda and Pest from the Neanderthal period to the Romans (second floor) and from the Romans to the Magyar conquest (first floor). For the subsequent history of Budapest, you should visit the excellent Kiscelli Museum in Óbuda (*see p61*).

Magyar Nemzeti Galéria (Hungarian National Gallery) Wings A, B, C, D

The National Gallery and its 70,000 pieces were moved to the reconstructed Royal Palace in 1975. Only Hungarian works (or those executed in Hungary) are displayed here (European masters and other antiquities may be found in the Museum of Fine Arts, *see p99*).

Permanent displays

• Medieval and Renaissance sculpture, including relics of the old Buda and Visegrád palaces – ground floor.
• Gothic wooden sculpture and panel painting from the 14th and 15th centuries, mostly from Upper Hungary (now Slovakia) – ground floor.
• Late Gothic triptychs, including a celebrated *Annunciation* (1506) by Master MS – first floor.

Late-Gothic triptychs in the Hungarian National Gallery

- Baroque art, dominated by Austrian artists who gained commissions in Hungary in the wake of the Counter-Reformation – first floor.
- Hungarian painting and sculpture of the 19th century. Look out for the charming Biedermeier genre and landscape paintings by Miklós Barabás, and the scenes from Hungarian history (works by Gyula Benczúr and Viktor Madarász) – first floor. In another wing (first floor) are Hungarian Post-Impressionists and rooms devoted to the most successful Magyar painter ever, Mihály Munkácsy.
- Hungarian painting and sculpture of the 20th century. The highlights here are the dreamlike work of Tivadar Csontváry Kosztka, the pointillism of József Rippl-Rónai and, especially, the output of the *plein-air* artists' colony at Nagybánya. Károly Ferenczy's *October* is perhaps the loveliest picture in the gallery – second floor.

The Palatinal Crypt

Every hour you can join a guided tour to see the vaulted crypt and sarcophagus of the popular palatine, Archduke Joseph of Habsburg. The crypt is the only section of Buda Castle that did not need reconstruction following the devastation of World War II.

Magyar Nemzeti Galéria (Hungarian National Gallery). Open: Tue–Sun 10am–6pm. Admission charge (free on 15 Mar, 20 Aug, 23 Oct). For English-speaking guides: Tel: (36) 20 439 7326. www.mng.hu

Monuments around the Royal Palace

In front of the palace's main entrance is József Róna's equestrian statue of Prince Eugene of Savoy, the hero of the Turkish wars, built in 1900. Emperor Franz Joseph paid for its erection after the town that had commissioned it (Zenta) ran out of money.

To the north is Gyula Donáth's *Turul Bird* (1903), the mythical begetter of the Árpád line of kings. In the western courtyard is Alajos Stróbl's *Matthias Fountain*, a sculptural representation of a ballad by Mihály Vörösmarty, which tells the story of 'beautiful Ilonka', who met and fell in love with King Matthias when he was out hunting incognito. She pined away and died when she realised that her love was hopeless.

Next to the fountain is György Vastagh's lively sculpture showing a *puszta* cowboy breaking in a horse.

Országos Széchenyi Könyvtár (Széchenyi National Library) Wing F

The library was founded in 1802 by Count Ferenc Széchenyi, father of the reform politician István Széchenyi. By law it receives a copy of every Hungarian book or journal and also collects scholarly works about Hungary. *Szent György tér 2. Tel: (36 1) 224 3700. Guided tours tel: (36 1) 224 3745. www.oszk.hu. Open: Tue–Sat 10am–9pm. Reader's ticket required. Check website for specials collections' availability.*

Walk: Rózsadomb and Víziváros

At the turn of the 20th century, elegant villas were built on the Rózsadomb (Hill of Roses), while the Víziváros (Water Town), so called for being constantly flooded, was settled by craftsmen and fishermen in the Middle Ages.

Allow 2½ hours. Start from the western end of the Margaret Bridge (Margit híd) and make your way to Frankel Leó útca via Vidra útca.

1 Lukács Gyogyfürdő and Malomtó

At Frankel Leó útca 25–27 is the Lukács spa (*see p53*) with a pleasant tree-shaded courtyard. Across the street is a ruined Turkish gunpowder mill and a millpond (Malomtó). If you walk through to the back of Lukács and turn left, you can see the Turkish Császár Bath, built by Pasha Sokollu in 1570. *Turn up Gül Baba útca at the junction of Török útca and Frankel Leó útca. Turn left up the steps.*

2 Gül Baba türbéje

This tomb of a famous Dervish scholar (*see pp53–4*) is reputedly the most northerly Muslim shrine in Europe. It is customary to remove your shoes before entering. There is a lovely view of Pest from here. *Climb up to the junction of Gül Baba útca and Vérhalom útca. Make your way down Apostol útca to Rómer Flóris útca, across Margit körút and along Fekete Sas útca.*

3 Bem szobor (József Bem Monument)

The Polish general Bem fought for the Hungarians in the 1848 War of Independence.

4 Flórián kápolna

The Baroque chapel of St Florian (1760) is nearby at Fő útca 90; peer

Statue of General Bem

through the glass entrance to see the frescoes and a finely carved pulpit.

5 Király Gyógyfürdő

These baths (*see p53*) were built for the garrison under the Turkish occupation. In the dimly lit interior the play of light beams in the rising steam is an aesthetic experience. The baths are a centre of the Budapest gay scene.

6 Öntödei Múzeum (Foundry Museum)

A sign next to the baths points to this unusual, wooden-roofed museum. The exhibits deal with metal working from the Bronze Age to that of steel.
Bem József útca 20. Tel: (36 1) 201 4370. www.omm.hu/ontode. Open: Tue–Sun 9am–5pm.
Return to Fő útca and continue south past the grim military prison (Nos 70–74) and Nagy Imre tér.

7 Batthyány tér

The Szent Erzsébet templom (Church of the Elizabethan Nuns) is on your left, just before the square. Their charitable tradition is maintained in the old people's home now occupying their convent. On the right is the rococo inn, at the Sign of the White Cross, behind which the post-chaise used to leave for Vienna. Szent Anna templom (St Anne's Church, *see pp56–7*) is to the south. Next to it is the Angelika coffee house (*see p166*), sometimes described as the favourite rendezvous for the 'society of old hens'.

8 Batthyány tér to Clark Ádám tér

Further along Fő útca is the Szilágyi Dezső teri templom (Calvinist Church) designed by Samu Pecz, whose statue stands beside it. Beyond it is the former Alsóvizivárosi plébánia templom (Capuchin Church) (*No 32*). Opposite the neoclassical No 20 is the graceful post-modernist Francia Kultúra Intézete (French Institute, built in 1992).
The siklό up to Buda Castle and buses for Pest and Buda leave from Clark Ádám tér.

Walk: Rózsadomb and Víziváros

Walk: Tabán and Gellért hegy

On this walk, the self-confident architectural elegance of the 19th century is interspersed with glimpses of a turbulent past.

Allow 2 hours.

Begin at Clark Ádám tér, reached by buses 16 and 105 from Pest or bus 86 along Fő útca on the Buda side.

1 Clark Ádám tér

The square, situated at the western end of the Széchenyi lánchíd (Chain Bridge, *see pp70–71*), is named after the bridge's Scottish builder. The northern side is flanked by two fine blocks made by Miklós Ybl (1814–91). In front of the funicular railway (*sikló*) up to the castle is the kilometre stone, whence all distances from the capital are measured. *Walk 100m (110yds) along Lánchíd útca. On your right you come to the Várbazár.*

Statue of Queen Elizabeth

2 Várbazár

This park complex of steps and terraces was designed by Miklós Ybl to link the castle with the Danube shore. Across the street is a statue of Ybl in front of the Kiosk (now the Vákert Casino, *www.vakert.com*), which he built in neo-Renaissance style to camouflage the castle's water-pumping station. *Continue south into Apród útca.*

3 Semmelweis Orvostörténeti Múzeum (Semmelweis Museum of Medicine)

At Apród útca 1–3 is the neoclassical house of the Semmelweis Museum of Medicine (*see p61*), named after the discoverer of puerperal fever, who was born here.

4 Török sírok (Turkish Graves)

Take the steps leading up between the museum and another Ybl-designed house where Adam Clark died. *From here, walk back southwards, passing the Aranyszarvas Étterem*

(Golden Stag) restaurant in a simple Baroque building.

5 Tabáni plébániatemplom (Tabán Parish Church)

The Tabán was a lively area of pubs and traders until its demolition in 1930. The parish church of St Catherine survives at Attila útca 11.

6 Erzsébet Királynö szobra (Statue of Queen Elizabeth)

South of the church is the monument to Emperor Franz Joseph's wife, the pro-Hungarian Elizabeth of Bavaria. A plaque recalls that the previous monument on this site, to the pro-fascist politician Gyula Gömbös, was blown up by the Communist resistance in 1944. *Make your way under the spaghetti junction to the steps at the foot of the Gellért Hill.*

7 Gellért emlékmű (Gellért Monument)

A stairway leads to this memorial (*see p66*) to the missionary St Gellért (Gerard of Csanád), allegedly martyred here. There is also a scenic waterfall.

8 Szabadság emlékmű (Freedom Monument)

The steep climb to the top of the hill is rewarded with stunning views. On the summit is the Freedom Monument (*see pp66–7*). The heroic Russian soldiers have been removed, leaving only an allegorical female figure and pieces of the permanent exhibition of military history.

9 Citadella (Citadel)

Above the monument is the Citadella, built by the Austrians in 1854 as barracks and fortress from which to keep a vigil on the unruly inhabitants of Budapest. It now has shops, a restaurant, a hotel and viewing terrace. *Descend through a pleasant park past the Gellérthegyi Sziklakápolna rock chapel (see p121) to the Gellért spa (gyógyfürdő) and the buses and trams on Szent Gellért tér.*

Walk: Tabán and Gellért hegy

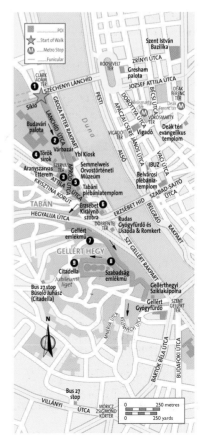

BUDA BATHS

There are many public baths in Buda and these have good facilities, interesting historical features and architectural charm. Admission charges work on a deposit system; part of it returned depending on length of stay; keep the receipt carefully.

The general website for the Budapest baths is *www2.budapestgyogyfurdoi.hu*

Gellért Gyógyfürdő (Gellért Spa)

The Buda spa most popular with visitors is where the earliest inhabitants exploited the mineral springs of the Gellért Hill; later, the poor of Buda bathed here (and watered their horses) during the Turkish occupation.

The present establishment goes back to a decision of the city council in 1901 to purchase the land and exploit the springs, whose outlet had been covered over when the Szabadság híd (Freedom Bridge) was built in 1896. Plans for a hotel and spa were finally approved in 1909. The building was completed and opened in 1918.

The architecture is in an agreeably over-the-top version of Jugendstil. The main indoor pool presents a fantasia of mosaics, columns and gargoyles. The entrance hall recalls the grandiosity of the Caracalla Baths in Rome.
XI, Kelenhegyi útca 2–4.
Tel: (36 1) 466 6166. Open: daily 6am–8pm; July–mid-Aug Fri & Sat 8pm–

The wave bath of Buda's most popular spa, the Gellért

midnight (with music). Treatment and therapies are available at slightly different times. Admission charge. Tram: 47, 49 and Bus: 7 (from Pest); Tram: 18, 19, 41 and Bus: 86 (from Buda).

Király Gyógyfürdő (King Spa)

The bath, built by Pasha Mustapha Sokollu, was completed in 1578. There was no thermal spring nearby, so water was piped in from the Lukács area.

The bath had several owners after the reconquest of 1686, the last (1796) being a certain Ferenc König (Király in Hungarian), from whom it takes its name. A charming neoclassical wing was added to the Ottoman baths in 1826 and the hydraulic system was renewed in 2007. (See p49.)
II, Fő útca 84. Tel: (36 1) 202 3688. Open: for men Tue, Thur, Fri & Sat 8am–8pm; for women Mon & Wed 8am–8pm; mixed Sun 8am–8pm. Last entry one hour before closing. Admission charge. Metro: M2 to Batthyány tér.

Lukács Gyógyfürdő (St Luke Spa)

Under the Turks, the spring here was used to drive a gunpowder mill, although a hospital spa named after St Luke had occupied the site of the present baths in the Middle Ages.

Lukács is an oasis of calm and charm with its outdoor pools in a huge courtyard under the shade of ancient plane trees. The clientele is intellectual and professional, and gossip as important here as bathing. (See p48.)

II, Frankel Leó útca 25–29. Tel: (36 1) 326 1695. Open: Mon–Sat 6am–7pm, Sun 6am–5pm. Admission charge. Tram: 17 (from Buda).

Rudas Gyógyfürdő és Uszoda (Rudas Spa & Turkish Bath)

Rudas' centrepiece, the fabulous Turkish bath, was built in the 16th century during the Ottoman occupation. The stunning 10m (33ft) dome is supported by eight pillars, underneath which is the octagonal pool that has been a men-only enclave since 1936. Today, however, women are allowed to use the pool on Tuesdays, and weekends are a mixed bag – when swimsuits are compulsory.
I, Döbrentei tér 9. Tel: (36 1) 356 1322. Open: daily 6am–6pm. Turkish vapour bath open: Mon–Fri 8am–8pm, men only (except Tue women only); mixed sessions Sat & Sun 6am–5pm; Fri & Sat 10pm–4am, mixed with music. Admission charge. Tram: 18, 19; Bus: 7, 86, 173 to the Buda bridgehead of Erzsébet híd.

CHURCHES AND CEMETERIES
Gül Baba türbéje (Tomb of Gül Baba)

The only significant Turkish monument to survive in Budapest, other than baths, is the tomb of Gül Baba, situated in a sunken rose garden at the top of the cobbled Gül Baba útca on Rózsadomb.

Gül Baba was a dervish, a luminary of the Bektashi mendicant order whose

Spa city

The spas of Buda and Pest evoke memories of a leisured age

In the prehistory of Buda, hundreds of spring-fed streams trickled off the hills into a riparian swamp, and thence into the Danube. When the Celtic Eravisci arrived, they occupied the Gellért Hill and, probably, other parts of the west bank. When the Romans took over, they retained the picturesque name the Celts had given to their settlement – Ak-Ink, meaning 'Abundant Waters' – and Latinised it to Aquincum.

There is still a Római fürdő (Roman bath) near the ruins of Aquincum, one of three fed by a source at nearby Csillaghegy. It seems that the Magyars, too, exploited the waters, for the newcomers divided Buda into areas known as Felsőhévíz (Upper Thermal Waters) and Alsóhévíz (Lower Thermal Waters).

In the Middle Ages, at least two hospitals based on spas were founded (at today's Gellért and Lukács baths) by the Knights Hospitallers of St John. For the Turks, bathing had a ritual significance and between 1541 and 1686 numerous Turkish baths were built; they remain today as almost the sole architectural and cultural legacy of Ottoman rule.

Budapest was officially designated a spa city in 1934 by the International Spa Congress (which subsequently moved its headquarters to the city). It certainly deserves the title, for there are 123 springs in Buda, Óbuda and Pest, spouting an estimated 70 million litres (15.4 million gallons) of water daily and supplying 47 baths, of which 12 have extensive medical facilities. The water temperature varies between 24°C and 78°C (75–172°F). Many of the springs are sulphurous or slightly radioactive: they are used to treat rheumatism, circulation disorders and gynaecological complaints.

Budapest baths have something for everybody: there are open-air and sports pools, artificial wave baths and bubble baths, medicinal and mud baths, warm, cool and Turkish baths. All those pounds put on from consumption of heavy Magyar dishes can (theoretically) be lost again in the city's 'abundant waters'.

For specific bath descriptions, see listings (pp52–3). For complete details of all Budapest's lovely bath houses, see www.budapestgyogyfurdoi.hu

One of the city's many baths

Springtime brings the city's parks into bloom

members cultivated the arts and engaged in agriculture in time of peace, but were ready to die as martyrs (*ghazi*) in time of war. He died during a thanksgiving service for the conquest of Buda, held in the Matthias Church (hastily transformed into a mosque) on Friday 2 September 1541. The Sultan himself is said to have been among the pallbearers as this distinguished Islamic scholar was laid to rest. Hungarians later credited him with the introduction of rose cultivation in Hungary. Later still, he entered popular mythology as a harmless figure of fun (he crops up in this role in an operetta by Jenő Huszka based on a story by Mór Jókai). The tomb was built on the orders of the pasha between 1543 and 1548. It is a modest octagonal building with a hemispherical copper dome topped by a crescent moon.

Originally, this was a place of pilgrimage for pious Muslims and there was also a *tekke* (monastery) next to it. The Jesuits turned it into a chapel in 1689 and kept it until their dissolution in 1773. The Turkish government acquired the shrine in 1885 and donated some of the furniture – the rest has been given by Hungarian Muslims. (*See p48.*)
II, Mecset útca 14. Tel: (36 1) 326 0062.
www.btm.hu/turbe/turbe.htm.
Open: Jan–Apr daily 10am–6pm;
May–Sept Tue–Sun 10am–6pm; Oct
Tue–Sun 10am–5pm; Nov–Dec daily
10am–4pm. Admission charge. Tram: 4,
6 to Márgit híd budai hídfő, then a short
walk uphill; or Bus: 191 from Nyugati
pályaudvar (M3) to Apostol útca,
then downhill.

Óbudai plébániatemplom (Óbuda Parish Church)

Károly Bebó is responsible for much of the notable interior of the charming Baroque church of St Peter and St Paul in Óbuda. The carved pulpit is especially fine rococo work, with depictions of the Good Shepherd, Mary Magdalene and allegories of Faith, Hope and Charity. (*See p65.*)
II, Lajos útca 168. Tel: (36 1) 368 6424.
HÉV: to Árpád híd; or Tram: 1 to
Szentlélek tér.

Szent Anna templom (St Anne's Church)

The original architect of the city's best-loved Baroque church (1761) is unknown, but the design is clearly Italianate. Above the doorway are sculptures representing Faith, Hope and Charity; further up are St Anne with Mary, the Buda coat of arms and a golden eye of God with angels. Inside, note the neo-Baroque ceiling frescoes by Pál C Molnár (1938) and the graceful pulpit by Károly Bebó.

II, Batthyány tér 7.
Tel: (36 1) 201 3404. Metro: M2 to Batthyány tér.

GARDENS AND PARKS
Európa liget (Europa Park)

This pleasant grove lies close to Ostrom útca below Bécsi kapu (Vienna Gate) on Castle Hill. In 1972, 100 years after the unification of Buda, Óbuda and Pest, mayors from various cities round the world planted trees here.

Bus: 16 from Moszkva tér or Deák Ferenc tér to Bécsi kapu tér.

Jubileumi liget, Gellért hegy (Jubilee Park on Gellért Hill)

On the southwestern side of the hill, below the Citadella and the Freedom Monument, the Jubilee Park was laid out in 1967 to mark the passage of 50 years since the Russian Revolution. The park is a delightful place for walking.

XI, Bus: 27 from Móricz Zsigmond körtér, Villányi útca to the stop Búsuló Juhász, then a 400m (440yd) walk. Or take Tram: 18, 19, 47, 49 or Bus: 86 to Szent Gellért tér and hike up.

Margit sziget (Margaret Island)

Margit sziget is named after Béla IV's daughter, who retired to a convent here. The Turks found the sanctuary a conveniently secure place to keep the pasha's harem. Palatine Joseph acquired possession in 1796, built a villa here and laid out a fine park with a rose garden. In 1869, it was opened to the public and became a favourite excursion area for Budapestians. The Habsburg governors sold it to the city in 1908. (*See pp58–9.*)

Bus: 26 from Nyugati pályaudvar.
Tram: 4, 6.

Inside Óbuda Parish Church

Buda

Walk: Margit sziget

Margit sziget (Margaret Island) is Budapest's loveliest park, with a history stretching back to Roman times. Originally, it was three islands, the largest of which (Rabbit Island) was long a royal hunting estate. Margaret was the daughter of King Béla IV. She retreated to a convent here in 1252, when only nine years old.

Allow 1½ hours.

The walk begins at the southern end of the island, reached by bus 26 from the east side of Margit híd (Margaret Bridge). Alight at the first stop on the island or take tram 4 or 6 to Margit híd and head north.

1 Centenáriumi emlékmű (Centennial Monument)

The large fountain, colourfully lit at night, was erected in 1972. It commemorates the centenary of the unification of Buda, Pest and Óbuda in 1872–73. A large restaurant, terrace, casino and stage are on the right.
Walk straight on, to the swimming pools on your left.

2 and 3 Hajós-Alfréd Sport Uszoda and Palatinus Strandfürdő

Serious swimmers can enjoy the massive indoor pool of the Hajós Baths, named after the gold medallist at the 1896 Athens Olympics. Hajós was also a successful architect and designed the pool and the building in 1930.

On the way to the Palatinus open-air baths and slides (which have a mechanism for making artificial waves), you pass through the attractive Rózsakert (Rose Garden).

4 Ferences kolostor romjai

Between the baths is a ruined Franciscan church dating from 1272. Palatine (viceroy) Joseph's splendid villa built next to the chapel in 1796 was destroyed in the 1838 flood. The archduke encouraged development of the island's spa and laid out gardens, but the public were not allowed in until 1869. There is a small zoo with birds of prey as well as chickens, deer and more.

The island boasts a gorgeous Japanese garden

Tel: (36 1) 474 2220. Open: mid-Apr–Oct 10am–6pm.
Wind your way past the open-air baths.

5 Dominikánus kolostor romjai/ Szabadtéri színpad

Northeast of the Palatinus Baths are the ruins of the Dominican convent where St Margaret lived a life of daunting asceticism (even washing was viewed with suspicion). Not far to the west is a water tower you can climb and an open-air stage used for opera performances in summer.

6 Szent Mihály templom (St Michael's Church)

To the northeast is the reconstructed Romanesque church of St Michael, which was built in 1930 using materials from the original 12th-century Premonstratensian church (the ruins of the Premonstratensian convent are nearby). In the church is a 15th-century bell, discovered in 1914 under a tree that had blown down in a storm. The monks had probably buried it before the arrival of the Turks to prevent it being melted down to make cannons.

7 Sculpture Avenue

Along the promenade to the Danubius Grand Hotel are busts of Hungary's greatest painters, poets and musicians. Among them is the 19th-century poet János Arany, who liked to sit under the island's trees in the evening composing his romantic lyrics.

8 Grand Hotel, Health Spa Resort

The beautifully restored Grand Hotel, designed by Miklós Ybl, is a true reflection of a more leisurely age and contrasts with the ugly Health Spa Resort; to the west is a charming Japanese garden.

At the northern end of the island, bus 26 can be boarded again either to Árpád híd metro (Pest side) or to Nyugati pályaudvar metro via Margit híd (Buda side). Otherwise climb on to Árpád híd for bus 106 to Árpád híd metro (Pest side) or further afield to Óbuda and Aquincum.

Walk: Margit sziget

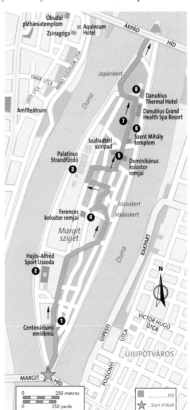

Millenáris park (Millennium Park)

The former industrial area of the Ganz-Fabrik was converted in 2001 to this lovely modern park and exhibition halls – an example of new city development.

II, Between Margit körút and Marczibányi tér (Buda side) behind the Mammut shopping mall.
www.millenaris.hu. Metro: Moszkva tér. Tram: 4, 6 to Szena tér.

Vérmező (Field of Blood)

The leader of the Jacobin conspiracy of 1795, Ignác Martinovics, was executed here, hence the name. The meadow on the western side of Buda Castle covers the site of a medieval village.
Bus: 5 from Március 15 tér.

MUSEUMS

Many of Budapest's more than 40 museums are in buildings of architectural interest. Museums in the complex of the Budavári Palota (Royal Palace) are dealt with on *pp44–7*. Many museums are closed on Monday and have free admission for the permanent exhibitions (but charge for temporary exhibitions).

Bartók Emlékház (Béla Bartók Memorial House)

The composer Béla Bartók (1881–1945) lived in this villa from 1932 until his escape from Hungary in 1940. In the garden is a life-size statue of him by Imre Varga. Bartók's furniture has been reinstated in the rooms, together with some of his collection of Hungarian ceramics and textiles. The former living room, with its painted wooden ceiling, is used for concerts.
II, Csalán útca 29. Tel: (36 1) 394 2100. www.bartokmuseum.hu. Open: Tue–Sun

Margaret Island is a popular recreational area

*10am–5pm. Admission charge. Bus: 5, 29
to Pasaréti tér, then 10 minute walk.*

Anyone interested in Bartók's
collaborator in the work of collecting
Hungarian folk music can visit the
Kodály Zoltán Emlékmúzeum (Zoltán
Kodály Memorial Museum, *see p100*).

Hadtörténeti Múzeum (Museum of Military History)

Based in the former Palatine Barracks
on Castle Hill, the display includes
rooms devoted to the War of
Independence (1848–49), World War I
and the 1956 revolution.
*I, Toth Árpád sétany 40.
Tel: (36 1) 356 9522. www.militaria.hu.
Open: Tue–Sun 10am–6pm, except
Oct–Mar closes at 4pm. Admission
charge. Bus: 16 from Moszkva tér or
Deák Ferenc tér to Bécsi kapu tér.*

Kiscelli Múzeum (Kiscelli Museum)

The most enjoyable of Budapest's
history museums chronicles the ages of
the city in displays combining nostalgia
with scholarship. A section on printing
shows the machine that printed Sándor
Petőfi's National Song, which roused
the populace in the 1848 revolution. It
is also worth lingering over the
paintings, mostly by 19th- and early
20th-century Hungarian masters.
(*See p63.*)
*III, Kiscelli útca 108. Tel: (36 1) 388 7817.
www.btmfk.iif.hu. Open: Tue–Sun
10am–4pm. Admission charge. Tram: 17;
Bus: 165 to Remetehegyi útca.*

Semmelweis Orvostörténeti Múzeum (Semmelweis Museum of Medicine)

Named after Ignác Semmelweis
(1818–65), the 'Saviour of Mothers',
whose father had a grocery shop here,
the museum has a fascinating display
on the history of medicine. There is
also a complete neoclassical pharmacy
designed by Mihály Pollack. (*See p50.*)
*I, Apród útca 1–3. Tel: (36 1) 375 3533.
www.semmelweis.museum.hu.
Open: Tue–Sun 10.30am–6pm,
until 4pm Nov–mid-Mar. Admission
charge. Bus: 5, 86 to Szarvas tér;
Tram: 18, 19, 41.*

ROMAN REMAINS

In the 1st century AD the Romans
created a garrison named Aquincum.
An outpost across the Danube was
known as Contra Aquincum (*see p84*).
The military camp, on what is now
Flórián tér (Óbuda), had its own baths
and a huge amphitheatre with seating
for 15,000. The civilian town was 2km
(1¼ miles) to the north and there were
other strategic *castra* and watchtowers,
components of the famous defensive
system along the Danube known as
'the limes'.

Aquincum

The town was a Pannonian Celtic
settlement named Ak-Ink (Abundant
Waters) and the Romans Latinised the
name to Aquincum. It originally existed
to service the military – in every sense
of the word. Including numerous

Buda

brothels and pubs, the extensive rest-and-recreation areas that surrounded the military *castrum* were collectively known as *canabae*.

At the beginning of the 2nd century, Trajan enhanced Aquincum's status by making it the provincial capital of Pannonia Inferior. Hadrian raised it to a *municipium* in AD 124, and in 194, under Septimius Severus, it became a *colonia*. The Roman governor (*legatus*) established his residence on the adjacent Óbuda Island.

Aquincum flourished during the 2nd and 3rd centuries, partly due to its proximity to the amber trade route that ran from the Baltic through western Hungary to Aquilea on the Adriatic. Decline set in during the 4th century, at the end of which Rome was forced to make concessions to the Huns and withdraw from the area.

An excellent publication in English detailing all these sights is the *Pannonia Hungaria Antiqua* (*Archaeolingua*). www.aquincum.hu

Sights of Aquincum

Substantial ruins of Aquincum remain, indicating the prosperity of a city numbering 40,000 inhabitants who enjoyed the benefits of an efficient water supply, sewage disposal and hypocaust heating. There were warm and cold baths, and houses were decorated with frescoes, mosaics and stucco. In the open-air part of the site are remnants of a forum, law courts, dwelling houses

Roman column

and religious (including Christian) sanctuaries.

Aquincum Museum contains everyday objects, either made locally or imported via the Rhine and the Danube from Germania and Gaul. Its star attraction is an organ worked by water pressure, a unique survival from Roman times.

Aquincum Museum, Szentendrei útca 135. Tel: (36 1) 250 1650. Open: May–Sept Tue–Sun 10am–6pm; Oct & end of Apr 10am–5pm; Nov–mid Apr 10am–4pm. The ruins open an hour earlier than the museum all year round except Nov–mid Apr when the ruins are closed. HÉV: to Aquincum; Bus: 34, 106 from Árpád híd metro (Pest side).

Remains around Aquincum

South of Aquincum is Óbuda, home to the so-called Herkules Villa, notable for mosaics depicting the labours of Hercules and Dionysian rites (wine production was encouraged in Pannonia from the 3rd century). One vivid scene shows Hercules about to loose an arrow at a centaur abducting a curvaceous nymph.

Nearby are the remains of a *cella trichora*, an early Christian chapel on a clover-leaf ground plan. It dates to the 4th century and was probably built over a martyr's grave. (For more on the Roman remains at Óbuda, *see pp30–31*.)

Herkules Villa: Meggyfa útca 19–21. Tel: (36 1) 250 1650. All visits must be made by prior arrangement. Open:

Oct Tue–Sun 10am– 5pm; May–Sept Tue–Sun 10am–6pm. Closed: Nov–Apr. Bus: 86, 109, 206 to Bogdáni útca.

The cella trichora *(view from exterior only), at the junction of Hunor and Raktár útca. Bus: 6, 84, 86; Tram: 1 to Flórián tér.*

Military Baths Museum: Flórián tér 3–5. Tel: (36 1) 250 1650. Open: Tue–Sun 10am–5pm, until 6pm in summer. Bus: 86, 109, 206; Tram: 1 to Flórián tér. Táborvárosi Múzeum (Roman Camp Museum): Pacsirtamező útca 63. Tel: (36 1) 250 1650. Open: Tue–Sun 10am–6pm: Closed: Nov–mid-Apr.

Just to the north of Aquincum are the remains of an aqueduct and of the civil amphitheatre, which is only half the size of the military one.

STATUES AND MONUMENTS

No free-standing monument from the Middle Ages has survived in Budapest, and most of those of the Baroque age have been taken to the Kiscelli Museum in order to conserve them. Today, the visitor sees mainly 19th- and 20th-century statuary, the best of it nobly commemorating men worthy of honour, the worst of it (socialist realism) now mostly consigned to the new park of Communist monuments near Nagytétény (*see pp136–7*). Described here are Buda's monuments of historical and/or aesthetic interest, although others are covered elsewhere, such as the Royal Palace (*see pp44–7*). For statues and monuments in Pest, *see pp72–114*.

Walk: Óbuda

High-rise blocks have ruined this once delightful area in District III, but there are still a few pockets of historic interest and charm that make this a lovely walk.

Allow 2 hours, or 3 hours if the Kiscelli Museum is included.

Take bus 29, 86, 109, 206 or the HÉV railway to Tímár útca, and walk back south.

1 Amfiteátrum

This Roman arena was built for the military in the 2nd century and could accommodate 15,000 spectators. According to the medieval epic *Das Nibelungenlied*, Attila the Hun ruled from 'Etzilburg', sometimes identified with this amphitheatre.

A longish detour is required for the Kiscelli Museum (*see p61*).

Turn right for Lajos útca and right again along Tímár útca. You emerge on a green

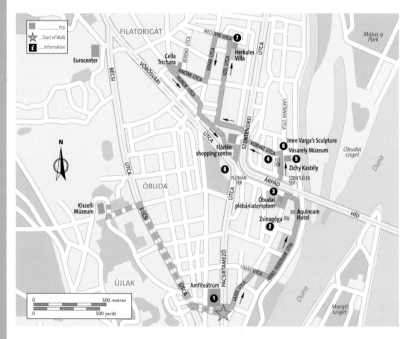

sward bordered by Lajos útca and Árpád fejedelem útja.

2 Zsinagóga

The fine neoclassical building of this former synagogue at Lajos útca 163 was designed by András Landherr in 1825 for the growing Jewish community.
Continue north and bear left before you reach the bridge.

3 Óbudai plébániatemplom (Óbuda Parish Church)

In front of the church (*see p56*) is a lawn and chestnut avenue lined with sandstone statues. The church stands on the site of the Roman military camp. The tomb of Count Peter Zichy, who was given the lands of Óbuda by the king following the expulsion of the Turks, lies beneath the pulpit.
Cross under Árpád Bridge to Fő tér.

4 Fő tér

The main square of Óbuda is flanked by Baroque houses. At No 4 is a collection of folk artefacts that comprises the Zsigmond Kun Collection and No 1 is the Óbudai Museum.
Zsigmond Kun Collection (Lakasmúzeum): Tel: (36 1) 386 1138. Open: Tue–Fri 2–6pm, Sat–Sun 10am–6pm. Óbudai Múzeum: Tel: (36 1) 250 1020). www.museum.hu/budapest/obudai. Open: Tue–Sun 10am–6pm.

5 Zichy Kastély (Zichy Mansion)

This Baroque family home was built in 1757. It contains the Lajos Kassák

Memorial Rooms, dedicated to Hungary's greatest avant-garde artist and writer. Adjoining it is the Vasarely Museum with art by Viktor Vasarely.
Kassák Múzeum: Tel: (36 1) 368 7021. www.museum.hu/budapest/kassak. Open: Wed–Sun 10am–5pm. Vasarely Múzeum: Szentlélek tér 6. Tel: (36 1) 388 7551. www.vasarely.tvn.hu. Open: Tue–Sun 10am–5.30pm.

6 Imre Varga's Sculpture

At the corner of Laktanya útca is *Strollers in the Rain*, Imre Varga's sculpture of ladies with umbrellas, which heralds the entrance to the Imre Varga Collection.
Tel: (36 1) 250 0274. Open: Tue–Sun 10am–6pm. Admission charge. Walk along Kórház útca, pass beneath Szentendrei útca and turn right along Szél útca to the Herkules Villa.

7 Herkules Villa

Covered in a blue awning, the Herkules Villa, at Meggyfa útca 21, evidently belonged to a well-to-do Roman. From the same period are the remains of a rare *cella trichora* (clover-leaf chapel) at the junction of Hunor útca and Raktár útca. (*See also p63.*)
Continue along Hunor útca to Flórián tér.

8 Flórián tér

The underpass and adjacent park area have many Roman pieces on show.
Trams run to Pest, or return to Szentlélek tér for buses to Buda and Pest.

Walk: Óbuda

Gellért emlékmű
(Gellért Monument)

On a dramatic site overlooking the Elizabeth Bridge rises the 6.76m (22ft) bronze statue of Hungary's first missionary. Gyula Jankovics' work (1904) is supposedly situated near the spot where Gellért was either hurled to his death or rolled into the Danube, nailed inside a barrel (versions differ). St Gellért (Gerard Sagredo) was born in Venice around 980 and martyred in 1046. He tutored King Stephen's son Emeric, and was made Bishop of Csanád in 1030. (*See p51.*)
XI, Bus: 5, 78, 86 or Tram: 18, 19 to Szarvas tér.

Kodály Zoltán szobor
(Statue of Zoltán Kodály)

In a grove on the northeast slopes of Castle Hill is Imre Varga's remarkable bronze (1982) of the composer Zoltán Kodály (1882–1967), which has been likened to pop art. Varga is a prolific creator of modern public monuments, highly naturalistic, and often with a touch of humour.
I, Europapark. Bus: 16A from Moszkva tér to Bécsi kapu tér.

Raoul Wallenberg emlékmű
(Raoul Wallenberg Monument)

Another bronze by Imre Varga (1987) is a belated tribute to the 'righteous Gentile' who saved thousands of Budapest Jews in 1944 by issuing them with Swedish ID cards. He probably died in a Russian gulag after the war.

Szilágyi Erzsébet fasor. Tram: 61 from Moszkva tér to Nagyajtai útca.

Szabadság emlékmű
(Freedom Monument)

As soon as the Russians had 'liberated' Budapest (and Vienna) they hastened to erect monuments in prominent places so that a grateful public should keep their contribution permanently in mind; the Freedom (formerly 'Liberation') Monument (1947) can be seen from most of Pest and much of Buda. Ironically, Zsigmond Kisfaludy-Stróbl's work was originally intended to honour Admiral Horthy's son, a pilot killed in a crash thought to have been engineered by the Germans. The addition of a Soviet soldier holding the red flag and one or two other touches adroitly made the iconographical switch from Horthyism to Communism. The massive female figure holding aloft a palm branch is

St Gellért (Gerard Sagredo), first missionary to Hungary

still there, but the Soviet soldier has gone, following the collapse of Communism. (*See p51.*)
I, Gellért hegy. Bus: 27 from Moricz Zsigmond korter, Villanyi útca to the stop Busuló Juhász, and then a 400m (440yd) walk.

Szoborpark (Sculpture Park)

The outlying new home for the city's Communist statuary (*see pp136–7*).
*Balatoni/corner XXII, Szabadkai útca. Tel: (36 1) 424 7500.
www.szoborpark.hu. Open: daily 10am–dusk. Admission charge. Tram: 4 to Fehérvári útca or Tram: 18, 41, 47 to Bocskai útca, then Bus: 150 from the corner of these two streets to Memento Park (30 minutes). Budapest local tickets and passes are valid. Or take Bus: 7E, 141, 173E to Kelenföldi pályaudvar then hop on Volánbusz Nos 710, 720, 721, 722 to Memento Park (10 minutes). You must buy a ticket for these yellow Volánbusz suburban buses at the station because Budapest local tickets, day passes and the Budapest Card are not valid on their routes. There is also an expensive but direct transfer bus from Déak Ferenc tér daily at 11am (also Jul–Aug 3pm).*

VIEWS FROM BUDA
Budai hegység (Buda Hills)

Just beyond Rózsadomb (Hill of Roses) is the lookout tower on József hegy, with one of the best upstream views of the Danube (take bus 191 from Nyugati pályaudvar to the end stop – Sarolta útca). The Árpád torony on Látó hegy

(bus 11 from Batthyány tér to Nagybányai útca, the end stop) is a lovely spot.

The highest Buda hill, János hegy (529m/1,736ft), can be reached by bus 90 from Moszkva tér (M2) to the Normafa stop, then walk through the forest. (You can also take the chairlift from Zugliget, the terminal station of bus 158 from Moszkva tér.) On the summit is the celebrated Erzsébet torony tower (1910), named after Queen Elizabeth.

Gellért hegy (Gellért Hill)

For dramatic views over the city and Danube, the best vantage points are from Gellért Hill.
Bus: 27 from the Villányi útca stop on Móricz Zsigmond körtér. Tram: 18, 19 to the Búsuló Juhász stop, then a 400m (440yd) walk.

Várhegy (Castle Hill)

Castle Hill is ringed by bastions. Those on the northern and western sides have been turned into pleasant promenades. Views of the Vérmező (*see p60*) and the residential quarter, Krisztinaváros, can be enjoyed from Tóth Árpád sétány.

On the other side of the hill you can see the Parliament from Fishermen's Bastion (*see p38*). Further along are excellent views from the terraces in front of the Castle Theatre and National Gallery.
The Castle Hill district can be reached by bus 16 from Deák Ferenc tér or bus 16A from Moszkva tér.

A city and its river

The Danube travels from its source, in the Black Forest in Germany, to empty into the Black Sea via the Danube Delta in Ukraine and Romania. On its journey, it also wends its way through (or along the borders of) Austria, Slovakia, Croatia, Serbia, Bulgaria and Moldova. The Danube is the second-longest river in Europe after the Volga: the Széchenyi lánchíd (Chain Bridge) in Budapest is not yet halfway along its 2,820km (1,752-mile) course. On the Budapest stretch it is generally around 5m (16ft) deep, although there are some holes near Szabadság híd where it plunges to 8 or 9m (26–30ft). The bed comprises pebbles, loam and sand with outcrops of rock. The flood period is in June, and lowest water levels are reached between October and December.

In Roman times, the river was the furthest boundary of the empire and, with its chain of fortresses (*limes*), a formidable barrier to threatening tribes from the east. Thereafter, its greatest value was as a trade route – the 'dustless highway' in one chronicler's picturesque phrase. Goods had to be dragged upstream by teams of horses – or convicts where the bank proved too treacherous for animals.

Things changed when the first steamship arrived in 1818. The journey from Pest to Vienna was cut from a month to three days and Hungarian agricultural exports boomed. The importance of Pest as a port was underlined by the scale of Miklós Ybl's imposing Customs House (1874 – now the University of Economics). In the 20th century, a free port was built on the edge of Csepel Island.

Until regulation in the 1870s, floods were a recurring hazard (there were 12 major ones between 1732 and 1838). To improve matters, the main channel was made deeper and narrower, and land was drained along the banks. Both the Parliament and the Technical University were built on reclaimed land. Floods are unlikely to occur nowadays, but, to make sure they don't, ice-breakers are deployed in winter. The bigger problem now is low water, which sometimes forces suspension of shipping.

During World War II all Budapest's bridges were destroyed, making ferries indispensable to cross-river traffic. Only two ferries operate today, in the northeastern part of the city, for use only by people, not vehicles. The Danube is now crossed by ten bridges (two railway and eight pedestrian). The red metro line also crosses it between the Parliament and the Batthyány tér.

Today's Danube is a largely tamed creature, the haunt of scullers and canoeists, and a few optimistic anglers on the lookout for some of the 51 species of fish reputed to reside in its grey (seldom blue) waters. Still, the river is the artery of Hungary, inextricably bound up with the nation's history. (*See also pp42–3.*)

The Jewish memorial on the Pest bank of the Danube

Széchenyi Chain Bridge

In 1820, a 29-year-old nobleman was returning hurriedly from Bihar County to Transdanubia for the funeral of his father. He reached Pest on 29 December, only to find that the pontoon bridge over the Danube had been dismantled for three weeks. It was not until 5 January – a full week later – that he could persuade a ferryman to negotiate the treacherous ice-floes.

The nobleman was Count István Széchenyi and his reaction was to begin lobbying for the building of a long-mooted bridge between Pest and Buda. On 10 February 1832, the Budapest Bridge Association was formed under Széchenyi's chairmanship. Following an old Central European tradition, it included not only enthusiasts, but also those

Looking through the famous triumphal arches

VIEWS FROM PEST

Duna *korzó* (between the Chain and Elizabeth Bridges) offers the best views of the Royal Castle and Castle Hill. For a vista of Pest from an unusual angle, climb the cupola of St Stephen's Basilica (*see p81*) – but be warned: there are over 300 steps.

who would otherwise have stymied the project out of jealousy, had they not been included.

Opposition came from the municipalities, who were unwilling to forgo the revenue of the pontoon toll, and from the nobility, who clung to their privilege of toll exemption which the owners of a privately built bridge were no longer prepared to indulge. However, the enlightened Palatine, Joseph, supported the project and the resistance was finally overcome. Széchenyi travelled to England to study bridge-building. He was impressed by William Tierney Clark's suspension bridge at Marlow in Buckinghamshire, and Clark was invited to design the Budapest bridge. A Scottish master-builder, Adam Clark (no relation), was engaged to supervise the construction work. The project was financed by Viennese bankers Georg Sina, Samuel

The Chain Bridge – the first to link Pest and Buda

Wodianer and Jakob Rothschild. Construction (1842–48) was not without difficulties: as the last component was being lowered into position, the chain of the hoist snapped, demolishing part of the scaffolding and pitching onlookers (including Széchenyi) into the Danube.

COUNT ISTVÁN SZÉCHENYI (1791–1860)

Called 'the greatest Hungarian' by his political rival Lajos Kossuth, Széchenyi was a reformer, a patriot and an enthusiast for technical innovation. He donated one year's income from his estates towards the foundation of the Academy of Sciences in 1827, and founded, *inter alia*, the National Theatre, the Danube Steamship Company and the Óbuda shipyard. He also organised the regulation of the Danube and the Tisza, and improved the quality of Hungarian livestock.

Although he served briefly as transport minister in the independent government of 1848, his last days were clouded by mental instability. In 1860, he committed suicide. His words sum up his political and social attitudes: 'We must struggle for the general good, as well as our own interest.'

The Chain Bridge was completed just before the outbreak of the War of Independence and survived an attempt by the Austrians to blow it up. It was officially inaugurated after the war (by which time Széchenyi was confined to a Viennese mental asylum). Its imposing triumphal arches instantly became Budapest's most characteristic landmark, but the sculpted lions by János Marschalkó were criticised for apparently lacking tongues. The sculptor was able to demonstrate in several learned articles that lions' tongues 'do not hang out of the mouth like those of dogs'.

The city had given an undertaking to the construction company not to build a competing bridge either side of the Chain Bridge closer than a distance of 8km (5 miles). Pressure of traffic soon made this condition intolerable and in 1870 the municipality bought the company out, so that construction of the Margaret Bridge could begin.

Pest

Pest, the eastern flat portion of Budapest, is ringed by two boulevards, the Kiskörút (Little Ringroad, running from Margit híd to Szabadság híd) and Nagykörút (Greater Ringroad, running in a wider arc from Margit híd to Petőfi híd). The historical centre is enclosed by the Kiskörút and contains major sights, although many lie between the two boulevards.

Although it was built on a Roman site, Pest was first referenced in 1061 as Contra Aquincum (*see p84*). Pest had remained mostly uninhabited until the economic boom of the 11th to 13th centuries. It was destroyed during the Mongol (Tartar) invasion in 1241 but it was rebuilt immediately due to its economic importance. By the 16th century, Buda, Pest and Óbuda constituted the largest conurbation between Vienna and Constantinople. After being linked by Széchenyi lánchíd, the three cities were unified in 1873 and by 1910, Budapest was the eighth-largest city in Europe, larger than Rome, Milan and Madrid. The population of Pest in particular grew thanks to migrants attracted by the industrial boom based on its port, the largest on the Danube.

The turn of the 19th century saw an intellectual boom and Pest benefited from the 1880 Council of Public Works' masterplan, which laid out a system of ring roads and radial boulevards, public transport links, building heights and green spaces still visible today.

In 1987, UNESCO granted Buda Castle, both banks of the Danube, Andrássy Avenue and the M1 metro line World Heritage List status. The historical yellow line was built in 1896, just six years after London's first underground lines were completed.

Today, Pest is the economic and political centre, although the president lives in Hungary's White House on Buda's Castle Hill (*see p32*). Buda's districts feature hills and villas, but the bulk of Budapest's population resides in Pest.

AROUND FERENCIEK TERE
Magyar Nemzeti Múzeum (Hungarian National Museum)

In 1802, the Széchenyi collection consisted of 11,884 documents, 1,150 manuscripts, 142 volumes of maps and engravings, and 2,675 coins. It was valued at the then enormous sum of 160,000 forints and constituted the

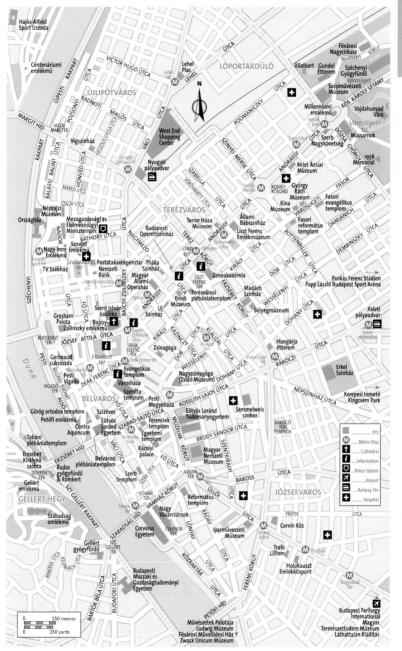

Hajós-Alfréd Sport Uszoda

Centenáriumi emlékmű

VICTOR HUGO UTCA

ÚJLIPÓTVÁROS

UPESTI RAKPART

RADNOTI

POZSONY

MIKLOS UTCA

MARGIT HID

JASZAI MARI TER

Vigszinház

SZALAY UTCA

BALASS

HONVED UTCA

MARKO UTCA

Néprajzi Múzeum

Országház

Mezogazdasági és Élelmezésügyi Minisztérium

BATHORY UTCA

Nagy Imre Emlékmű

Szovjet

Kossuth Lajos ter

Szabadság ter

TV Székház

Postatakarékpénztár

Nemzeti Bank

Magyar Állami Operaház

Aranykezu utca

Szent István bazilika

Gresham Palota

Bajcsy-Zsilinszky emlékmű

ROOSEVELT TER

JÓZSEF ATTILA UTCA

Gerbeaud cukrászda

Erzsébet ter

Pesti Vigadó

VIGADÓ TER

BELGRAD RAKPART

ALSO

Duna

Görög ortodox templom

Petőfi emlékmű

Contra Aquincum

Szizéves

Eötvös Loránd Egyetem

Tabáni plébániatemplom

Erzsébet Királynő szobra

ERZSÉBET HID

Belvárosi plébániatemplom

DÖBRENTEI TER

Rudas gyógyfürdő & Römkert

Gellért emlékmű

GELLÉRT HEGY

SZT GELLERT RAKPART

Szabadság emlékmű

Gellért gyógyfürdő

SZT GELLERT TER

KELENHEGY UTCA

MINERVA UTCA

BARTOK BELA UTCA

BUDAFOKI UTCA

Budapesti Műszaki és Gazdaságtudományi Egyetem

West End Shopping Center

Nyugati pályaudvar

Nyugati pályaudvar

UTCA

IZABELLA

VÖRÖSMARTY UTCA

TERÉZVÁROS

Budapesti Operettszinház

NAGYMEZO

TEREZ

Thália Szinház

Terézvárosi plébániatemplom

Ernst Múzeum

ANDRASSY

Uj Szinház

DEAK FERENC UTCA

KIRALY

Bajcsy-Zsilinszky utca

Zsinagóga

KAZINCZY UTCA

WESSELENYI

Evangelikus templom

Városháza

Szervita templom

Pesti Megyeháza

DEAK FERENC UTCA

Astoria

KOSSUTH LAJOS UTCA

BELVÁROS

VACI UTCA

SZABAD SAJTO UTCA

Ferenciek templom

Ferenciek tere

Egyetemi templom

Károlyi palace

FO UTCA

VACI UTCA

SZERB UTCA

Szerb templom

FOVAM TER

VAMHAZ KORUT

Nagy Vásárcsarnok

Corvinus Egyetem

SZABADSÁG HID

CSARNOK TER

Református templom

LONYAI

KORAKTAR UTCA

Museum of Applied Arts

PETOFI HID

Művészetek Palotája

Ludwig Múzeum

Fővárosi Művelődési Ház

Zwack Unicum Múzeum

LÖPORTÁRDÜLÖ

N

Lehel Piac

Lehel ter

LEHEL UTCA

UTCA

PODMANICZKY

SZINYEI MERSE UTCA

Terror Háza Múzeum

Állami Bábszinház

Liszt Ferenc Emlékmúzeum

Zeneakadémia

Madách Szinház

WESSELENYI KORUT

Bélyegmúzeum

DOHANY UTCA

Hungária étterem

Blaha Lujza ter

RÁKÓCZI

Erkel Szinház

NÉPSZINHAZ UTCA

Semmelweis szobor

Eötvös Loránd Tudomanyegyetem

BRODY SANDOR UTCA

SZENTKIRALYI

Magyar Nemzeti Múzeum

KALVIN TER

Kalvin

BAROSS

ÜLLOI UTCA

RADAY

Iparmuvészeti Múzeum

Ferenc korut

Trafo Lilliom

FERENC KORUT

Holokauszt Emlékközpont

Fővárosi Nagycirkusz

ALLATKERTI KORUT

Állatkert

Gundel Étterem

Széchenyi Gyógyfürdő

Városliget

Szépmüvészeti Múzeum

KÓS KAROLY SÉTÁNY

Millenniumi emlékmű

Hösök tere

Vajdahunyad Vára

Városligeti tó

Szerb Nagykövetség

Műcsarnok

1956 Memorial

DOZSA GYÖRGY UTCA

FASOR

Kelet Ázsiai Múzeum

KODÁLY KÖRÖND

György Ráth Múzeum

Kina Múzeum

VAROSLIGETI UTCA

Fasori evangélikus templom

Fasori református templom

DAMJANICH UTCA

ROTTENBILLER UTCA

DEMBINSZKY UTCA

Puskás Ferenc Stadion

Papl László Budapest Sport Aréna

STEFANIA UTCA

Keleti pályaudvar

Keleti pályaudvar

Kerepesi temető Kingcsem Park

RÁKÓCZI TERI CSARNOK

JÓZSEFVÁROS

PRÁTER UTCA

Corvin Köz

Klinikák

Nagyvárad

Budapest Ferihegy International

Magyar Természettudom Múzeum

Láthattalan Kiállitás

	POI
M	Metro Stop
†	Cathedral
i	Information
⊖	Police Station
✈	Airport
🚉	Railway Stn
✚	Hospital

0   250 metres

0   250 yards

Statue of poet János Arany in front of the Hungarian National Museum

The leading neoclassical architect of the day, Mihály Pollack, was chosen to design the building, which was completed in 1837. Its façade recalls the Erechtheion on the Athens Acropolis, while the interior stairway sweeps up to a domed area reminiscent of the Pantheon in Rome.

The collection

The collection shows the history of the Hungarian people. Highlights include a room devoted to the 1848 revolution, the tent of a Turkish commander and Renaissance stalls with marquetry from the church at Nyírbátor (northeast Hungary).

The panelled Széchenyi Memorial Room contains a portrait of the founder by the Viennese artist Joseph

third most important national museum in Europe (after the Louvre and the British Museum). The museum enjoyed the support of the Palatine Archduke Joseph, who became one of the trustees.

Expansion was at first hampered by application of an archaic law under which all objects discovered on Hungarian soil belonged to 'the state' and were transferred to Vienna. Then, in 1832, the great collection of the scholar Miklós Jankovich was acquired, marking the 'second founding' of the museum. At the same time, the Palatine persuaded the Diet to allocate half a million forints (to come from the pockets of the nobility) for the construction of an edifice sufficiently splendid to be the repository of the nation's heritage.

COUNT FERENC SZÉCHENYI (1754–1820)

The story of the Hungarian National Museum begins with Ferenc Széchenyi, father of 'the greatest Hungarian', István Széchenyi, and like him a patriot and moderniser.

Emperor Joseph II appointed him viceroy of Croatia, but Széchenyi realised that Joseph's centralising and authoritarian approach left no room for national aspirations and resigned his post in 1786. He devoted himself to collecting artefacts and books with a view to donating them to the Hungarian nation; but even this gesture had to receive permission from Joseph's successor, Franz I, before it could be put into effect.

In his old age, Ferenc Széchenyi became fanatically conservative and seems to have suffered from religious melancholy, foreshadowing the mental instability that overtook his son in his final years.

Ender; round the top of the walls are the coats of arms of all the Hungarian counties.

VIII, Múzeum körút 14–16.
Tel: (36 1) 338 2122. www.mnm.hu.
Open: Tue–Sun 10am–6pm.
Admission charge, although permanent exhibition is free. Metro: M2 to Kálvin tér; Tram: 47, 49 to Kálvin tér.

Fő útca & Váci útca (District V)

Váci útca incorporated Lipót útca in the 18th century and became a pedestrian zone resplendent in high-end shops. Over-commercialisation of Váci útca has resulted in the Hungarian government, with financial aid from the EU, renovating and rejuvenating an alternative: Fő útca.

Fő útca

This was completed in the spring of 2010 and begins at Október 6 útca just south of the new 'intelligent' fountain on Szabadság tér (*see pp110–11*). It continues along in front of St Stephen's Basilica and past Elizabeth Square where it becomes Bécsi útca then morphs again into Petőfi Sándor. At No 5 is FUGA, the Budapest Centre of Architecture, a wonderfully eclectic venue for music, exhibitions and film. Beyond the underpass, Fő útca continues as Károly Mihály útca past the Centrál Kávéház (*see p167*) and Café Alibi by the imposing Law Faculty, then comes to an end by the Old City wall at Kálvin tér as Kecskeméti útca (*see p76*).

Váci útca

This was always a fashionable promenade, as 19th-century etchings show, but most of its fine neoclassical buildings have disappeared. No 9 is the Pest Theatre, built by József Hild in 1840 on the site of a famous hotel and ballroom where the 11-year-old prodigy Franz Liszt once gave a concert. No 11a is faced with colourful Zsolnay ceramics and was built in the Jugendstil style by Ödön Lechner and Gyula Pártos (1890). Also worth a glance is the postmodernist Taverna Hotel (No 20) by József Finta and Associates (1987), which is now another Mercure hotel.

The cross street of Déak Ferenc útca is known as Fashion Street. But as you continue south along Váci útca, designer names ebb into overpriced cafés and tourist shops.

Vörösmarty tér

This marks the start of Váci útca at a point where the inner-city gate for the road to Vác (*see p127*) once stood. Under the trees in the centre of this spacious square is a monument of Carrara marble (by Ede Telcs and Ede Kallós, 1908) to the Romantic poet Mihály Vörösmarty (1800–55). The poet is shown reciting his *Szózat* (Appeal) to the Hungarian masses, a line of which is etched on the plinth: 'Be faithful to your land forever, O Hungarians!' Although *Szózat* contains more optimistic passages, the

(*Cont. on p79*)

Walk: Szabadság híd to Ferenciek tere

This is one of two walks exploring the historic core of Pest. It begins just outside the former old city wall.

Allow about an hour.

Start at the Pest side of Szabadság híd (see p43).

1 Corvinus Egyetem (University of Economics)

The former Karl Marx University at Fővám tér 8 was one of the more liberal institutions under Communism. Miklós Ybl's building (1874) was originally the Customs House. Its grandeur reflects Pest's importance as a centre of trade in the late 19th century.
www.corvinusegyetem.hu
Walk straight on to the central market.

2 Nagy Vásárcsarnok (Central Market)

This is the largest of Pest's five market halls (*see p141*), opened in 1897 after the 1896 Millennial celebrations.
Walk east along Vámház körút towards Kálvin tér.

3 Református templom (Calvinist Church)

This rather plain neoclassical church (*see p79*) took 14 years to build due to funding problems. Inside is the tomb of Countess Zichy.

From Kálvin tér, it is a few minutes' walk on Múzeum körút to the Magyar Nemzeti Múzeum (Hungarian National Museum, see pp72 & 74–5). Otherwise turn left into Kecskeméti útca.

4 The Old City Wall

The Mercure Hotel stands on the site of the city gate. Walk along Kecskeméti útca, which has been converted, along with the streets it morphs into, all the way from Kálvin tér to Szabadság tér (*see pp110–11*) into Fő útca, literally Main Street. This 2010 EU/Hungarian development has created a pedestrian street dotted with large stone markers. It is succeeding in its aim to create a more authentic alternative to the commercial Váci útca. (*See p75.*)
Turn left down Szerb útca.

5 Szerb templom (Serbian Church)

This church (*see p79*) was built in 1698. It is said that at the beginning

of the 19th century every fourth house in Pest was owned by a Serb merchant.
Retrace your steps to Károlyi Mihály útca.

6 Jogi Kar and Egyetemi templom (Faculty of Law and University Church)

On your left on the open square is the elegant Faculty of Law and the University Church (1742, *see p80*), probably the work of Andreas Mayerhoffer. In the early 19th century, it was a centre of the reform movement.

7 Károlyi palota (Károlyi Palace)

This was the city residence of Count Mihály Károlyi, first president of the Hungarian Republic in 1918. His widow, known as the 'red countess', kept an apartment here. Today it houses the Petőfi Museum of Literature (*see p80*).

8 Egyetemi Könyvtár (University Library)

The University Library is an impressive neo-Renaissance building (1876) with superb *sgraffito* murals. (*Open Mon–Fri 10am–6pm; tours at 11am & 5pm.*)

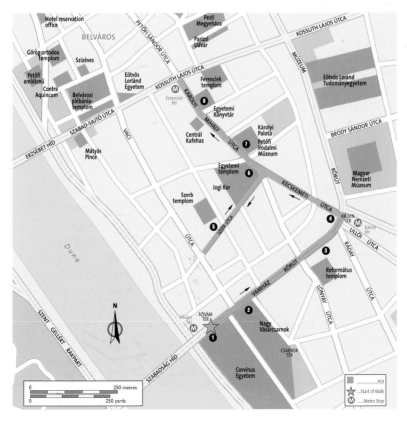

Stunning detail in the Museum of Applied Arts's interior

nightmare vision it evoked of *nemzethalál* (national extinction) spoke directly to the hearts of Hungarians, then as now.

On the north side of the square is a block built by József Hild, long known as the 'cutters' house' because a wealthy tailor, a surgeon, a slaughterer and a banker lived here. On the ground floor is the celebrated café and confectioner, Gerbeaud (*see p85*).

Iparművészeti Múzeum (Museum of Applied Arts)

This lovely museum was founded in 1872 and was the third museum of its kind in Europe. The superb Jugendstil building was designed by Ödön Lechner with Gyula Pártos in 1896 (*see pp18–19*) and provides a suitable exterior for Hungarian furnishings and *objets*. The opening, attended by Franz Joseph himself, was part of the Millennial celebrations of that year (*see p97*). Its oriental style of ornamentation reflected the architect's view that Magyars had originally come from the East.

IX, Üllői útca 33–37. Tel: (36 1) 456 5100. www.imm.hu. Open: Tue–Sun 10am–6pm (Dec–Mar until 4pm). Admission charge. Metro: Ferenc körút. Tram: 4, 6 to Üllői útca.

Holokauszt Emlékközpont (Holocaust Memorial Centre)

Housed in the award-winning new wing of the adjoining Páva Synagogue. *IX, Pava útca 39. Tel: (36 1) 455 3333.*

www.hdke.hu. Open: Tue–Sun 10am–6pm. Admission charge. Metro: Ferenc körút; Tram: 4, 6 to Üllöi útca.

Református templom (Calvinist Church)

József Hofrichter's rigid neoclassical, somewhat provincial church of 1830 is not much enhanced by the portico added in 1838. The inside is more pleasing, with long galleries by József Hild and stained glass by Miksa Róth, the latter showing Protestant Hungarian heroes and Calvin himself. The treasury contains goldsmiths' work of the 17th to 19th centuries. (*See p76.*) *V, Kálvin tér 7. Tel: (36 1) 217 6769. Metro: M3 to Kálvin tér.*

Szerb templom (Serbian Church)

The Serbian merchants and craftsmen of Pest had their own printing house and other institutions, including this

Moorish influence in the Museum of Applied Arts

attractive Baroque church (1698). The architect is thought to have been Andreas Mayerhoffer. The iconostasis dates from 1850. Paintings of scenes from the life of Jesus, the saints and the apostles are by Károly Sterio. (*See pp76–7.*)
V, Szerb útca 2–4. Metro: M3 to Kálvin tér.

Egyetemi templom (University Church)

It is thought that the Dominicans had a church on this site in the Middle Ages, later turned into a mosque by the Turks. The Hungarian order of Paulites acquired it in the 1720s. Their church was not completed until 1742 (the towers in 1770) and was probably designed by the Salzburg architect Andreas Mayerhoffer.

The rococo ceiling frescoes of the Adoration of the Virgin (1776) are by the Bohemian Johann Bergl, while the beautifully carved pews are the work of Paulite monks. The adjacent theological library also contains finely carved shelves and galleries, but may be difficult to access. (*See p76.*)
V, Egyetem tér 5–7/Papnövelde útca. 7. Tel: (36 1) 318 0555. Metro: M3 to Kálvin tér.

Petőfi Irodalmi Múzeum (Petőfi Museum of Literature)

Housed in the architecturally stunning and historically important Károlyi palace, this series of rooms lovingly presents preserved documents, art, relics and books showcasing Hungarian literature. In addition to Petőfi, there are dedicated exhibitions for Mór Jókai, Attila József and Endre Ady.
V, Károlyi Mihály útca 16. Tel: (06 1) 317 3611. www.pim.hu. Open: Tue–Sun 10am–6pm. Admission charge. Metro: M3 to Ferenciek tere or Kálvin tér.

The Baroque Serbian Church

Ferenciek templom (Franciscan Church)

The Italianate Baroque church of the Franciscans in Pest was finished in 1758, but its fairy-tale tower was added in 1858. The 19th-century frescoes of the interior are by Károly Lotz. A marked pew shows where the composer Franz Liszt used to sit.

V, Ferenciek tere 9. Tel: (36 1) 317 3322. Metro: M3 to Ferenciek tere.

Semmelweis szobor (Semmelweis Statue)

The marble statue (1906) of Ignác Semmelweis, the 'Saviour of Mothers' (*see also p61*), is by Alajos Stróbl. The sculptor depicted his own wife and baby as part of the ensemble in recognition of Semmelweis's improvements in medical practice that had saved them after a difficult birth. (*See p50.*)

VIII, Rochus Hospital, Gyulai Pál útca. Metro: M2 to Blaha Lujza tér.

AROUND DEÁK FERENC TÉR
Szent István bazilika (St Stephen's Basilica)

Budapest debtors say, 'I'll settle up when the Basilica is finished', an allusion to the 54 years (1851–1905) it took to build the church. After the dome of the neoclassical original collapsed (January 1868), Miklós Ybl rebuilt the church to a neo-Renaissance plan. Franz Joseph, attending the consecration, is said to have cast anxious eyes at the dome, whose previous fall, according to an eye-witness, made a 'horrible roar' and broke 300 windows in the neighbourhood. After Ybl's death, József Kauser completed the work. St Stephen's is not basilical in form, but was granted basilical status by Pope Pius XI on the occasion of the Eucharistic Congress held in Budapest in 1938.

Ybl's replacement dome is one of the most striking features of the interior, 22m (72ft) in diameter and 96m (315ft) high, the same height as the Parliament. Leading artists of the day contributed to the church's decoration. Károly Lotz designed the dome mosaics, while Gyula Benczúr painted the popular *St Stephen Dedicating his Country to the Virgin Mary* (south transept). The marble statue of St Stephen on the high altar is by Alajos Stróbl.

The star attraction is the Szent Jobb, claimed to be the mummified right hand of St Stephen (in the chapel to the left of the altar). In 1938, it was paraded round Hungary in a gold-painted train, but nowadays its excursions are limited to a circuit of the church on 20 August, St Stephen's Day in Hungary.

V, Szent István tér 1. Tel: (36 1) 317 2859. www.bazilika.biz. Metro: M3 to Arany János útca or M1 to Bajcsy-Zsilinszky útca.

Evangélikus templom (Lutheran Church)

Emperor Joseph II's Tolerance Patent (1781) allowed the building of

Protestant churches (but without towers) in areas where a minimum of 100 Protestant families existed to form a parish. The Lutheran Church of Pest, designed by Mihály Pollack, was completed by 1809 and József Hild added the neoclassical portico in 1856. The adjacent Evangélikus Országos Múzeum (Lutheran Museum) is also worth a visit: its most treasured possession is Martin Luther's will, acquired in 1804. Around 4 per cent of Hungarians are Lutherans.

V, Deák Ferenc tér 4. Tel: (36 1) 317 4173. www.evangelikusmuzeum.hu. Museum open: Tue–Sun 10am–6pm, to 4pm in winter. Admission charge. Metro: M1, 2, 3 to Deák Ferenc tér.

Belvárosi plébániatemplom (Inner City Parish Church)

The history of Pest is reflected in the many-layered architecture of the *plébániatemplom.* Succeeding a church built on the ruins of Roman Contra Aquincum, a burial chapel for St Gellért was erected here in 1046. Parts of a subsequent 12th-century basilica survived Gothic reconstruction in the 15th century. The Turks turned the choir into a mosque, as a *mihrab* (prayer niche) in the south wall testifies. Baroque conversion under György Paur was begun in 1725 and two further alterations took place in the 19th century. Twentieth-century restorers have laid bare medieval details such as the sedilia in the sanctuary and the Italian-style 15th-century fresco of the Crucifixion.

The modern panels of the altar, depicting the life of the Virgin Mary, are the work of Pál C Molnár. At the end of the side aisle are two beautiful Renaissance tabernacles in red marble, probably made by craftsmen at the

The magnificent dome of St Stephen's Basilica

court of Matthias Corvinus. The statue of St Florian recalls fires that badly damaged Pest several times in the early 18th century. (*See p84.*)
V, Március 15 tér 2. Tel: (36 1) 318 3108. Metro: M3 to Ferenciek tere.

Szervita templom (Servite Church)

The Servites, one of the religious orders invited to Hungary during the Counter-Reformation, hung on in Pest, although the city council once forced them to move, and on another occasion compelled them to rebuild on their own land in a manner the council thought fitting to the metropolis. Their church is in a pleasantly harmonious Baroque style and contains some fine sculpture, notably János Thenny's statues of St Stephen, St Joachim, St Anne and St Ladislas.
V, Szervita tér 6. Tel: (36 1) 318 5536. Metro: M1,2 & 3 to Deák Ferenc tér.

Nagyzsinagóga (Great Synagogue)

The largest synagogue in Europe is still a centre of liberal Judaism. It was built by the Viennese architect Ludwig Förster (1859) and enlarged in 1931 in Moorish style. Imre Varga's moving weeping willow Monument to the Holocaust Victims in the rear courtyard recalls the terrible events of the mid-20th century. The attached **Zsidó Múzeum** (National Jewish Museum) is situated where Theodor Herzl (1860–1904), the founder of Zionism, was born. It contains disturbing

The top of the Great Synagogue tower

documentation of Jewish persecution.
VII, Dohány útca 2–8. Museum: Tel: (36 1) 342 8949. Open: May–Oct Mon–Thur 10am–5pm, Fri & Sun 10am–2pm; Nov–Apr Mon–Thur 10am–3pm, Fri & Sun 10am–2pm. Closed: Sat. Synagogue: Tel: (36 1) 342 1335. www.dohany-zsinagoga.hu. Open: Mon–Fri 10am–3pm, Sun 10am–1pm (except during ceremonies). Closed: Sat. There are combined tickets for the synagogue and the museum. Metro: M2 to Astoria.

Zsinagóga (Orthodox Synagogue)

The rival to the liberal synagogue was the (moderately) Orthodox one, two streets away, which also has a vividly

(*Cont. on p86*)

Walk: Erzsébet híd to Deák Ferenc tér

The walk begins outside Mátyás Pince, a restaurant to be experienced. The Roman fort where Pest originated is just under the bridge and the walk includes the shopping area of Váci útca and its environs.

Allow 1 hour. Start in front of Mátyás Pince restaurant at Március 7 tér at the Pest end of Erzsébet híd (see p43).

1 Mátyás Pince

If you want to experience a typical (if touristy) Hungarian restaurant with stained-glass windows, mural paintings and gypsy music, there's no place like Mátyás Pince, an institution since it opened in 1904.

Walk under Erzsébet híd to the other half of Március 15 tér.

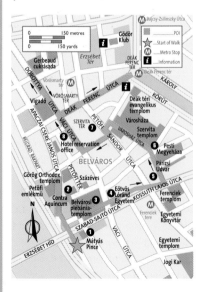

2 Contra Aquincum

This diminutive, now sunken fortress (*see p61*), with walls 3m (10ft) thick, was a 4th-century outpost in barbarian territory that protected the main town of Aquincum on the far side of the river. *A detour to the north takes you to the Görög Orthodox templom (Greek Orthodox Church) at Petőfi tér 2 (drop in to hear the singing at 6pm on Saturdays). In the parallel Pesti Barnabás útca, at No 2, is the Százéves (100 Years) restaurant, located in one of the few remaining Baroque palaces of Pest.*

3 Belvárosi plébániatemplom (Inner City Parish Church)

The most historic church of Pest (*see p81*). It has had an eventful history: the Romanesque and Gothic churches were both largely destroyed, while the Turks turned the diminished building into a mosque. Highlights of the interior are the two lovely Renaissance tabernacles made of red marble.

4 Eötvös Loránd Egyetem (Loránd Eötvös University)

Named after the distinguished physicist (1848–1919), this is Budapest's main university. You pass under the building's connecting archway on your way to Kigyó útca and thence to Ferenciek tere.

5 Párizsi Udvar (Paris Arcade)

Flanking Ferenciek tere to the north is the striking Jugendstil (Art Nouveau) arcade designed by Henrik Schmahl (1911), with its oriental-looking stained-glass cupola. The arcade is undergoing changes and seriously needs a revamp. Jégbüfé, on Ferenciek tere, is a good place to stop for light refreshments before carrying on across Kossuth Lajos útca to the Ferenciek templom (Franciscan Church, *see p81*). On the north wall is a relief showing Count Wesselényi rescuing Pest inhabitants by boat during the floods of 1838.

Turn left on Városház útca.

6 Pesti Megyeháza, Városháza (County and City Halls)

The Pest County Hall (No 7 Városház útca) is a simple neoclassical building (1830), while the City Hall (Nos 9–11) is an elegant Baroque structure designed by Antonio Martinelli in 1735 as a hospital for the war-wounded. It was established by Emperor Charles VI. An imposing Atlas bearing a globe stands over the entrance.

The statue of Vörösmarty, rich in detail

7 Szervita tér (Servite Square)

Városház útca leads to the square which was recently renamed after the Servite Order, whose church stands on the corner (*see p83*). Two restored Jugendstil houses (*see pp90–91*) at Nos 3 and 5 are worth a glance, especially the mosaic (a representation of 'The Transfiguration of Hungary') in the gable of No 3.

Turn left into Petőfi Sándor útca, right immediately into Régiposta útca, where the folk-art craftsman's shop is pinpointed by a copper peacock above the door, then right again into Váci útca.

8 Váci útca to Vörösmarty tér & Gerbeaud Cukrászda

This shopping area is always bustling. An alternate route to Vörösmarty tér is by staying on Petőfi Sándor útca, also known as Fő útca (*see p75*). On the square is the monument to the poet Mihály Vörösmarty (1800–55) and the celebrated 1870 Gerbeaud coffee house, with its enticing menu of Viennese and Hungarian pastries (*see p167*).

Deák Ferenc tér, the junction of all three metro lines, lies to the east.

oriental look about it. Currently, the synagogue is under restoration and difficult to visit.

Rumbach Sebestyén útca 11–13. M2 to Metro: Astoria.

Pesti Vigadó (Pest Concert Hall)

Mihály Pollack's original *redoute* (ballroom) on this site fell victim to Austrian cannon fire from the Buda Hill during the 1848 War of Independence. Between 1858 and 1865, Frigyes Feszl built a new concert hall in a romantic style that incorporates oriental elements, reflecting the Asiatic roots of the Magyars. One of the figures in the frieze along the top of the façade is Attila the Hun, though the descent of the Hungarians from the Huns is more than doubtful. Further emphasis is placed on Magyar identity by the interior frescoes, scenes from Hungarian folk tales painted by Károly Lotz and Mór Than. 'Vigadó' is coined from *vigad* (to make merry – or have a ball), but, while the exterior has just seen an extensive renovation, the interior will not be seeing any balls or performances until the long-running funding and development issues are solved.

V, Vigadó tér 1–2. Tram: 2 along the Pest embankment to Vigadó tér.

Bajcsy-Zsilinszky emlékmű (Bajcsy-Zsilinszky Monument)

The sculpture (by Sándor Győrfi, 1986) shows the politician who headed the non-Communist resistance to the Nazis at the moment of his arrest by Hungarian fascists in 1944. He was shot

Romantic Pest Concert Hall

shortly after his arrest. On the base of the monument is a quotation from Ferenc Kölcsey: 'A haza minden előtt' ('The homeland before everything').
V, Deák Ferenc tér. Metro: M1, 2, 3 to Deák Ferenc tér.

József Nádor Szobor (Palatine Joseph Monument)

Johann Halbig's elegant bronze figure (1869), draped in the cloak of St Stephen's Order, honours the younger brother of Emperor Franz I. Archduke Joseph (1776–1847) headed the Embellishment Commission (*see pp99 & 102*) that transformed the face of 19th-century Pest. He was one of the few Habsburgs to be loved by Hungarians.
V, József Nádor tér. Metro: M1 to Vörösmarty tér.

Roosevelt tér (Roosevelt Square)

The best surviving architectural feature of the square, which was once ringed by fine neoclassical buildings, is the Magyar Tudományos Akadémia (Academy of Sciences) at the northern end. A statue of István Széchenyi stands before it; he put up the initial construction funds, with the rest of the money raised from public subscription. On the plinth are figures of classical deities – Minerva, Neptune, Vulcan and Ceres – symbolising his multifarious achievements.

Adolf Huszár's monument (1887) honours a lawyer and shrewd politician who was minister for justice in the independent government of 1848–49

and whose 'Easter Essay' in the *Pesti Napló* (16 April 1865) gave the impetus for the political Compromise of 1867 and the setting-up of the Austro-Hungarian Dual Monarchy. Also on the square are Ferenc Deák, a man of outstanding integrity, who lived for years as a bachelor in a suite of rooms in the nearby English Queen Hotel (the Gresham Palace was subsequently built on the site). József Eötvös (1813–71), an educational reformer.
V. Metro: M1 to Vörösmarty tér; Tram: 2 to Roosevelt tér.

Magyar Kereskedelmi és Vendéglátóipari Múzeum (Museum of Trade and Tourism)

The emphasis at this museum is on everything to do with the railway catering and retail trades. The re-created interiors of 19th-century food trolleys and outlets have a great deal of charm, and attractive period posters are on sale.
V, Szent István tér 15. Tel: (36 1) 212 1245. www.mkvm.hu. Open: Wed–Mon 11am–7pm. Closed Tue. Admission charge, although permanent exhibition is free. Metro: M3 to Arany János útca, M1 to Bajcsy-Zsilinszky útca.

AROUND ANDRÁSSY ÚTCA
Budapesti Operettszínház (Budapest Operetta Theatre)

Designed in 1894 by Viennese architects Fellner and Helmer, the fabulous Art Nouveau exterior housed exquisite balls
(*Cont. on p90*)

Operetta

Operetta was very popular during the period of the Austro-Hungarian Empire (1867–1918). Its origins were various: Austrian composers were inspired by the smash hits of Jacques Offenbach in Paris and by the tradition of the Wiener Volksstück (Viennese Popular Theatre). The Hungarian equivalent of the latter was the *Népszínmű*. A musical rendering of Sándor Petőfi's poem about the life and love of a peasant boy from the Great Plain (*János Vitéz*) is a classic example of it. The characteristic figures represented in Hungarian *Népszínmű* became the romantic clichés associated with a world that was already passing: the *csikós* (cowboy from the Great Plain), the *betyár* (a sort of Robin Hood), the *huszár* (hussar), the *táblabíró* (provincial judges with feudal attitudes), together with a cast of peasants, *heyducks* (personal gendarmerie of the magnates) and sentimentally portrayed gypsies.

The classic operetta is Johann Strauss's *Die Fledermaus* (1874), a witty and melodious satire on the decadent world of late 19th-century Vienna. The more strait-laced public in Budapest were initially slow to

The Hungarian State Opera House

Composer Franz Lehár at work

accept this, but then came the *Gypsy Baron* (1885), a work that symbolically united the two halves of the empire. The libretto was based on a story by the greatest Hungarian novelist, Mór Jókai, and Johann Strauss wrote the music. It was an instant success.

The final period of operetta, which was increasingly a vehicle of escape from the realities of imperial decline and war, was dominated by Hungarian composers. Franz Lehár wrote two works that conquered the world – *The Merry Widow* (1905) and *Land of Smiles* (1929). The prolific Emmerich Kálmán had enormous success with the *Csárdás Princess* (1915). The frenetic energy and brittle glamour of its dance routines, set in the nightclub milieu, seem in retrospect to be the dance of death of the empire itself:

Every pulse is racing faster
While we dance and flirt and play:
The world outside is all disaster;
What care we till break
of day . . . ?

and banquets. The original chandelier overshadows the row of boxes that comprise some of the renovated theatre's 917 seats. Operettas (*see pp88–9*) and musicals take place all year except mid-July to mid-August.
VI, Nagymező útca 17.
Tel (36 1) 312 4866.
www.operettszinhaz.hu. Metro: M1
to Opera.

Magyar Állami Operaház (Hungarian State Opera)

In the 1870s, it was decided to build an opera house in Pest of comparable grandeur to those in other European cities. Miklós Ybl won the commission and the opera house went up between 1875 and 1884. Built in a graceful neo-Renaissance style, the technically sophisticated building embodies national pride combined with allusions to musical history. In niches on either side of the main entrance are statues of Hungary's two greatest 19th-century composers: Ferenc Erkel (left) and Ferenc (Franz) Liszt (right). Four Muses are represented at the corners of the first storey, while famous composers line the balustrade above. The interior was decorated by Bertalán Székely, Mór Than and Károly Lotz (note Lotz's cupola fresco of Apollo on Olympus). Technical innovations included new fire precautions as several European theatres had recently burnt down with loss of life. It was also something of a feat to install the auditorium's bronze chandelier weighing all of three tonnes.

MIKLÓS YBL (1814–91)

The Hungarian State Opera is probably the finest work of this great Hungarian architect, one of the best practitioners of so-called historicism.

He built many handsome apartment blocks in Pest, constructed around an internal courtyard, and offered spacious, high-ceilinged flats for the well-to-do. His public works reflect the grandeur and elegance of the Italian Renaissance. They include the second phase of St Stephen's Basilica and the huge Customs House (now the University of Economics). A statue of Ybl stands on the Danube bank below the castle, opposite his Várbazár complex (*see p50*).

The cost ran to one million forints, most of it personally contributed by Emperor Franz Joseph.

Famous directors of the opera include Gustav Mahler (1888–91), Arthur Nikisch (1893–95) and Otto Klemperer (1947–50). In the 1930s (surprisingly, in view of the right-wing political climate), a number of modern operas were staged, including works by Stravinsky. (*See p115.*)
VI, Andrássy útca 22. Tel: (36 1) 353 0170.
www.opera.hu. Daily one-hour guided tours in various languages at 3pm & 4pm; reservations necessary (tel: (36 1) 332 8197). Metro: M1 to Opera.

Új Színház (New Theatre – formally Parisiana)

This gem of theatre architecture was built as a cabaret venue by Béla Lajta in 1909. Alterations in the 1920s transformed Lajta's original Jugendstil into something closer to Art Deco.

Its complete renovation won it the 1998 Europa Nostra Prize and has resulted in a glittering array of gilding, glasswork and coloured marble.

VI, Paulay Ede útca 35.
Tel: (36 1) 269 6021. www.ujszinhaz.hu.
Metro: M1 to Opera.

Zeneakadémia (Music Academy)

The first music academy was founded in 1875 by Franz Liszt and occupied three rooms above his flat in Irányi útca (Pest); there were then 38 students of piano and composition. After four years, demand was such that expansion became necessary, and the academy moved to Andrássy útca (then Sugár útca), where it occupied several floors and had its first auditorium. At the turn of the century, the city decided to buy land for a much bigger music conservatory, subsequently built between 1904 and 1907 to plans by Flóris Korb and Kálmán Giergl.

The Liszt Ferenc Zenemüvészeti Főiskola (Franz Liszt High School for Music), to give it its official title, is a remarkable example of Korb and Giergl's idiosyncratic style, sometimes called 'Baroque Jugendstil'. Liszt is honoured with a huge statue (by Alajos Stróbl) over the main entrance and there are reliefs of two other founding professors, Ferenc Erkel and Róbert Volkmann. The building's exterior is pompous and heavy, but the interior is striking, particularly in the iridescent colours of the Zsolnay ceramic fittings. In the first-floor lobby is Aladár

The New Theatre is a dazzling example of Art Deco

Körösfői-Kriesch's weird fresco *The Fountain of Youth*, with the sententious inscription: 'Those who search for life make a pilgrimage to the wellspring of art.' Its painter was a member of the artists' colony based in the village of Gödöllő (*see pp129–30*), north of Budapest, whose members drew inspiration from Hungarian folk motifs and the English Pre-Raphaelites. Above the entrances to the auditorium on the ground floor Körösfői-Kriesch painted two further frescoes representing sacred and profane music.

The large auditorium of the Music Academy seats 1,200 and is famous for its excellent acoustics. On the walls are images (painted by István (*Cont. on p96*)

Jugendstil architecture

In Central Europe, the German term *Jugendstil* is applied to the Art Nouveau architecture that had its roots in the Paris of the 1890s. In Budapest, the word *szecesszió* – 'Secession style' – is also used, reflecting the influence of the famous Viennese Secession movement, established in 1897 in opposition to the conservative and academic elements that prevailed in the arts.

Jugendstil/Art Nouveau was a liberating force: sensual, richly ornamental and prepared to draw eclectically on the world of nature and folklore for its motifs. Coming as it did with the upsurge of national consciousness in the countries of the Austro-Hungarian Empire, it is not surprising that idiosyncratic versions arose at local level.

Hungarian Jugendstil drew on current ideas about ethnic roots; in the works of Ödön Lechner this was carried further and developed into a so-called 'national style' (*see pp18–19*). However, all Jugendstil architects, whether leaning towards the approach of Lechner, or that of the Viennese Secession, or even that of the English Arts and Crafts Movement, shared a common enthusiasm for exploiting

materials such as ceramics, glass and wrought iron. A determination to avoid pattern-book repetition of forms was another characteristic principle.

Though in public buildings individuality sometimes had to give way to official or commercial considerations, private villas for the wealthy (of which the vast majority were built at the beginning of the 20th century) provided an opportunity for architects to give free rein to their imagination and ingenuity.

Anyone interested in seeing some of these private houses should spend some time on either side of the outer reaches of Andrássy útca. Examples of fine Jugendstil villas can be seen at Városligeti fasor 24 and 33, both designed by Emil Vidor; further out, at Ajtósi Dürer sor 25, is the villa built for the sculptor György Zala (co-organiser of the Millennium Memorial project), to a modified Lechner design (*see p97*).

Although Ödön Lechner and his partner Gyula Pártos (*see pp18–19*) overshadow the rest, there were many interesting architects in early 20th-century Budapest who built their own more or less idiosyncratic versions of Jugendstil. Their public and commercial buildings are all near the centre of Pest.

Gresham palota (Gresham Palace)

This richly ornamented (and beautifully restored) block was built for the English insurance company of the same name by Zsigmond Quittner between 1905 and 1907. It has splendid stairways, stained glass by the Gödöllő artist Miksa Róth, and a marvellous wrought-iron gate with peacock motifs. The palace is now the Four Seasons Hotel.

V, Metro: M1 to Vörösmarty tér; Tram: 2 to Roosevelt tér.

Párizsi udvar (Paris Arcade)

Henrik Schmahl's 1911 arcade has elaborate ornamentation on the façade as well as inside, where the coloured glass lights in the roof create an atmosphere of Alhambra-like mystery. The building is still awaiting restoration. (*See p85.*)

V, Ferenciek tere 5. Metro: M2 to Ferenciek tere.

Török bankház (former Turkish Bank)

The glassed façade of the house (Henrik Böhm, Ármin Hegedűs, 1906) recalls French Art Nouveau. Miksa Róth made the striking mosaic in the gable, showing the Magyars offering allegiance to the Virgin Mary in her capacity as Patrona Hungariae. On the same square, Béla Lajta's Rózavölgyi Ház (No 5) betrays the influence of

The gable mosaic of the former Turkish Bank

the controversial Viennese architect Adolf Loos. There is another Jugendstil façade at No 2.

V, Szervita tér 3. Metro: M1, 2, 3 to Deák Ferenc tér.

Tomb of the Schmidl family

It is well worth the trek to the Jewish Cemetery in Kőbánya to see the loveliest combined effort of Ödön Lechner and Béla Lajta, a gleaming gem of green and turquoise ceramic with gold edging, setting off delicate floral and star motifs. Inside is a stylised mosaic of the Tree of Life.

X, Izraelita temető, Kozma útca. Tram: 37 from Blaha Lujza tér (M2) to Izraelita temető; journey time 35mins. Or Bus: 68.

Walk: Andrássy útca

This walk takes you along the grandest boulevard of Pest, with a diversion through theatreland. Andrássy útca is the dividing boulevard between districts VI and VII.

Allow 1½ hours.

Walk from the metro stop at Deák Ferenc tér across the east side of Erzsébet tér to the corner of Bajcsy-Zsilinszky útca and József Attila útca.

1 Bajcsy-Zsilinszky útca 12

Fans of postmodernist architecture will appreciate the reflecting glass and futuristic sculpture of this building by József Finta and associates.
A short detour down Bajcsy-Zsilinszky útca brings you to St Stephen's Basilica (see p81). Otherwise, bear diagonally to the right.

2 Andrássy útca

This boulevard has reflected political events in its many name changes. It was named Andrássy in 1885 after the distinguished prime minister and foreign minister (1823–90). Under Communism it was called Stalin Avenue, then Avenue of Hungarian Youth during the 1956 revolution, then Avenue of the People's Republic, and now Andrássy útca again.

3 Magyar Állami Operaház (Hungarian State Opera)

This is one of Miklós Ybl's most opulent public buildings (*see pp90*). Emperor Franz Joseph financed it and attended the opening on 27 September 1884, when Ferenc Erkel's national opera *Bánk Bán* was performed.
Opposite is a building by Ödön Lechner (see pp18–19), that was the Budapest ballet school. Walk down Dalszínház útca to Új Színház.

4 Új Színház (New Theatre)

The beautifully restored Art Deco theatre is worth a visit simply to marvel at the interior, which has been re-created entirely in the spirit of the original (*see p90*).
Walk back to Andrássy útca, turn right and continue to Nagymező útca.

5 Nagymező útca

Nagymező útca was once the Broadway of Budapest. On the left is Budapesti Operettszínház (*see p87*) – another restored Art Nouveau masterpiece. At No 8 is the revived **Ernst Múzeum**, containing modern Hungarian and foreign art (*Tel: (36 1) 341 4355.*

www.ernstmuzeum.hu. Open: Tue–Sun 11am–7pm. Admission charge). The Jugendstil house was partly designed by Ödön Lechner, and the stained-glass window is by József Rippl-Rónai.

Check out the restored Art Nouveau splendour of the 1911 Párizsi Nagy Áruház at No 39, now home to Alexandra Bookshop and a beautiful café in its Károly Lotz ballroom (see p167).

Continue down Nagymező útca to the junction with Király útca, where you will see the late Baroque Terézváros Parish Church (1809). Inside are two fine neoclassical altars designed by Mihály Pollack. Across the junction at Király útca 47 is the Pékary-ház (National Savings Bank). Note the statues of fierce Magyar chieftains over the portals.

Turn left along Király útca until you reach the southern end of Liszt Ferenc tér, which has one of Budapest's highest concentrations of bars.

6 Zeneakadémia (Music Academy)

The Music Academy (1907) at Liszt Ferenc tér 8 (see pp91 & 96) is a bizarre mixture of Hungarian national style and eclectic features. Symphonic, chamber and choral works are performed in the auditorium.

Walk north, passing the modern statue of Franz Liszt (László Marton, 1986) and (at the Andrássy útca end) a statue of the poet Endre Ady. There is a tourist information bureau at Liszt Ferenc tér 9–11. Turn right on Andrássy útca for Oktogon (M1).

Walk: Andrássy útca

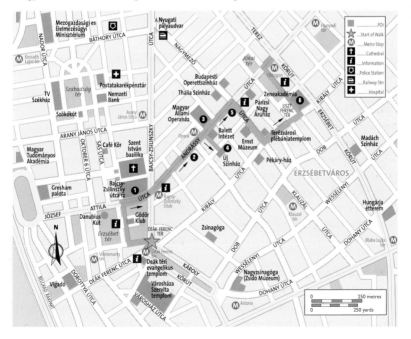

Gróh and Ede Telcs) suggesting musical movements – *allegro, andante, adagio* and *scherzo.* The smaller auditorium is used for chamber music and seats 400. The foyer has frescoes by János Zichy illustrating Hungarian musical history.

The academy has had a distinguished past; many world-famous performers such as Antal Doráti, George Szell and Sir Georg Solti are numbered among its pupils. Its professors included all the great Hungarian composers: Ferenc Erkel, Béla Bartók, Zoltán Kodály, Leó Weiner and, of course, Liszt himself. The musical tradition here is unbroken, except for a bizarre interlude at the end of World War II when the building was used for the trial of Ferenc Szálasi, the Hungarian fascist leader and psychopath. *VI, Liszt Ferenc tér 8. Tel: (36 1) 342 0179. www.zeneakademia.hu. Metro: M1 to Oktogon; Tram: 4, 6 or Trolleybus: 70, 78 to Király útca.*

Terror Háza Múzeum (Terror House Museum)

Four floors of terror courtesy of the 1956 revolution and general Communist rule. Particularly poignant are the underground cells. (*See p100.*) *VI, Andrássy útca 60. Tel (36 1) 374 2600. www.terrorhaza.hu. Open: Tue–Sun 10am–6pm. Admission charge. Metro: M1 to Vörösmarty útca.*

Liszt Ferenc Emlékmúzeum (Franz Liszt Memorial Museum)

The former apartment of Franz Liszt contains photographs and documents illustrating the composer's stormy life (1811–86). Liszt's books, musical scores and much of his furniture have been preserved and there is a bronze of the great man's right hand by Alajos Stróbl. *VI, Vörösmarty útca 35. Tel: (36 1) 322 9804. www.lisztmuseum.hu. Open: Mon–Fri 10am–6pm, Sat 9am–5pm. Closed: Sun. Admission charge. Metro: M1 to Vörösmarty útca.*

Hősök tere (Heroes' Square)

The 2.6km (1²⁄₃-mile) long boulevard of Andrássy útca ends in the east at Heroes' Square, the site chosen at the end of the 19th century for the Millennium Monument (*see opposite*). The site was selected to commemorate the millennium that had passed since the seven Magyar tribes arrived to settle the area. Every monument on the square relates to the theme of national identity, along with the triumphs and catastrophes of Magyar history.

Hősök tere, as well as its metro station on the antique M1 line, is part of Budapest's World Heritage List site. The various elements to the memorial were not completed until 1926 and then were promptly damaged in World War II. Along with the rest of Budapest, Hősök tere was carefully rebuilt. In 1989, the square swarmed with 250,000 patriots for the memorial and reburial of Imre Nagy. The emotive arrow-shaped metal-and-rust memorial to the southeast of Heroes' Square has the rather Soviet-sounding moniker: 'the

Central Monument of the 1956 Hungarian Revolution and War of Independence'. For more on the 1956 revolution, *see pp10–11*.

Millenniumi emlékmű (Millennium Monument)

In the vast square that confronts you as you enter from the west, the dominant object is György Zala's 36m (118ft)-high Millennium Monument. At the

Relief of battling Hungarians In Heroes' Square

top of an elegant Corinthian column is a representation of the Archangel Gabriel, holding the Crown of St Stephen in one hand and the Apostolic Cross in the other. According to legend, the Archangel appeared to King Stephen in a dream and told him to convert the Hungarians to Christianity. The Apostolic or Patriarchal Cross (with two horizontal bars) signifies King Stephen's role as converter of the nation.

At the base of the column are Zala's romantic representations of the leaders of the seven Magyar tribes who entered the Carpathian Basin in AD 896. The depiction of these fearsome-looking chieftains astride their horses represents the apotheosis of romantic historicism at the turn of the 20th century. In front of the column and the seven chieftains is a simple memorial to the Hungarian soldiers who fell in the two world wars, with a guard of honour on political anniversaries.

The Colonnade Behind the Archangel Gabriel column is a crescent-shaped colonnade with statues of significant figures in Hungarian history placed above friezes showing crucial historical events. From left to right the statues represent: St Stephen, St Ladislas, Kálmán Könyves (Beauclerc), Andrew II and Béla IV (all of the Árpád dynasty); the Angevin rulers Charles Robert and Louis the Great; János Hunyadi (Regent 1445–52) and Matthias Corvinus; then four Transylvanian princes (replacing Habsburgs who had ruled Hungary when the memorial was first built); and finally, the 19th-century revolutionary leader Lajos Kossuth (*see p107*). Above are allegorical sculptures of War and Peace, Work and Wealth, Knowledge and Glory.

Symbolism and politics on Heroes' Square Following the Austro-Hungarian defeat in the 1866 Austro-Prussian War, Déak Ferenc signed the Ausgleich (Compromise) with Austria in 1867. With it came a degree of sovereignty at last restored to Hungary after centuries of absolute rule from

The pantheon of great Hungarians in the Colonnade

Vienna. But the fact that the king-emperor (Franz Joseph) was still a Habsburg posed delicate problems for those constructing a monument to national achievement which, on the one hand, had to make concessions to Magyar pride and, on the other, had to avoid any offence to the ruling house.

Habsburg rule effectively began in 1526 following defeat by the Turks at the Battle of Mohács. In dealing with the period before this, national glory under native and foreign dynasties could be confidently asserted – sometimes providing a salutary historical reminder for the Habsburgs at the same time. An example is the frieze under the colonnade statue of

Charles Robert of Anjou which depicts the battle of the Marchfeld (1278); it was here that Rudolf of Habsburg's victory over Ottakar of Bohemia was secured by the Hungarian king Ladislas IV and his Cumanian cavalry.

Originally, the colonnade contained the statues of five Habsburgs: Ferdinand I, Charles VI, Maria Theresa, Leopold II and Franz Joseph himself. These were generally the ones least offensive to Hungarian sensitivities, or even, like Maria Theresa, held in some affection. Under the Communist Republic of Councils (1919), the Habsburg statues were removed and the Millennium Monument turned into a giant obelisk, the front of which featured Karl Marx being fawned upon by grateful workers. Under the regent, Miklós Horthy, the Habsburgs were returned to their niches, but were once again removed by the Communists after World War II, to be replaced by the independent Transylvanian princes of the 17th and 18th centuries, István Bocskai, Gábor Bethlen, Imre Thököly and Ferenc Rákóczi.

The harsh, Stalinist Rákosi regime (1945–56) would have liked to sweep away the whole monument, since its symbolism was not appropriate to their historical script. Luckily, this was never allowed to happen.

Műcsarnok (Hall of Art)

Schickedanz and Herzog were the architects for the building on the south side of Heroes' Square, the Hellenistic Műcsarnok (1895). It proved useful during World War I, when it was requisitioned as a military hospital. The mosaic on the pediment, *St Stephen as Patron of the Arts*, was a later addition. The gallery mostly shows work by modern Hungarian artists.
XIV, Dózsa György útca 37.
Tel: (36 1) 460 7000. www.mucsarnok.hu.
Open: 10am–6pm except Thur 10am–8pm. Closed: Mon.

Szépművészeti Múzeum (Museum of Fine Arts)

On the north side of Heroes' Square is the Museum of Fine Arts, devoted to non-Hungarian art. This imposing piece of Hellenistic historicism (1906) was

THE MILLENNIAL CELEBRATIONS

In 1881, the Budapest Council submitted a proposal to the National Assembly for a monument to mark the arrival of the Hungarians in the Carpathian Basin some 1,000 years earlier. Scholars were unable to agree on the exact date of their arrival. In the end, a millennium of 1896 was chosen. György Zala and Albert Schickedanz were given the task of preparing a monumental scheme to celebrate the millennium and 'inspire a sense of continuity and permanence'.

The statues and monuments were actually erected after the millennial celebrations (for which the first stretch of underground railway was also built). The 1896 exhibition celebrating Magyar achievements took up the whole area of the Városliget (*see pp99 & 102–5*) and was approached by a triumphal arch on Heroes' Square. It attracted over six million visitors.

Pest

also designed by Zala's co-worker on the Millennium project, Albert Schickedanz, with Fülöp Herzog.

This is one of Europe's most substantial art collections, with 2,500 paintings on display, many derived from the Esterházy Collection purchased by the Hungarian state in 1870. The Italian school is particularly well represented, with important pieces by Bellini and Titian and no fewer than five striking El Grecos.
XIV, Dózsa György útca 41.
Tel: (36 1) 469 7100;
www.szepmuveszeti.hu. Open: Tue–Sun 10am–5.30pm (until 4pm Jan–Mar). Admission charge, but free for permanent exhibitions. Metro: M1 to Hősök tere.

Walk: Oktogon to Gundel Étterem

This walk is mostly concerned with the legacy of the Millennial celebrations of 1896, held 1,000 years after the Hungarians first entered the Carpathian Basin.

Allow 2 hours.

Start from the metro station (M1) at Oktogon, which is fast-food central, and walk east along Andrássy útca.

1 Terror Háza Múzeum

The ÁVH, the secret police of the Communist regime, had their headquarters in this building, which they took over from their Nazi counterparts. A plaque on the wall recalls that Cardinal Mindszenty was tortured here. The building is now home to the Terror Háza Múzeum (*see p96*).

Andrássy útca 60. Tel (36 1) 374 2600. www.terrorhaza.hu. Open: Tue–Sun 10am–6pm. Admission charge.

2 Kodály körönd

The roundabout is named after the composer Zoltán Kodály, whose Memorial Museum is at No 1. At each exit of the roundabout are statues of Hungarian heroes of the Turkish wars.

Zoltán Kodály Memorial Museum: Tel: (36 1) 352 7106. www.kodaly-inst.hu. Open: Wed 10am–4pm, Thur–Sat 10am–6pm, Sun 10am–2pm. Turn right down Felső erdősor útca then left into Városligeti fasor.

3 Városligeti fasor

All along the tree-lined avenue are elegant early 20th-century villas, one of which belonged to the family of the Marxist philosopher György Lukács. At Városligeti fasor 5–7 is Aladar Árkay's curious **Fasori református templom** (Calvinist Church, 1913), combining Hungarian vernacular with Finnish influence. No less remarkable, at Városligeti fasor 17, is Samu Pecz's neo-Gothic **Fasori evangélikus templom** (Lutheran Church, 1905). Gyula Benczúr painted the *Adoration of the Magi* on the high altar. At No 12 is the **György Ráth Múzeum**, containing Chinese and Japanese artefacts. Other highlights include Nos 23, 24 and 47.

György Ráth Museum: Tel: (36 1) 342 3916. www.hoppmuzeum.hu. Open: Tue–Sun 10am–6pm, 4pm in winter. Turn left on Dózsa György útca, passing the area where the Communists held their propaganda rallies and which is now home to a striking new 1956 Memorial (see pp10–11) and the idökerék *(time wheel) which takes one year to make a full turn. You will then reach Heroes' Square.*

4 Hősök tere (Heroes' Square)

The square (*see pp96–9*) is a national focus of identity created for the Millennial celebrations. East of the square is the Műcsarnok (*see p99*), devoted to modern art; north is the Szépművészeti Múzeum (Museum of Fine Arts, *see p99*). The column in the centre of the square is topped by a statue of the Archangel Gabriel.

Beyond Heroes' Square, cross Városligeti tó (lake) on to Kós Károly sétány and turn right down the Vajdahunyad sétány. Rowing boats are available on the lake in summer, and in winter it becomes an outdoor ice rink.

5 Vajdahunyad vára (Vajdahunyad Castle)

Ignác Alpár's architectural fantasy (*see p104*) boasts a replica of Vajdahunyad Castle in Transylvania. Other features include a replica of the cathedral at Ják (western Hungary), the Agricultural Museum and the statue of King Béla III's anonymous chronicler (*see p103*).

6 Széchenyi Gyógyfürdő, Állatkert, Gundel Étterem

Back across the Városliget are the Széchenyi Spa (*see p104*), Vidám Park (amusement park, *see p153*), the Gundel Étterem (restaurant) at Állatkerti útca 2 and the zoo (Állatkert).

Metro: M1leaves from Hősök tere or Széchenyi fürdő.

Walk: Oktogon to Gundel Étterem

The façade of the Museum of Fine Arts

Városliget (City Woodland Park)

The 1km (²/₃-mile) square Városliget is a playground for Budapestians, young and old, a historic landmark and a veritable paradise for lovers of trees, of which the park has over 6,900, including several rare species. The area was once a hostile swamp through which meandered the stagnant waters of the Rákos Creek.

In 1240, the Tartar army of Batu Khan inflicted a crushing defeat on the Magyars here by feigning a retreat and luring their opponents on to the marsh. In 1259, Béla IV granted what had now become pastureland, known as the *ukur* (ox land), to the Dominicans of Margit sziget.

The sandy meadows were annexed to Pest by Leopold I, and Maria Theresa instigated systematic tree planting in 1751. The Embellishment Commission of the city further improved the park, after holding a competition (won by a Bavarian landscape gardener, Henrik Nebbien) for the best ideas to beautify it.

The popular Palatine Joseph threw his weight behind an imaginative 26-point plan for improving and beautifying Pest according to a proposal by the architect János Hild. A commission set up to realise Hild's ideas first met in November 1808. Its primary business was urban planning to integrate the city core with fast-developing new districts. The Commission laid down regulations concerning the maximum height of houses and their exterior decoration. It was these that subsequently determined the unified aspect of neoclassical Pest. The Commission also gave its attention to the greening of the city through tree planting and landscaping, which created Margit sziget and Városliget, among other green spaces.

The ever-increasing financial burden it placed on citizens, who had to pay for the projects, contributed to the Commission's decline after 1830 and it was finally dissolved in 1856. In 1880, it was succeeded by the highly successful Council of Public Works, which planned the next and greatest phase of city expansion.

The park contains several sights and museums including: the Széchenyi Spa, the Museum of Transport, the Agricultural Museum, the Amusement Park and the Zoo (*see p153*).

Anonymus emlékmű (Anonymous Monument)

This is understandably the capital's best-loved monument (1903). The sculptor, Miklós Ligeti, was the beneficiary of money given by Emperor Wilhelm II of Germany, who visited Budapest in 1897 and remarked on the need for more statues in the city. He had in mind more bombastic representations of warriors, but the city authorities contented themselves with a few muscle-bound Turk-killers on Andrássy útca. Ligeti's subject is very different. Master P was the anonymous monkish chronicler of

Béla III, and his *Gesta Hungarorum* (1204) was the first history of the Magyars. The sculptor has respected the historian's anonymity by hiding his face under his cowl.

XIV, Courtyard of Vajdahunyad Castle. Metro: M1 to Hősök tere.

Közlekedési Múzeum (Museum of Transport)

The origin of the collection lies in the grand Millennial Exhibition of 1896 (*see p97*). Features include the history of the Hungarian railway, historical vehicles and displays on urban, water and road transportation.

XIV, Városligeti körút 4. Tel: (36 1) 273 3840. www.km.iif.hu. Open: May–Sept Tue–Fri 10am–5pm, Sat & Sun 10am–6pm; Oct–Apr Tue–Fri 10am–4pm, Sat & Sun 10am–5pm. Admission free for the permanent collection; admission charge for the temporary exhibitions. Tram: 1 and Trolleybus: 72, 74 to Erzsébet királyné útja.

In the Petőfi Hall nearby is a permanent display on the history of aviation. (*Open: May–Oct Tue–Fri 10am–5pm, Sat & Sun 10am–6pm. Closed Nov–Apr.*)

The museum has an outlying branch: the Földalatti Múzeum (Millennium Underground Museum) in the Deák Ferenc tér metro station, which displays the history of the M1, the first underground railway in continental Europe, in a disused tunnel section with original vehicles.

www.bkv.hu. Open: Tue–Sun 10am–5pm. Admission charge. Entrance from the pedestrian underpass.

Széchenyi Gyógyfürdő (Széchenyi Spa)

The most impressive spa on the Pest side opened in 1913 (enlarged in 1927). It is a rambling neo-Baroque establishment supplied by a thermal spring discovered in 1876. The water rises from a depth of 1,256m (4,120ft) at a temperature of 70°C (158°F).

XIV, Állatkerti körút 11, Városliget. Tel: (36 1) 363 3210. www.budapestgyogyfurdoi.hu. Open: daily 6am–7pm (last entry 6pm) and until 10pm in high summer. Admission charge (deposit system, part returned depends on length of stay; keep receipt). Metro: Széchenyi fürdő.

Vajdahunyad Vára (Vajdahunyad Castle)

One of the most popular features of the 1896 Millennial Exhibition held in the City Woodland Park was Ignác Alpár's

JÁNOS HUNYADI (c.1407–56)

János Hunyadi was Hungary's greatest general in the early wars against the Turks, and the father of King Matthias Corvinus. He was regent between 1446 and 1453.

Hunyadi rose to prominence at the court of King Sigismund, whose illegitimate son he was rumoured to be. His greatest triumph was at Nándorfehérvár (Belgrade) in 1456, a battle that stopped the Turkish advance for 70 years. To mark this victory, Pope Calixtus III ordered the church bells of Christendom to be rung each day at noon in perpetuity.

architectural phantasmagoria, originally a temporary structure, but by popular demand it was subsequently rebuilt in stone (1904–08). It presented a stylistic cross-section of architecture in Hungary through the ages. The Romanesque is represented by a replica of its best-preserved example, the cathedral at Ják in western Hungary, and the Baroque by the somewhat heavy neo-Baroque of the Agricultural Museum. The *pièce de résistance*, however, is Vajdahunyad Castle, which gave its name to the whole complex (its famous original was the seat of the Hunyadi clan in Transylvania). In the courtyard is Miklós Ligeti's impressive statue of Béla III's chronicler, *Anonymous* (*see p103*). Additional Gothic and Renaissance sections copied from other buildings create a bizarre Hollywood effect, so that you half expect Errol Flynn to jump out of a castle window. The castle replica itself is one-third of the size of the original in Romania.
Metro: M1 to Hősök tere or Széchenyi fürdő.

Magyar Mezőgazdasági Múzeum (Agricultural Museum) This educational museum is another legacy of the Millennial Exhibition. Of the 18 permanent displays, those on wine production, animal husbandry and fishing are perhaps the most interesting. Horse breeding, also featured, is another field where Count István Széchenyi was active, importing English horses and methods to Hungarian studs and instituting the first horse races.
XIV, Vajdahunyad Castle on Széchenyi-sziget, Olof Palme sétany, Városliget. Tel: (36 1) 363 1117. www.mezogazdasagimuzeum.hu. Open: Tue–Sun 10am–5pm (Nov–Mar until 4pm). Admission charge. Metro: M1 to Hősök tere or Széchenyi fürdő.

Vajdahunyad Castle

AROUND KOSSUTH LAJOS TÉR
Országház (Parliament)

Feudalism endured in Hungary up to the 19th century, in some respects even into the 20th. The first glimmerings of modern parliamentarianism are contained in a memorandum submitted to the 1790–91 session of the Diet by a legal historian, József Hajnóczy. EU citizens can join the queue and take a free tour of the building and see the Hungarian Crown jewels.

The parliamentary tradition

Leading politicians of the Reform Era (István Széchenyi, Ferenc Deák, József

Statues on the façade of the Agricultural Museum

'If I were the ruler of Hungary, I would order all ships passing by on the Danube to stop for two minutes in front of the Houses of Parliament, so that travellers on board can admire, enjoy and learn from the beauty of the best Hungarian building.'

József Keszler, writing in *Magyar Nemzet* when the Parliament was completed in 1902.

Eötvös) advocated a dilution of noble privilege, and the revolutionary government of 1848 actually raised the proportion of the population enjoying political rights from 2.5 per cent to 8 per cent.

The franchise was effectively narrowed again through tax qualifications in the 1870s and it was not until 1918 that universal suffrage briefly arrived. The Horthy period (partially) and that of Communism (totally) eclipsed democracy, although, in between, free elections were held in 1947. Governments are elected for five-year terms; the next election is due to be held by May 2015.

The building of the Parliament

A competition to design the proposed Parliament building was held in 1883. Only 19 plans were submitted (in contrast to the Berlin Reichstag, which attracted 180 entries); the small number may have been due to the specifications. Imre Steindl (1839–1902) won with a neo-Gothic design, attacked by some as a 'German style', alien to the Hungarians; its supporters pointed out that Magyar and German culture had interacted fruitfully for centuries. In its style, river position and cruciform layout, the building showed the influence of Barry and Pugin's new Palace of Westminster on the Thames in London.

The exterior presents a dazzling array of finials, buttresses, towers and a mighty dome. The gilded, marble-clad interior lives up to its role as a national shrine. In the Speaker's Hall is Mihály Munkácsy's vast historical picture showing the Hungarians under Árpád receiving the homage of the Slav tribes of the Carpathian Basin.

You can also see the Crown of St Stephen in the Parliament building since its move from the Hungarian National Museum.

Tel: (36 1) 441 4904 Mon–Thur 8am–4.30pm, Fri 8am–2pm to arrange group tours. Individuals do not need to make any advance booking. The ticket office is at Gate X; open: Mon–Fri 8am–6pm, Sat 8am–4pm, Sun 8am–2pm. Admission charge for non-EU citizens. www.parlament.hu. Metro: M2 or Tram: 2 to Kossuth Lajos tér.

LAJOS KOSSUTH (1802–94)

A provincial lawyer and journalist, Kossuth made his first major political move by founding Pesti Hírlap, which (illegally) reported the proceedings of the Diet. He was briefly president of Hungary in 1848, but was forced into exile by the failure of the revolution. The rest of his life was spent abroad – in England, America and Italy, where he died. He remains a potent symbol of the Hungarian struggle for freedom.

Statue of Ferenc Rákóczi II, with the Parliament beyond

Statuary around the Parliament

To the south is a statue of the 20th-century poet Attila József, overlooking the Danube river he celebrated in verse. To the north is Mihály Károlyi, briefly prime minister of a democratic Hungary in 1918. On the square is the 18th-century freedom fighter Ferenc Rákóczi II, and Lajos Kossuth to the north.

ST STEPHEN'S CROWN

In the middle of the Parliament building (*see pp106–7*) is the historic Holy Crown (which actually post-dates the reign of St Stephen). It was returned to Hungary in 1978 from America, where it had been held in safekeeping since the end of World War II.

The crown is that of a Byzantine empress (*corona graeca*), to which an upper part (*corona latina*) was added, perhaps under Béla III (1172–96). The famous leaning cross on the top replaced an earlier one, a reliquary probably containing a fragment of the True Cross.

The *corona graeca* features portraits of the Byzantine emperor Michael Ducas, flanked by his son and the Hungarian king, Géza I (1074–77). The precious stones symbolise the four elements – sapphire for air, almandine (a kind of garnet) for fire, green glass for earth and the rim of pearls for water.

The Parliament in statistics

One thousand workers took 17 years to build the Parliament. It is 265m (869ft) long, 123m (404ft) wide and 96m (315ft) high (including the dome). It required 40 million bricks and 30,000 cubic metres (over 1 million cubic ft) of stone cladding and has 691 rooms, 17 gates, 29 staircases and 12 lifts. Only 23 years after completion, renovation had to begin, as the stone chosen by Steindl was too soft.

Néprajzi Múzeum (Ethnographical Museum)

This museum opposite the Parliamant is worth visiting to view the neo-Renaissance interior of Alajos

Hauszmann's building (1896). It began life as Hungary's Supreme Court, hence Károly Lotz's emblematic fresco on the ceiling, depicting Justitia enthroned among the clouds, flanked by allegories of Justice, Peace, Sin and Revenge. The first floor is devoted to the traditional culture of the peoples of Hungary and was opened only in 1991. On the second floor, with the help of material from the museum's marvellous photographic archive, primitive cultures are documented, including that of the Ob-Ugrian Hanti and Manszi tribes in the Urals, ancestors of the Hungarians.
V, Kossuth Lajos tér 12.
Tel: (36 1) 473 2400. www.neprajz.hu.
Open: Tue–Sun 10am–6pm. Admission charge, but free for permanent exhibitions. Metro: M2 or Tram: 2 to Kossuth Lajos tér.

Nyugati pályaudvar (Western Railway Station)

The first train on the first stretch of railway built in Hungary left for Vác on 15 July 1846 from the wooden predecessor to the present Western Railway Station. The architect responsible for this gracious example of industrial architecture (1877) was a Frenchman, August de Serres, and it was built by the famous Eiffel Company of Paris. In order to ensure that train services were not disrupted during construction work, the new station was built above and around the old one, which was demolished only when the work was complete.

The station has been restored, not quite authentically, since the (nonetheless attractive) blue paint on the ironwork is a postmodernist conceit. The former Royal Waiting Room, built for the arrival of Franz Joseph and Elizabeth when they attended the Millennial celebrations of 1896, is in the east wing. Its ceiling features the coats of arms of the Hungarian counties served by trains from this station. To the right of the main entrance a sumptuous restaurant, redolent of the bourgeois comforts of the railway age, still stands … as probably the most elegant McDonald's in Europe.
VI, Teréz körút 109–111. Metro: M3 to Nyugati pályaudvar.

Vígszínház (Comedy Theatre)

The charming neo-rococo theatre was built by the Viennese firm of Fellner and Helmer. When it opened in 1896, the public were sceptical of its chances
(*Cont. on p113*)

Walk: Deák Ferenc tér to Fehér ház

The walk explores the political and economic quarter of Pest.

Allow 2 hours.

Under Deák Ferenc tér is the Millennium Underground Museum. On the edge of Erzsébet tér, walk towards the Danube past the Corvinus Kempinski Hotel and turn right at the British Embassy on Harmincad útca.

1 Danubius kút (Danubius Fountain)

This triple-basined fountain on Erzsébet tér is a copy of Miklós Ybl's beautiful original. The ladies perched on the lower bowl represent Danube tributaries – the Tisza, Dráva and Száva. To the east is the Gödör Klub, a varied cultural centre located in the pit dug for initial plans for the new National Theatre.

Dog-leg from Bécsi útca back on to Harmincad útca then turn right on to József nádor tér.

2 József Nádor szobor

Johann Halbig's statue of Archduke Joseph of Hungary stands in the square. The sixth son of Emperor Leopold II, the archduke was Palatine of Hungary from 1796 until his death 50 years later. He did much to realise Hungarian aspirations and moderate the policies of the Habsburg court in Vienna.

Turn left down József Attila útca and right into Roosevelt tér.

3 Roosevelt tér

The square (*see p87*) is flanked by hotels at the southern end, and the elegant Magyar Tudományos Akadémia (Academy of Sciences) to the north. There are statues of 19th-century statesmen – József Eötvös (who reformed public education), Ferenc Deák (who organised the 1867 Compromise with the Habsburgs) and István Széchenyi (*see p71*). On the east side are the Ministry of the Interior, and the Jugendstil Gresham Palota (Palace), now a Four Seasons Hotel.

Walk along Akadémia útca and turn right down Széchenyi útca, which leads to Szabadság tér.

4 Szabadság tér

The Intelligent Fountain (*Szökőkút*) is a thoroughly entertaining addition to the square. The former stock exchange on the west side was TV Székház (Hungarian Television Centre); it is currently vacant. The Soviet Memorial is the last of its kind remaining in

Budapest (*see pp136–7*). Opposite is Ignác Alpár's eclectic **Nemzeti Bank** (National Bank, 1905). Don't miss the *Látogatóközpont* (Visitor's Centre). It's an interesting exhibition about the history of the forint where you can mint coins, print your own banknote with your photo on it and see your weight in gold forints or euros. (*Tel: (36 1) 428 2752. www.mnb.hu. Open: Mon–Fri 9am–4pm. Free admission.*)

North of that is the Jugendstil American Embassy, where Cardinal Mindszenty took refuge during the brief 1956 revolution then remained for 19 years. Ödön Lechner's marvellous Postatakarékpénztar (Post Office Savings Bank, *see p19*) is round the corner (*Hold útca 4*). Just to the north is the *Batthyány örökmécses* (Batthyány Eternal Flame) commemorating the prime minister of the independent government, Count Lajos Batthyány, who was shot on this spot.

Turn left on Báthory útca to the monument of Imre Nagy gazing at the Parliament from his bridge on Vértanúk tere adjacent to Kossuth Lajos tér.

5 Kossuth Lajos tér

This vast space is dominated by Imre Steindl's Országház (Parliament, *see pp106–8*), the most ambitious construction project ever undertaken in Hungary. From 1885, some 1,000 labourers and craftsmen worked on it for 17 years. Alajos Hauszmann's Supreme Court, now the Mezögazdasági es Elelmézesügyi Minisztérium

(Ministry of Agriculture) and the Neprazji Múzeum (Ethrographical Museum) occupy the southeastern side. The statues on the square represent heroes of the struggle for independence. A statue of executed prime minister Imre Nagy stands alone on a small bridge on adjacent Vértanúk tere.

Walk up to Fehér ház (White House), formerly the sinister headquarters of the Communists, or browse the antique galleries on Falk Miksa útca. Tram and bus stops are on Szent István körút.

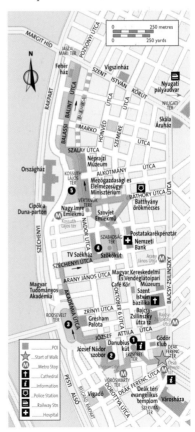

The neo-Renaissance exterior of the Eastern Railway Station

of survival (it was too far out from the centre and had no funding from the state). In fact, a diet of Hungarian and European comedies, played in naturalistic style, soon had audiences flocking to it. Ferenc Molnár was one dramatist who began his career here. Between the wars the staging of modern playwrights' work and visits by guest companies from abroad built up the theatre's reputation.
XIII, Pannónia útca 1.
Tel: (36 1) 329 2340. www.vigszinhaz.hu.
Metro: M3 or Tram: 4, 6 to Nyugati pályaudvar.

OTHER SIGHTS
Keleti pályaudvar
(Eastern Railway Station)

Budapest's Eastern Railway Station (designed by Gyula Rochlitz and János Feketeházi, 1884) has a 44m (144ft) steel framework behind a rather grandiose, recently renovated neo-Renaissance façade. Two British engineers are honoured with statues high up on the triumphal arch that spans the main entrance: on the right is James Watt (1736–1819), inventor of the steam engine; on the left, George Stephenson (1781–1848), builder of the famous *Rocket* locomotive in 1829.

Despite the station's name, many trains from the west arrive here, just as trains for the north and east leave from the Western Railway Station.

The square in front of Keleti pályaudvar is named after Gábor Baross (1848–92), who was transport minister in the 1880s. He rationalised the Hungarian railway system by nationalising the six existing private railway companies.
VIII, Baross tér. Metro: M2 to Keleti pályaudvar.

Kerepesi temető
(Kerepesi Cemetery)

Beyond the Eastern Railway Station (Keleti pályaudvar), Pest begins to spread itself with sports stadia, race tracks and the huge (90,000sq m/ 970,000sq ft) Kerepesi Cemetery. The cemetery, Hungary's national pantheon, is no longer in use. Its status as a patriotic shrine was scarcely enhanced by the inclusion of Communist worthies, buried with full honours traditionally supplied by the unsavoury Workers' Militia. The last to be entombed in the 'Pantheon of the Working Class Movement' was János Kádár in 1989.

Perhaps it was the disagreeable company that prompted the son of László Rajk to have his father's remains removed from the area: Rajk Senior (who was just as unscrupulous as his tormentors, but spoke well) was executed after a show trial in 1949, Kádár himself having successfully extracted his 'confession' in prison. His reburial in 1956 after his rehabilitation was attended by 250,000 and lit the fuse for the revolution of that year. Another notable absentee from Kerepesi is Imre Nagy, the ill-fated prime minister of

Inside the Kerepesi Cemetery

graves of honour here include Lajos Batthyány (prime minister of the independent government of 1848) and Ferenc Deák (architect of the Compromise with Austria, 1867). József Antall, the first post-Communist prime minister, was buried here, next to Kossuth, on 18 December 1993. The world of the arts is represented by Ferenc Erkel, the actress Lujza Blaha and Zsigmond Móricz (an early 20th-century writer in the Zola mould).
VIII, Main entrance in Fiumei útca. Metro: M2 to Keleti pályaudvar; Tram: 24 to Dologház útca.

1956, who was reburied in the Pest Municipal Cemetery in 1989 after a ceremony in his honour on Heroes' Square. Previously, he had lain in an unmarked grave.

Some distance from the burial place of those who enslaved their fellow-countrymen is that of Lajos Kossuth, who led the enslaved temporarily to freedom in 1848. The tomb is a rhetorical monument crowned by a figure holding aloft the torch of liberty. Other major public figures who have

Láthatatlan Kiállítás (Invisible Exhibition)
On the edge of a park is this not-for-profit museum guided by the visually impaired and designed to allow the seeing to feel life without sight. See how gadgets are adapted, then feel your way around seven zones. Book in advance for an English guide.
VIII, Népliget útca 2. Tel: (36) 20 771 4236. www.lathatatlan.hu. Open: noon–8pm, Sat & Sun 10am–8pm. Admission charge. Metro: M3 to Népliget.

Művészetek Palotája (Palace of Arts)
In Millenniumi Kulturális Központ (Millennium City), this building houses the Ludwig Collection (*see below*), the Béla Bartók National Concert Hall, which has world-class acoustics and can seat 1,700 people, and the Festival

Theatre. The new concert organ, the largest pipes of which were installed during initial construction, has 92 registers and five manuals. Free guided tours should be arranged in advance, (*tel: (36 1) 555 3005*).
IX, Komor Marcell útca 1.
Tel: (36 1) 555 3000. www.mupa.hu.
Tram: 2, 24 to Millenniumi Kulturális Központ.

Ludwig Múzeum (Ludwig Collection)
This museum contains a collection of contemporary art, donated by the German industrialist Peter Ludwig, and features Picasso, Warhol and Lichtenstein among others. It was originally housed in the Buda Castle, but moved to the Művészetek Palotája (Palace of Arts) in the 2005 development, Millennium City. The location houses the Ludwig Múzeum, the Nemzeti Hangversenyterem (National Concert Hall), the Fesztivál Színház (Festival Theatre), a restaurant, a funky pop-art café and a stylish bookshop. (*See above.*)
IX, Komor Marcell útca 1.
Tel: (36 1) 555 3444.
www.ludwigmuseum.hu. Open: Tue–Sun 10am–8pm, last Sat of each month 10am–8pm. Closed: Mon. Admission charge. Tram: 2 to Millenniumi Kulturális Központ.

Zwack Unicum Múzeum
Along Dandár útca, adjacent to the main factory site, is the home of Hungary's national drink. Trace the

---

FERENC ERKEL (1810–93)

First director of the National Theatre, Erkel composed the quintessential Hungarian opera *Bánk Bán* (1861), a musical setting of József Katona's patriotic play about a murder at the medieval Hungarian court. Erkel's music combined elements of the 18th-century *verbunkos* (played on military recruiting drives), folk themes and pre-Verdian opera. He also wrote the remarkably moving Hungarian national anthem (1844).

---

history of this herbal *digestif* before and after the Zwack family's exile to the USA during Communist rule, then sample the tipple. Always call to make tour arrangements.
IX, Soroksári útca 26.
Tel: (36 1) 476 2383. www.zwack.hu.
Open: Mon–Fri 9am–6pm. Closed Sat & Sun. Admission charge. Tram: 2 to Haller útca.

Erkel Színház (Erkel Theatre)
Renovation has left little of the building's original Jugendstil ornamentation intact, but its modern styling is itself attractive. In particular, the first-floor buffet area boasts two spectacular wall paintings by the Hungarian painter Aurél Bernáth. At one end is *A Midsummer Night's Dream* and at the other a representation of Imre Madách's Faustian drama *The Tragedy of Man* (1861). Bernáth worked on the paintings between 1972 and 1973. This is also the alternate venue of the Hungarian State Opera. (*See p90.*)
VIII, Köztársaság tér 30. Tel: (36 1) 333 0540. Metro: M2 to Blaha Lujza tér.

Pest

Hungarian lifestyle

For centuries, Hungary was an agrarian feudal society, and many a city-dweller is still provided by country cousins with home-made fare, vegetables and fruit. A popular 'rustic' tradition among young Budapestians today is the *szalonnasütés* (bacon barbecue). In a suitably rural environment, such as Szentendre Island, bacon is roasted with peppers and potatoes, and Magyar folk songs are sung.

A more genuine peasant tradition is the December *disznóölés* (pig-killing); every part of the pig is used to make *kolbász* (sausage), *hurka* (black pudding), *sonka* (ham), *disznósajt* (pickled feet and ears), *kocsonya* (pork in aspic), *szalonna* (bacon) and *zsír* (lard).

While life in the country is still geared to the rhythm of the seasons, urban Hungarians often juggle their waking hours between two jobs in order to make ends meet. Life is hectic; by Western standards it is also uncomfortable for most, due to a perennial shortage of accommodation. Young married couples are often condemned to live with in-laws, and most families have bedrooms that double as sitting rooms. In the inner city, many live in hideous concrete panel-housing blocks, notorious for their poor quality and lack of privacy. In the suburbs, life is more agreeable for those who live in family bungalows with lovingly tended vegetable gardens. Suburbanites may keep fit by gardening, but city-dwellers must turn to other means. Swimming in the spas is a popular pastime, combining as it does opportunities for gossip with healthy exercise. During the summer, and especially the weekends, most of Budapest flees to Lake Balaton, where many people have built holiday homes. Once the winter departs, street cafés

Traditional *kolbász*

and outdoor areas of bars and clubs fling open their doors so locals can absorb some much-needed vitamin D.

More space, more cash and more attention to diet are beginning to have an impact on Hungarian lifestyle for the younger generations, and although a more 'European' lifestyle, with chain hotels, cafés, etc, is becoming more noticeable, Budapest very much remains a Hungarian city.

Unlikely to change are the gregarious habits of the Magyars, their capacity to make much out of little, and their ability to fill the calendar with excuses for celebration. Every day, it seems, is somebody's name day, and therefore an excuse for a visit that begins with the enigmatic greeting: *'Isten éltessen sokáig, füled érjen bokáig'* ('May God grant you a long life and may your ears reach your ankles').

Lake Balaton is popular among locals for a weekend getaway

Getting away from it all

'Travel is more than the seeing of sights; it is a change that goes on, deep and permanent, in the ideas of living.'

MIRIAM BEARD

Budapest

The main excursion outside Budapest's city centre is based on natural phenomena. A series of caves exists under the Buda Hills, comprising ancient and long inactive vents for hot springs. The caves have been formed along tectonic fractures. The same hills are criss-crossed with hiking trails as well as a small mechanical railway and chairlift. Budapest's comprehensive public transport network provides excellent connections. For details, *see pp183–5.*

Around Budapest, whether you opt for the charms of nearby Lake Balaton or the further afield reaches of the Hungarian Plain, there are many sights to keep you occupied. Lake Balaton is Budapest's favourite destination and in the summer, the extensive rail and road links become stretched. Its slender finger-shaped shores begin just 100km (62 miles) from the city but it stretches to its southwest point at the medicinal lake at Hévíz 190km (118 miles) from Budapest.

The Danube Bend provides dramatic scenery and picturesque riverside towns from Szentendre just 23km (14 miles) north of Budapest, to Esztergom 64km (40 miles) downriver. Trains, buses and boats in the summer provide easy and comfortable travel choices to all destinations. Also, within the Budapest metropolitan area is Gödöllő, home to the Royal Palace, a favourite summer residence of Sissy, Emperor Franz Josef's wife. For further details, *see pp129–30.*

At approximately 268km (167 miles) by 528km (328 miles), Hungary is small enough to make most regions accessible from Budapest, but these destinations, due to distance and interest, can't be fully appreciated in a day. Further afield, the ancient town of Eger has a castle, thermal baths and some of the best red and white wines in Hungary just 140km (87 miles) northeast of Budapest. Similarly, Tokaj's renowned sweet wines make this more distant northeastern region of Hungary

Hungary

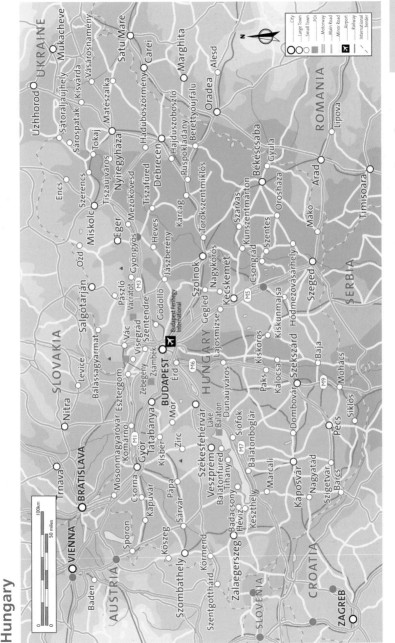

'Budapest and the Danube present one of the most beautiful river-town landscapes anywhere: perhaps the most beautiful in Europe, on a par with London and the Thames or Paris and the Seine.'

Jules Romains 1926

another popular wine-tasting destination. Kecskemét in the southern plain known as the Alföld is famous for its fabulous horsemanship, while Pécs, in the far south close to the border with Serbia and Croatia, was European City of Culture in 2010. Tokaj, the Alföld and Pécs are all UNESCO World Heritage Sites. For detailed information and travel options, *see pp133–5.*

BUDAI HEGYSÉG (THE BUDA HILLS)

The easiest way of seeing the Buda Hills is to make a tour with the cogwheel railway and the Children's (formerly 'Pioneer') Railway (*see p152*).

The cogwheel railway (*Fogaskerekű Vasút*) ascends from Városmajor along wooded slopes past the Svábhegy (a Swabian village founded under Maria Theresa), and the Pető Institute for brain-damaged children, to Rege útca on Széchenyi-hegy. Nearby is the end-station for the Children's Railway (Gyermekvasút), staffed by children under the supervision of adults. You can take it to the terminus at Hűvösvölgy, or get off at Normafa (first stop) or János hegy (fourth stop) for rambles with convenient return connections. From Normafa, a 2km

(1¼-mile) walk (bear left) brings you to the Budakeszi Vadaspark (Game Park), with return buses to Moszkva tér. From János hegy (529m/1,736ft, lookout tower), a chairlift (*libegö*) descends to Zugligeti útca (bus 155 to Moszkva tér).

Cogwheel Railway: Tram: 59, 61 from Moszkva tér along Szilágyi Erzsébet fasor to Városmajor. The Children's Railway (www.gyermekvasut.hu) runs every 45–60 minutes 9am–6.30pm in summer, 9am–5pm in winter. Budapest local tickets and passes are not valid on the Children's Railway. Budakeszi Game Park open: daily 9am–5pm. Bus: 22 from Moszkva tér to Szanatórium útca.

Rock Chapel in the caves in Gellért Hill

The János hegy chairlift operates 9am–5.30pm or 9.30am–4.30pm according to season.

Buda Caves

A number of exciting caves have been discovered in the Buda Hills, and four of them can be visited without difficulty. At the ticket offices for the Pál-völgyi and Szemlőhegyi caves you can apply to join special tours of several other caves not normally open to the public. Appropriate dress will be provided. It is essential that you are fit and in sound health.

Budavári Labirintus
(Buda Castle Labyrinth)

The unique calcareous tufa caves under Castle Hill were created by hot-water springs almost half a million years ago. In the 1930s, as part of the war-time defence programme, the complex of cellars was converted into a shelter large enough to accommodate as many as 10,000 people at a time. Extensive restoration is removing the concrete slapped on when the labyrinth served as a secret military base during the Cold War.

I, Úri útca 9; a wheelchair-accessible entrance is at Lovas útca 4/A. Tel (36 1) 212 0207. www.labirintus.com. Open 9.30am–7.30pm. Admission charge.

*Adjacent is the entrance to the **Hospital in the Rock**, the top-secret military hospital and bunker used from World War II.*

I, Lovas útca 4/C. Tel: (36) 70 701 0101. www.sziklakorhaz.hu. Open Tue–Sun 10am–10pm. Admission charge. Bus: 16 to Dísz tér.

Gellérthegyi Sziklakápolna
(Rock Chapel)

The earliest human habitation of the region was probably in the Gellért caves. A chapel consecrated here in 1926 was walled up by the Communists but restored and reopened in 1990. The acoustics and views are superb.

XI, Szent Gellért rakpart 1. Open: 9am–8pm. Tram: 18, 19, 41, 47, 49. Bus: 86 to Szent Gellért tér.

Pál-völgyi Barlang

This 7km (4-mile)-long cave came to light in 1902 when the son of the local quarry manager squeezed himself through a gap in the rocks. The highlight of the three-hour tour is the 'zoo', so called because the drip formations bring to mind elephants and crocodiles. Book to ensure an English guided tour, which are scheduled for Monday, Wednesday and Thursday afternoons.

II, Szépvölgyi útca 162. Tel: (36 1) 325 9505. www.barlangaszat.hu. Open: Tue–Sun 10am–4pm. Admission charge. Bus: from Kolosy tér, Óbuda to Pál-völgyi cseppkőbarlang.

Szemlőhegyi Barlang

This is renowned for its 'peastone' formations, like bunches of grapes with

little stalactites suspended from them. Part of the cave is used for treating people with respiratory diseases. There is a small exhibition about local speleology in the reception building.
II, Pusztaszeri útca 35.
Tel: (36 1) 325 6001. Open: Wed–Mon 10am–4pm. Admission charge. Bus: 29 from Árpád híd to Szemlı-hegyi-barlang.

DANUBE ISLANDS

Of the islands on the Budapest stretch of the Danube, the small Óbuda Island is largely of historical interest: a shipyard was founded here in 1836 on the initiative of Count Széchenyi and worked until the 1990s. At the north end are the ruins of the Roman governor's palace. Margaret Island is the city's loveliest park (*see p57*). Csepel Island begins in Budapest and extends to the Great Hungarian Plain.

Csepel sziget (Csepel Island)

This elongated sliver of land begins as Budapest's industrialised XXI district and ends 54km (34 miles) to the south. The origins of the district's heavy industry go back to 1882 when Manfred Weiss founded a factory producing ration tins for troops of the Austro-Hungarian army. He moved to Csepel in 1890 and expanded into armaments. The Communists nationalised the business after the war, and the workers of 'Red Csepel' were supposed to be a bulwark of proletarian solidarity (they even had the somewhat dubious

pleasure of being represented by the Stalinist dictator Rákosi). Nevertheless, they were the last to hold out against Russian tanks in the 1956 revolution.

Csepel's industry is now largely obsolete and it is planned to use some of its vacant plots for exhibitions and the like. Across the Danube on the Buda side can be seen the restored Baroque Nagytétényi Castle which has a good display of the history of European furniture.
XXII, Kastélypark útca 9–11. Tel: (36 1) 207 0005. www.nagytetenyi.hu. Open: Tue–Sun 10am–6pm. Admission charge. Bus: 33 from Móricz Zsigmond körtér to Petőfi Sándor útca (30 minutes), from Csepel, bus 138 to Campona shopping mall, and then bus 3 to the Petőfi Sándor útca stop.

You can see Nagytétényi Kastélymúzeum, the Tropicarium (an aquarium and tropical rainforest complex, *www.tropicarium.hu*) and Szoborpark in a day or half-day, because bus 33 stops at the Campona mall (Lépcsős útca, where the Tropicarium is) on the way to Nagytétényi. From Campona, bus 150 goes to the Szoborpark (Statue Park, *see pp136–7*).

Ráckeve

The place most worth visiting on Csepel Island lies to the south, where the ugly industrial suburbs give way to cottages and gardens. *Rác* means 'Serb' in Hungarian, and the small town was originally populated by Serbs from Keve, who fled here in the 15th century. Today, of Ráckeve's 8,500 inhabitants, only a handful are Serb. The Gothic Szerb templom (Serbian Church, *Viola útca 1*) dates to 1487, but the two side chapels were added later, with the Baroque spire. Inside are colourful frescoes (1771) in Byzantine style by Tódor Gruntovic (who was apparently an Albanian from Kosovo). The sequence begins to the right of the entrance with the Nativity and continues round the church walls, ending with the Resurrection. The Baroque iconostasis (1768) is also striking. The Savoyai Kastélyszálló, the Baroque mansion belonging to Prince Eugene of Savoy, is now a luxurious hotel and restaurant (*Kossuth Lajos útca. Tel: (36 24) 485 253*). Prince Eugene was Central Europe's greatest general, and was responsible for clearing Hungary of the Turks after the reconquest of Buda in 1686.

Aqualand Ráckeve harnesses thermal waters into a huge complex of indoor and outdoor pools, spas, slides and rides.

Strand útca 1. Tel: (36 24) 423 220. www.aqua-land.hu. Open Mon–Thur 6am–9pm; Fri 6am–1am, Sat 8am–1am, Sun 8am–9pm.

Ráckeve is 46km (29 miles) south of Budapest. The Ráckeve HÉV suburban train leaves Vágóhíd in Pest and takes 70 minutes. Tram: 2, 24 end at Vágóhíd.

WEKERLE TELEP (WEKERLE SETTLEMENT)

In the XIX district (Kispest), a remarkable experiment in 20th-century social housing reflects the ambitious plans for city expansion developed by Budapest's mayor, István Bárczy. Inspired by the principles of the English garden suburb, the Wekerle Housing Estate was built over 20 years from 1909 as a completely self-contained village for employees of the municipality. Sándor Wekerle was the far-sighted and liberal prime minister between 1892 and 1895, and again between 1906 and 1910. The principal architect for the estate was the polymath Károly Kós who invested the wooden, gabled and balconied houses with a Transylvanian charm (albeit pseudo). Four ornamental gates stand at the entrances to the central Kós Károly tér. The west gate is particularly interesting, consisting of a huge planked gable rising over rusticated plinths. Another gate mixes vernacular decoration with Renaissance features.

The houses have their own vegetable gardens – a rarity within the city – and the different quarters are divided by leafy avenues and squares.

Metro: M3 to Határ út; then Bus: 194 or 199 to Kós Károly tér. Or Bus: 99 from Blaha Lujza tér metro (M2), Népszínház útca to Kós Károly tér.

Getting away from it all

The Serbian Church, Ráckeve

DUNAKANYAR
(THE DANUBE BEND)

The Danube enters Hungary flowing west to east, but at Esztergom it is forced into an S-shape in a narrow valley between the Pilis and Börzsöny Mountains. After Visegrád it completes a final loop, thereafter settling on a north–south course. This whole stretch of the river – from Esztergom to Szentendre Island – is known as the Danube Bend, an area of enchantingly dramatic scenery.

Szentendre

Szentendre (St Andrew), the closest town to Budapest on the Danube Bend, has a Balkan charm rarely encountered in Hungary. It was founded as a town for Serbian refugees after the catastrophic defeat of Serbia by the Turks at Kosovo in 1389. A second wave of immigrants came in 1690, fleeing the wrath of the Turks after an abortive uprising. Both the earlier Hungarian kings and the Habsburgs favoured these refugees from the south. The settlers were able to exploit their trading privileges and the town's proximity to the Danube to become wealthy. Several Orthodox churches were built here in the 18th century, usually on the site of wooden predecessors, each representing a community drawn from a common provenance in the Slav homeland.

The Serb population dwindled during the 20th century and now only about 100 are left out of Szentendre's 20,000 inhabitants. Some of the churches have been sold and are difficult to access. Szentendre's other claim to fame is the artists' colony started here in the early years of the 20th century and still going strong. At weekends, the riverside restaurants are packed with day-trippers arriving by car, bicycle, motorbike, bus and train.

Go for vanilla or branch out to beetroot at Margaretta Cukrászda (*Görög útca 4*), home to hundreds of ice creams. Alternatively, grab a pint at the Red Lion Pub (*Szerb útca 4*) or settle in for superb coffees from across the globe at Café Frei (*Bogdányi útca 40*).

Belgrád székesegyház
(Belgrade Cathedral)

The episcopal church is open only at times of Mass (*Sat 5pm in winter, 6pm in summer, Sun 10am, 4pm*). The iconostasis (1777), the bishop's throne and the pulpit are notable. Do not miss the nearby Szerb Egyházművészeti Gyűjtemény (Collection of Ecclesiastical Treasures), which contains fine icons and other works by Orthodox masters. *Pátriárka útca 5. Tel: (36 26) 312 399. Open: Mar–Sept Tue–Sun 10am–6pm; Oct–Dec Tue–Sun 10am–4pm; Jan & Feb Fri–Sun 10am–4pm. Admission charge.*

Blagoveštenska templom
(Church of the Annunciation)

Commissioned by Greek merchants and built by Andreas Mayerhoffer (1754), this church has a fine iconostasis (1804) by a Serb artist from Buda.

Church of the Annunciation

Edge of Fő tér. Open: most days 9am–5pm. Admission charge.

Ferenczy Károly Múzeum (Károly Ferenczy Museum)

The museum is devoted to artistic works by the Ferenczy family, of whom the father, Károly (1862–1917), was the leading figure in the Nagybánya artists' colony.

Fő tér 6. Tel: (36 26) 310 244. Open: mid-Mar–Sept Tue–Sun 9am–5pm. Admission charge.

Kovács Margit Múzeum (Margit Kovács Museum)

Billed as Hungary's leading ceramicist, Margit Kovács (1902–77) drew on the traditions of folk art and fine art. The claims made for her work have been recklessly inflated.

Vastagh György útca 1. Tel: (36 26) 310 244. Open: mid-Mar–Sept Tue–Sun 9am–5pm. Admission charge.

Marcipán Múzeum (Marzipan Museum)

Fő tér 2–4, entrance through the cake shop. Tel: (36 20) 452 3875. www.szabomarcipan.hu. Open: daily 10am–6pm.

Plébániatemplom (Parish Church of St John)

Steps lead up from Fő tér to Templom tér, on which stands the church of the Catholic Dalmatian community. You can only view it from the porch, but it is worth the climb for the marvellous panorama of the town from the square.

Pozarevacka Church
(Church of St Michael the Archangel)

The church was built in 1763 on the site of a wooden predecessor. Here and in the Blagoveštenska an atmospheric tape of Orthodox chanting is played for the benefit of visitors.

Kossuth Lajos útca. Open: in summer, Fri–Sun 11am–5pm. Admission charge.

Szabadtéri Néprajzi Múzeum
(Village Museum or Skanzen)

Known as a skanzen after a pioneering Swedish ethnographical reconstruction of village life, the museum shows typical peasant dwellings, churches and functional agricultural buildings from ten regions of Hungary. At weekends there are often demonstrations and folklore programmes.

5km (3 miles) west of Szentendre on Szabadságforrás útca.
Tel: (36 26) 502 500. www.skanzen.hu.
Open: Apr–Oct Tue–Sun 9am–5pm (until 4pm in winter). Bus: 7 from HÉV station. Admission charge.

Városi Tömegközlekedési Múzeum
(Museum of the Hungarian City Public Transport)

Very interesting for tram fans – next door to the HÉV terminus (turn right as you exit the HÉV).

Dózsa György útca. Tel: (36 26) 314 280.
www.bkv.hu/muzeum/szentendre.html.
Open: Apr–Oct Tue–Sun 10am–5pm.

Szentendre (www.szentendre.hu) is 23km (14 miles) northwest of Budapest. Take the suburban rail network (HÉV) direct from Batthyány tér or hourly buses from Árpád híd bus terminus. Boats leave from Vigadó tér (twice daily in summer, otherwise weekends only; see www.mahartpassnave.hu). Budapest local tickets, passes and the Budapest Card are valid only to Békásmegyer and not to Szentendre on the HÉV. You should buy a supplementary ticket at the station or on the train from the conductor.

Vác

Mentioned by Ptolemy in his *Geographia*, the ancient town of Vác on the left bank of the Danube was made an episcopal see by King Stephen. The town was rich – the Vác silver mark was the main local currency of the 14th century – and the bishops were powerful. One of them, Kristóf Migazzi, had the Triumphal Arch near Március 15 tér erected for Maria Theresa's visit in 1764. Its architect, Isidore Canevale, built the imposing neoclassical cathedral on Konstantin tér in 1777. It contains a fine fresco (*The Trinity* by Franz Anton Maulbertsch) in its cupola. Worth seeing also are the finds in the crypt of the Dominican church.

34km (21 miles) north of Budapest. Frequent trains from Nyugati pályaudvar. Szentendre and Vác can be seen in one day. Buses run hourly from Szentendre to Váci Rév, where a ferry meets the bus and takes you to the centre of Vác, from where buses return at regular intervals until 10.30pm.

Visegrád

The smallest town in the country (population 1,700) is famous for King Matthias Corvinus's early Renaissance summer palace and the medieval citadel. The Fellegvár (Citadel) is well worth the climb. The Hungarian Crown jewels were once kept in this powerful fortress on a 350m (1,148ft)-high peak. The views over the river and of the Börszöny Mountains are superb. Visegrád celebrated its millennium in 2009.
Tel: (36 26) 398 101. Open daily 10am–6pm, to 4pm in winter. Admission charge on the path from Nagy Lajos útca. Taxis are available in summer, and from April to September there is a direct bus from Árpád híd terminus.

Királyi palota (Royal Palace)

Charles Robert of Anjou put Visegrád on the map by building a palace here in 1316. Enlarged and embellished by Sigismund of Luxembourg and Matthias Corvinus in the 15th century, it was rediscovered in the 1930s. You will notice Matthias's coat of arms on the Herkules Fountain. The Lion Fountain (a replica) is so called because sleeping lions support the five columns of the baldacchino.
Fő útca 23. Tel: (36 26) 398 026. Open: Tue–Sun 9am–4.30pm. Free admission.

Solomon torony (Solomon's Tower)

In the Lower Castle of the citadel, the tower was actually built two centuries after Solomon, son of Andrew I, was imprisoned in Visegrád, so the name is a romantic invention. It houses a museum with remnants from the Royal Palace.
Mátyás Király Múzeum (King Matthias Museum). Tel: (36 26) 398 026. www.visegradmuzeum.hu. Open: May–Oct, Tue–Sun 9am–5pm. Free admission.

Visegrád (www.visegrad.hu) is 40km (25 miles) from Budapest and reached by hourly buses from Árpád híd (Pest side), or via Road 11 by car. Boats run from Vigadó tér twice daily in summer (www.mahartpassnave.hu).

The Danube at Visegrád

Zebegény

Károly Kós's vernacular church is the main sight in this artists' haunt on the left bank of the Danube. The stylised frescoes (Emperor Constantine's *Vision of the Cross*, *St Helena Discovering the True Cross*) are by the Gödöllő artist Aladár Körösfői-Kriesch (*see p91*).
50km (31 miles) north of Budapest.
Roads 2 & 12 via Vác; boats from Vigadó tér (see www.mahartpassnave.hu); the Szob- or Sturovo-bound trains via Vác from Nyugati pályaudvar.

Esztergom

Esztergom is where King Stephen was born (c. 975) and where he was crowned on Christmas Day, 1000. He founded Esztergom's archbishopric the following year; Hungarian primates were based here until the Turkish conquest and returned only in the 19th century.
Esztergom is 64km (40 miles) from Budapest on Road 11. Half-hourly buses from Árpád híd (Pest side). Trains from Nyugati pályaudvar. A boat leaves at 8am daily in summer (weekends in low season) from Vigadó tér, Budapest (www.mahartpassnave.hu).

The Basilica

Hungary's largest church, begun in 1822 and completed in 1869, is more imposing than pleasing, but do not miss the red marble funerary chapel (1507) of Archbishop Tamás Bakócz, a relic of the original cathedral. The crypt contains some fine Renaissance sarcophagi and

the *kincstár* (treasury) has exquisite gold- and silversmiths' work.
Szent István tér 1. Tel: (36 33) 402 354. www.bazilika-esztergom.hu. Open: daily Mar–Oct 8am–5pm; Nov–Feb 8am–4pm. Free admission to the basilica; admission charge to the Treasury, Crypt, Cupola and Bell Tower.

Keresztény Múzeum (Christian Museum)

This is in Esztergom's Víziváros (Water Town). Its greatest treasure is the Lord's Coffin of Garamszentbenedek (c. 1480), which was paraded in Easter processions carrying the figure of Christ crucified.
Mindszenty tér 2. Tel: (36 33) 413 880. www.keresztenymuzeum.hu. Open: Mar–Oct 10am–5pm. Closed: Jan–Apr Mon & Tue. Admission charge.

Vármúzeum (Medieval Royal Castle)

The old castle is just to the south of the basilica. It includes a 12th-century chapel with a fine rose window, the Hall of Virtues and the room where King Stephen was born.
Szent István tér 1. Tel: (36 33) 415 986. Open: Tue–Sun 10am–6pm (until 4pm in winter). Free admission.

GÖDÖLLŐ

Count Antal Grassalkovich I (1694–1771) began construction of the Baroque Királyi Kastély in 1733. The Crown designated it a royal residence in 1867 and it became known as the Sissy Mansion after Queen Elizabeth (popularly known as Sissy), wife of the Austro-Hungarian emperor Franz Joseph I (*see pp8–9*), who loved coming here. After 1945 it became a home for aged people and later a Soviet military barracks; it is now a museum.

Take the HÉV from Örs Vezér tere until the Szabadság tér stop. Budapest local tickets, passes and the Budapest Card require a supplementary ticket, which can be bought at the Örs Vezér tere and Szabadság tér ticket office or on the train from the conductor. The palace is right across the street. Tel: (36 28) 410 124. www.kiralyikastely.hu. Open: daily 10am–6pm (5pm in winter); last tour at 5pm.

VÁCRÁTÓT

This fascinating botanic garden comprises 12,000 species of plants and trees, artificial lakes, follies and a watermill.

Alkotmány útca 2–4. Tel: (36 28) 360 122. www.botkert.hu. Open: Apr–Oct 8am–6pm; Nov–Mar until 4pm. Greenhouses are closed on Mondays. Admission charge.

25km (16 miles) north of Budapest. Hourly trains from Nyugati pályaudvar or take Volánbusz from Újpest-Városkapu (M3). By car, take Road 2 to Szödliget and turn right.

ZSÁMBÉK

The ruined Romanesque and late Gothic church here was built for the Premonstratensians in the 13th century and later taken over by the Paulites. Another attraction here is the Lamp Museum, housed in a typical Swabian cottage (the village was Swabian until the expulsion of many Germans following World War II).

Tihany Abbey, on the northern shore at Lake Balaton

*33km (21 miles) west of Budapest.
Buses from Széna tér (next to Moszkva
tér). www.zsambek.hu. Lamp Museum:
Magyar útca 18. Tel: (36 23) 342 212.
Open: daily 8am–6pm. Admission
charge.*

LAKE BALATON

Approximately 100km (62 miles)
southwest of Budapest is Lake Balaton,
Central Europe's largest inland sea. Its
warm waters (30°C/86°F in summer)
make it Hungary's most popular resort.
Sailing, windsurfing and horse riding
are additional attractions, as is fishing:
there are 40 different species of fish in
the lake, the most famous being the
indigenous *fogas* (pike-perch).

Vines at Badacsony

Tihany

The Benedictine abbey of Tihany was
founded by Andrew I in 1055 and its
Baroque church contains beautiful
carvings by Sebestyén Stulhoff. The
ample-bosomed angel on the Altar of
the Virgin Mary is supposed to be a
portrait of the artist's beloved, a local
fisherman's daughter. The Romanesque
crypt contains the simple gravestone of
King Andrew, who died in 1060.

Other sights of interest include the
Abbey Museum. The display covers
local topography and the origins of the
Magyars; one room is devoted to the
physicist Lóránd Eötvös (1849–1919),
who conducted experiments on the
Balaton ice-sheet.
*I, Andras tér 1. Tel: (36 87) 538 200.
Open: May–Sept, Tue–Sun 9am–6pm;*
*Nov–Mar 10am–4pm; Apr & Oct
10am–5pm.*

The rustically furnished House
of the Fishermen's Guild, off Pinsky
Promenade, has material on the life of
the Balaton fishermen. To the north is
the Visszhangdomb (Echo Hill), and
beyond that the Óvar (old earthern
castle ruin). In its rock base Orthodox
monks carved out their hermit cells.
www.tihany.hu

Badacsony

A little further west is the table-top
volcanic mountain of Badacsony
(*www.badacsony.hu*). Its vine-clad
slopes produce some of the region's
best wines, notably Szürkebarát (Pinot
Gris) of the Pauline monks. The
southeastern face has impressive basalt
columns over 50m (164ft) high. In the
town centre, just north of the main
road, is the József Egry Memorial
Museum, devoted to the Balaton's
famous local painters.
*Egry sétány 12. Tel: (36 87) 431 044.
www.vmmuzeum.hu. Open: May–Sept,
Tue–Sun 10am–6pm.*

Keszthely

At the lake's western end is the town of Keszthely (*www.keszthely.hu*) where Count György Festetics (1755–1819) lived in 'retirement' (semi-exile) after taking part in a failed rebellion against the Habsburgs. While here, he founded the Helikon circle of reform-minded intellectuals and an agricultural university known as the Georgikon. The high point of the tour of the country mansion is the Helikon Library, beautifully constructed from Slavonian oak by a local carpenter. *Festetics Country Mansion, Kastély útca 1. Tel: (36 83) 312 191. Open: Tue–Sun 10am–5pm; July & Aug daily 9am–6pm. Admission charge.*

The delightful country house in Keszthely

In the town, the Balaton Museum covers zoological, ethnological and archaeological aspects of the region. *Múzeum útca 2. Tel: (36 83) 312 351. Open: May–Oct Tue–Sun 10am–6pm; Nov–Apr Tue–Sat 9am–5pm. Admission charge.*

Other places of interest

Hévíz is 8km (5 miles) from Keszthely and is home to the world's second-largest thermal lake. It is fed by a source 1km (²/₃ mile) below the surface (*www.heviz.hu. Baths open: summer 8.30am–5pm; winter 9am–4pm*). Frequent buses leave from Keszthely railway station for Hévíz.

The marshy **Kis-Balaton** at the lake's western tip, where the River Zala runs into it, is good for birdwatchers. Along the southern shore there are many resorts, of which Siófok is the biggest and most popular.

The 5km (3-mile)-long **Csodabogyo's Cave** near Balatonederics is open for 2- and 4-hour tours. (*Tel: (36 20) 454 7034. www.csodabogyos.hu*)

The best way to reach Lake Balaton is by intercity train, which requires reservation (well in advance in summer). See the Thomas Cook European Rail Timetable for times (see p178). Trains leave from Déli pályaudvar (Southern Railway Station) or Keleti pályaudvar (Eastern Railway Station). For bus timetables, see www.balatonvolan.hu or www.menetrendek.hu. For more information, see www.balaton-tourism.hu

KECSKEMÉT

Kecskemét flourished as part of the Sultan's personal possessions during the Turkish occupation. In the 19th century, its vines were the only ones in Hungary to escape the phylloxera plague, and the town's wealth is reflected in its architecture. The birthplace of the composer Zoltán Kodály and the father of Hungarian drama József Katona, it is also the production centre of the celebrated *barackpálinka* (apricot schnapps).

The main sights are clustered around three central squares. Where Rákóczi útca enters Szabadság tér, on the left is Géza Márkus's Cifra palota (Ornate Palace, 1902), a dazzling Jugendstil building. Opposite it is the Moorish-looking former synagogue (1862), converted in 1966 into a 'House of Science and Culture'. The Town Hall, designed by Ödön Lechner and Gyula Pártos, should not be missed. Its carillon of 37 bells plays the works of Kodály, Erkel and Beethoven every hour.
Kecskemét is 85km (53 miles) south of Budapest and reachable by train (from Nyugati pályaudvar) and bus (from Népliget terminal). By car, take M5 and the motorway (toll road – vignette necessary) or the old Road 5.
www.kecskemet.hu

THE ALFÖLD

Commonly referred to as the *puszta* (abandoned), the once-forested Great Plain was heavily depopulated under the Turks and during the 18th century.

The traditions of *puszta* – a UNESCO cultural landscape on the World Heritage List – may be savoured at Lajosmizse and Bugac where the *csikósok* (cowboys) give displays of horsemanship daily in the summer season. At Bugac there is a Pásztor Múzeum (*www.knp.hu. Open: daily May–Oct 10am–5pm*) and a famous country inn (*csárda*).
Lajosmizse is also home to a Farmhouse Museum (Tanyamúzeum). Tel: (36 76) 356 166. Open: May–Oct Tue–Sun 10am–5pm. Closed: Nov–Apr.

PÉCS

The attractive city of Pécs was founded by the Celts, and subsequently (as Sopianae) became the capital of the Roman province of Pannonia Valeria. King Stephen established a bishopric here in 1009. The early Christian cemeteries here are on the UNESCO World Heritage List and the town is known as the gateway to the Balkans. Under the Turkish occupation, Pécs was a centre of Islamic culture, boasting five madrasahs (seminaries) and 17 mosques. In the 18th century, viticulture thrived and coal deposits were discovered, then in the 19th century the city boomed as a result of leather-making and other industries. Uranium deposits were discovered close by in the 1950s. Pécs is home to the characteristic Zsolnay ceramic tiles so beloved of Ödön Lechner and the Hungarian national style (*see pp18–19*).

Getting away from it all

The cathedral

The huge neo-Romanesque cathedral above Szent István tér was given its present form by the Viennese architect Friedrich Schmidt between 1882 and 1891, but there are 11th-, 12th- and 14th-century remnants. Inside are 19th-century frescoes by Bertalan Székely, Károly Lotz and others. In the Corpus Christi Chapel, look for the Pastoforium of Bishop Szatmáry, a lovely Renaissance altar (1521) in red marble.

Remains of the early Christian church in Pécs

Christian Roman remains

Pécs has some of the earliest Christian sanctuaries in Hungary. The Roman tombs at Apáca útca 9 and the remains of the *cella trichora* (clover-leaf chapel) on the opposite side of the street are not always accessible; but the mausoleum (AD 350), just to the north on Szent István tér, is open (*tel: (36 72) 312 719. Open: Apr–Oct 10am–6pm; Nov–Mar 10am–4pm*). The mausoleum contains underground burial chambers richly decorated with frescoes depicting Christian themes such as The Fall and Daniel in the Lion's Den.

Turkish remains

Hungary's best-preserved Turkish monuments are at Pécs. The most impressive is the Mosque of Gazi Kasim Pasha (*Széchenyi tér. Open: summer Mon–Sat 10am–4pm, Sun 11.30am–4pm; winter Mon–Sat 11am–noon, Sun 11.30am–2pm*), built in 1579, using the stones of an earlier Christian church. It has since reverted to a Catholic church again. To the west of the town centre is the Mosque of Jakovali Hassan Pasha (*Rákóczi útca 2. Open: Apr–Sept 10am–6pm*) with a finely carved *minbar* (pulpit).

At Nyár útca 8, also to the west, is a *türbe* (sepulchral chapel, 1591). Nearby is the only surviving Turkish fountain. The Tomb of Idris Baba on Nyár útca 8 is closed to visitors but visible in the garden of a children's hospital.

The cathedral at Pécs

Other sights

The Bishop's Palace, on Dóm tér, is fronted by a modern statue of Franz Liszt. From the other side of the square you enter Káptalan útca through an archway. The street contains no fewer than five museums, of which the Zsolnay Museum (*Káptalan útca 2. Tel: (36 72) 324 822. Open: Tue–Sun 10am–6pm. Admission charge*) is the most interesting. The Zsolany Museum has produced the world-famous colourful ceramics since 1853. The other museums – except the one featuring 20th-century Hungarian art – are devoted to individual artists. Walk along Kossuth Lajos útca to see the restored Jugendstil Hotel Palatinus and the neo-rococo theatre, home to Péc's Ballet. In Jókai útca is a splendid Zsolnay well, whose lion's-head spout is copied from the so-called Treasure of Attila discovered in Romania (now in Vienna). The works of Tivadar Csontváry Kosztka (1853–1919), in the Csontváry Museum, express a mystical vision of self and nation. Don't miss his great Baalbeck canvas and the poignant *Lonely Cedar.*

Pécs is 180km (112 miles) south of Budapest. See www.pecs.hu. Direct trains run from Budapest's Déli or Keleti pályaudvar. Buses leave from the terminal beside the Népliget metro.

Where are they now?

The Communists stamped their presence all over Budapest in the form of street names and monuments, and newly elected city councils have been assiduous in removing these since the toppling of the regime in 1989.

Scores of names have been changed. Many were obvious candidates for oblivion – Engels Square or Lenin Avenue, for instance. Some were names associated with the obsessive Communist quest for legitimacy (Liberation Square, People's Army Square, First of May Avenue); others immortalised little-known minor functionaries.

In the autumn of 1992, work began on the removal (at huge cost) of 56 Communist statues from squares and parks, spurred on by activists of the Hungarian Association of Freedom Fighters of 1956. They announced that if any were left *in situ* on

A statue at Szoborpark

A statue from the Communist era relegated to the Sculpture Park near Nagytétény

23 October (the anniversary of the 1956 revolution), they would tear them down with their own hands – a fate that befell the mega-statue of Stalin during the revolution itself.

Many of the socialist realist sculptures have been placed in a specially built park outside Budapest, Szoborpark – a 'Disneyland of old Communism' as the deputy mayor described it. The presentation is dramatic: as you walk through a pedimented gateway flanked by larger-than-life statues of Lenin, Marx and Engels, a vista opens before you of heroically depicted groups of toiling workers or fighting soldiers, powerfully evoking the mixture of ideology and kitsch

that passed for Communist art. In the view of the deputy mayor, their preservation is itself an assertion of civilised values. Only one Communist monument remains in Budapest, and regular springtime demonstrations on Szabadság tér (*see pp110–11*) illustrate the wholehearted Hungarian wish that the Soviet Memorial be consigned to this park as well.

Meanwhile, someone has discovered a warehouse full of Habsburg monuments that miraculously survived destruction in the 1950s. There is, of course, space for these now …
For location and details see p67.
www.szoborpark.hu

Shopping

In the commercialised Váci útca in the heart of Pest (see pp75 & 85) you will find long-established shops selling folk art and books alongside newcomers like Adidas and Zara. Souvenir-hunters will find plenty to interest them on Castle Hill, while the Fortuna Passage opposite the Hilton has a good bookshop and antiques. Other items to look out for are Herend porcelain and Zsolnay faience. Food delicacies include salami, goose liver and Tokaji wine.

Card use and acceptance is widespread. Most larger shops and petrol stations accept Visa, Visa Electron, Eurocard/MasterCard and Maestro cards. American Express and Diners Club seem less used by Hungarians.

Antiques

Bizományi Áruház Vállalat (BÁV)

The state-owned auction-house chain is good for antiques and vintage *objets*.
V, Ferenciek tere 10.
Tel: (36 1) 318 3733.
www.bav.hu. Also at V,
Szent István körút 3.
Tel: (36 1) 473 0666; and other locations.

Központi Antikvárium

Antique and second-hand books. Múzeum körút, being close to many university faculties, is rich with second-hand bookshops.
V, Múzeum körút 13–15.
Tel: (36 1) 317 3514.

Montparnasse French Art Deco Gallery

Falk Miksa útca is the unofficial antique street of Budapest and twice a year (May & Sept) the shops on the street throw open their doors for a street fair.
V, Falk Miksa útca 10.
Tel: (36 1) 302 6444.
www.montparnasse.hu

Art galleries

BÁV Galéria

V, Falk Miksa útca 21.
Tel: (36 1) 353 1975.
www.bav.hu

Kogart-Ház

VI, Andrássy útca 112.
Tel: (36 1) 354 3820.
www.kogart.hu

Koller Gallery

I, Táncsics Mihály útca 5.
Tel: (36 1) 356 9208.
www.kollergallery.com

Delicatessens

Culinaris

V, Balassi Bálint útca 4.
Tel: (36 1) 373 0028.
www.culinaris.hu. Also at VI, Hunyadi tér 3 & III, Perc útca 8.

La Boutique des Vins

V, József Attila útca 12.
Tel: (36 1) 317 5919.
www.malatinszky.hu

Pick

The house of the famous Hungarian salami.
V, Kossuth Lajos tér 9.
Tel: (36 1) 331 7783.
www.pick.hu

T Nagy Tamás Cheeses

V, Gerlóczy útca 3.
Tel: (36 1) 317 4268.
www.tnagytamas.hu

Shopping

Department stores
Corvin
Check out the summer
bar/club scene on the
roof.
VIII, Blaha Lujza tér 1.
Tel: (36 1) 266 7788.

Folk art
Embroidery, lace, faience,
wax figures and painted
Easter eggs.
Folkart Centrum
V, Váci útca 58.
Tel: (36 1) 318 5840.
www.folkartcentrum.hu
Holló Folkart Gallery
V, Vitkovics Mihály útca
12. Tel: (36 1) 317 8103.

Foreign-language
bookshops
Alexandra (Párizsi Nagy
Áruház)
V, Andrássy útca 39.
Bestsellers
V, Október 6 útca 11.
Tel: (36 1) 312 1295.
www.bestsellers.hu
Libra Books
VIII, Kölcsey útca 2.
Tel: (36 1) 267 5777.
www.nyelvkonyvbolt.hu

Maps
Cartographia
V, Bajcsy-Zsilinszky útca
37. Tel: (36 1) 312 6001.
www.cartographia.hu

Térképkirály (Mapking)
XIV, Szugló útca 83–85.
Tel: (36 1) 221 9707.
www.utikonyv.eu

Music
Rózsavölgyi Zeneműbolt
V, Szervita tér 5.
Tel: (36 1) 318 3500.
www.rozsavolgyi.hu

Shoes
Vass Handmade Shoes
V, Haris köz 2.
Tel: (36 1) 318 2375.
www.vass-cipo.hu

Shopping centres
Budapest now also has
numerous new shopping
centres (malls). Every
mall has various outlets
plus a supermarket,
restaurants, toilets and
often a cinema.
Allee
XI, Október 23 útca.
www.allee.hu
Arena Plaza
VIII, Kerepesi útca, next
to Keleti pályaudvar.
Tel: (36 1) 880 7000.
Campona
With tropicarium,
oceanarium and indoor
rainforest.
XXII, Nagytétényi útca
37–45. Tel: (36 1) 424
3000. www.campona.hu

Dome Árkád Center
XIV, Örs Vezér tere 25.
Tel: (36 1) 433 1414.
Duna Plaza
V, Váci útca 178.
Tel: (36 1) 465 1666.
www.dunaplaza.net
Europark
VIII, Üllői útca 201.
Tel: (36 1) 347 1607.
www.europark.hu
Mammut I and II
II, Széna tér.
Tel: (36 1) 345 8020.
www.mammut.hu
Westend City Center
VI, Váci útca 1–3, next to
Nyugati pályaudvar.
Tel: (36 1) 238 7777.
www.westend.hu

Urban Art
Bolt
VII, Rumbach Sebestyén
útca 10.
www.boltmuhely.hu
FUGA Budapest Centre
of Architecture
V, Petőfi Sándor útca 5.
Tel: (36 1) 266 0837.
www.fuga.org.hu
Korcsma
VI, Király útca 28.
Tel: (36) 20 377 2334.
www.korcsma.com
Retrock
V, Ferenczy István útca
28. Tel: (06) 30 678 8430.
www.retrock.com

MARKETS
Flea markets

The legendary flea markets (*bolhapiac*) of Budapest, though not for the faint-hearted, are a paradise for junk fanatics. Since the collapse of Communism, the amount of Marxist-Leninist bric-a-brac to be found in them has increased; there are even Russian army uniforms and caps, sold off by impoverished Soviet troops before their departure. Some listings are available from the Hall & Market Management of Budapest (*www.csapi.hu*).

Ecseri Piac (Ecseri Flea Market)

This was officially renamed *Használtcikk* (used items) market after one of its several moves from its original location on Ecseri útca, but everyone uses the old name. The outer stalls (*kirakodó*) are

loaded with knick-knacks – most of them uninspiring, the good stuff having been sold to dealers in the early hours. These dealers (many of them Slavs or Roma) occupy booths in the centre, and it is here that you might find bargains. Much of their stock comes from peasants, persuaded to part with their family heirlooms when the dealers canvassed a village.

The most interesting goods at Ecseri are decorative silver and Russian icons. Unfortunately, the silver is usually being sold illegally (under Hungarian law a permit is required to deal in it), while the icons may well have been looted from Ukrainian churches. Not long ago the police confiscated some icons that had been stolen from somewhere near Chernobyl – on the grounds that they were contaminated with radiation, not

Vegetables on display

because they were stolen! Other items of interest said to crop up include bentwood chairs made by the Viennese Thonet company, old radios and copper lamps. It is best to go to Ecseri with a Hungarian who knows the ropes and you should beware of pickpockets.
XIX, Nagykőrösi útca 156. Open: Mon–Fri 8am–1pm, Sat 6am–3pm. Bus: 54, 55 from Boráros tér to Alvinc útca (20 mins).

Józsefvárosi Piac
(Market in the Józsefváros)
The self-styled Worldwide Business Centre is really a Third World souk. Traders come from as far afield as China and Vietnam, but chiefly from the former Soviet Union, Bulgaria and Romania. They trade cheap goods for things not available back home. American kitsch is big here, as is liquor of uncertain provenance, used car parts, cigarette lighters – anything, in short, that might have fallen off the back of a lorry or turned up in the attic.
X, Kőbányai útca 9. Open: daily until 1pm. Tram: 28, 62 from Blaha Lujza tér or Bus: 9 (from Deák Ferenc tér), 109 (from Óbuda) to Kőbányai útca 31.

Another interesting flea market is held outside the Petőfi Hall (Petőfi Csarnok) in the Városliget.
XIV, Zichy Mihály útca 14. Tel: (36 1) 251 7266. www.bolhapiac.com. Open: Sat & Sun 8am–2pm. Metro: M1 to Hősök tere or Tram: 1 to Erzsébet királyné útja.

Food and general markets
Nagy Vásárcsarnok (Central Market)
This is a fabulous 19th-century covered market. It was one of five opened in the 1890s (*see p76*) and is a protected monument (*műemlék*). There are over 100 stalls on three floors selling fresh local produce, flower seeds, lace and pottery; note that most stalls close around noon. Cheap local eateries line the top floor and the market spills out on to the street at weekends.
IX, Vámház körút 1–3. Tel: (36 1) 366 3300. Open: Mon–Thur 6am–5pm, Tue–Fri 6am–6pm, Sat 6am–2pm. Tram: 47, 49 to Fővám tér.

Lehel Piac (Lehel Market)
Futuristic market hall opened in 2002 in an old market location.
XI, Váci útca 9–15. Metro: M3 to Lehel tér.

Rákóczi Téri Csarnok (Market Hall on Rákóczi tér)
Another market hall from the 1890s.
VIII, Rákóczi tér 7–8. Tel: (36 1) 210 2565. Tram: 4, 6 to Rákóczi tér.

Western supermarkets like Spar and Tesco have moved in on Budapest and every shopping mall has a large and well-stocked supermarket. Local supermarket names include Match and Kaiser's.
24-hour Tesco supermarkets
XIV, Fogarasi útca. Tram: 62 from Blaha Lujza tér to Fogarasi útca or Metro: M2 or Trolleybus: 80 to Pillangó utca. XIII, Gács útca 3. Metro: M3 to Újpest-Városkapu.

Hungarian folk arts

Hungary's folk traditions have long reflected diverse ethnic groups (Ruthenians, Slavonians, Slovaks, Romanians and Serbs, as well as Magyars). Despite commercialisation, beautiful handicrafts are still produced, and the charm of folk song and dance is undimmed. Surviving peasant homes provide a fascinating insight into a way of life not totally extinct.

Folk art shops are found at all popular tourist spots. Visitors to Budapest may first glimpse folk embroidery as they pass the Transylvanian women who sell their wares at the entrance to any metro, on Castle Hill or around any of the major tourist sites. Their speciality is the lovely red (or sometimes blue) tulip or heart pattern on a white background. Other regions produce delicate open work, wool-embroidered cushion ends, and beautifully ornamented aprons, tablecloths or handkerchiefs. Dense, multicoloured needlework for folk costumes is a Matyó speciality from northern Hungary.

Hand-painted dolls

Pottery is a traditional wedding gift. From the Great Plain come water jars with an ochre glaze and attractive coloured pitchers, or plates with flower, bird or star patterns. Look out, too, for the smoky black pottery of Nádudvar in the Hajdúság region. Another popular souvenir is the beautiful Zsolnay ceramics used to decorate so many of Hungary's secessionist buildings.

The horsemen, shepherds and swineherds of the Great Plain specialise in carved artefacts such as whip handles, crooks, axes, mirror frames or tobacco boxes. Look out for beautiful folk carving if you visit the Protestant churches of Southern Transdanubia and the Upper Tisza.

The place to see rural architecture is a *skanzen* (an open-air museum village such as the one at Szentendre; *see p125*). The houses often had wattle-and-daub walls and roofs thatched with reeds.

Folk entertainment – dancing, singing and seasonal celebrations – may be seen all over Hungary, but especially at Hollókő in the north, home of the Palóc people. Easter time

Traditional Hungarian pottery

A colourful brochure of folklore events and performances is obtainable from TourInform, *Sütő útca 2*, or *Liszt Ferenc tér 11*. *Tel: 800 36 000 000 (toll free) or (361) 438 8080.* *(Also see pp139 & 147.)*

here harks back to pagan purification and fertility rites. The girls paint beautiful floral designs on eggs, and must run the gauntlet of young men sprinkling them with well water.

Entertainment

Entertainment in Hungary covers everything from traditional folk music and festivals to more highbrow events such as the ballet, opera and classical music concerts. Cinema is a long-standing art form in this part of the world, too, and both home-grown and mainstream Hollywood films can be seen.

CINEMA

The cinematic tradition is strong in Hungary. Works by directors such as Miklós Jancsó, Pál Sándor and István Szabó will be well known to Western film buffs. Although the big co-productions such as *Colonel Redl* or *Mephisto* have been widely exposed abroad, the occasional Budapest summer season of home-grown films affords a chance to see more obscure works with English subtitles.

Most multiplexes show films in the original language – be aware that even in English-language films, any foreign-language dialogues will be subtitled in Hungarian. Check out **Corvin Budapest Filmpalota** (*www.corvin.hu*), where a walkway commemorates the fierce fighting that went on in the area in the 1956 revolution. Another large multiplex is **Palace Cinemas** (*www.palacecinemas.hu*), which has screens in shopping centres across the city. Classics are shown at the **Örökmozgó Filmmúzeum** (*VII,*

Erzsébet körút 39. Tel: (36 1) 342 2167. Tram: 4, 6 to Király útca). Also, **Szimpla Kert** has a small outdoor cinema.

The best sources of information are *Budapest Week* (*www.budapestweek.hu*) and *The Budapest Sun* (*www.budapestsun.com*). See also *www.xpatloop.com*

PERFORMANCE
Ballet & dance

Ballet is not a major feature of the Budapest scene but the *corps de ballet* is resident at the State Opera House and foreign companies make guest appearances at Budapest arts festivals (*see p147*). Ballet, musicals and modern dance performances are also staged in the **Thália Theatre** (*Thália Szihaz, VI, Nagymezö útca 22–24. Tel: (36 1) 312 4230. www.thalia.hu. Metro: M1 to Opera*) and the new **Palace of Arts** (*IX, Komor Marcell útca 1. Tel: (36 1) 555 3000. www.mupa.hu. Tram: 2, 24 to Millenniumi Kulturális Központ*).

Opera

Opera is popular in Hungary and has a distinguished tradition going back to the opening of Miklós Ybl's opera house in 1882 (*see p90*).

If you want Hungarian opera, look for Bartók's *Kékszakállú herceg vára* (Bluebeard's Castle), Erkel's *Bánk Bán*, Goldmark's *Sába királynöje* (The Queen of Sheba) and Kódaly's *Háry János*.

To see opera in the environs for which they were written, aficionados should not miss a performance at the **State Opera House** (*Magyar Állami Operaház, VI, Andrássy útca 22. Tel: (36 1) 353 0170. www.opera hu. Metro: M1 to Opera*). Similarly, despite extensive renovations to what was the Jungenstil delight of the **Erkel Theatre** (*Erkel Színház, VIII, Köztársaság tér 30. Tel: (36 1) 333 0540. Metro: M2 to Blaha Lujza tér*), it still makes a lovely setting for some dramatic arts. The new **Palace of Arts** (*see opposite*) holds within its lofty roof the enormous Béla Bartók National Concert Hall and the more intimate Festival Theatre (*see www.mupa.hu for programme details*).

Operetta and musicals

The heyday of operetta (*see pp88–9*) followed the formation of the Austro-Hungarian Empire in 1867 and lasted until the end of World War I. It has been largely superseded by the musical, of which two popular Hungarian examples are the rock-operas *István, a király* (*Stephen the King*) and *Attila*.

Venues include the **Operetta Theatre** (*Fövárosi Operett Színház, VI, Nagymezo útca 17. Tel: (36 1) 353 2172. www.operettszinhhaz.hu*) and the Palace of Arts (*see opposite*). Hopefully, the **Pesti Vigadó** will reopen as a venue; lack of funds means only the exterior renovations have been completed to date (*V, Vigadó tér 2. Tel: (36 1) 354 3755*).

Theatre

The obvious problem about visiting the theatre in Budapest is the language barrier. **Merlin Theatre** (*V, Gerlóczy útca 4. Tel: (36 1) 317 9338. www.merlinszinhaz.hu. Metro: M1, 2, 3 to Deák Ferenc tér*) is currently the only venue for English-language productions – the venue also converts into a club after theatre shows. The latest on the city scene is the new **National Theatre** (*Nemzeti Színház*) within the Palace of Arts complex (*see opposite*).

Ballet performances are well attended

MUSIC

In Hungary, the classical tradition, nurtured by the Music Academy (*see pp91, 95 & 96*), is very strong.

The new generation includes outstanding soloists such as Dezsö Ránki and Zoltán Kocsis (piano), Vilmos Szabadi (violin) and Miklós Perényi (cello). Distinguished composers of the past such as Franz Liszt, Ferenc Erkel, Béla Bartók, Zoltán Kodály, Ernö Dohnány, as well as individuals such as György Ligeti and György Kurtág, have left their mark on the modern music scene.

See classical music at the modern **Budapest Convention Centre** (*Budapest Kongresszusi Központ, XI, Jagelló útca 1–3. Tel: (36 1) 372 5700. www.bcwtc.hu. Tram: 61 or Bus: 8, 40, 112, 139, 212 to BAH-csomópont*) and within the exotic architecture and sublime acoustics of the **Music Academy** (*Zeneakadémia, VI, Liszt Ferenc tér 8. Tel: (36 1) 342 0179. www.zeneakademia.hu. Metro: M1 to Oktogon; Tram: 4, 6 or Trolleybus: 70, 78 to Király útca*). State-of-the-art acoustics at the **Palace of Arts** (*see p144*) means musical performances here are hard to beat.

Frequent organ and choral music performances are also held in the Matthias Church, St Stephen's Basilica and other churches around Pest.

Modern music

If you're looking for modern, new wave and contemporary performances, then

INFORMATION AND BOOKING FOR MUSICAL PERFORMANCES

Tickets for classical music (symphony concerts, chamber music, recitals and rock concerts) are sold at the **Cultur-Comfort Central Ticket Office** (*Cultur-Comfort Központi Jegyiroda, VI, Paulay Ede útca 31. Tel: (36 1) 322 0000. www.cultur-comfort.hu. Metro: M1 to Opera*). Tickets for all performances, whether classical, modern or outdoor, are sold via **Ticket Express** (*VI, Andrássy útca 18. Tel: (36) 30 303 0999. www.tex.hu; and from various partner outlets including IBUSZ, Media Market, Tourinform and TUI*). Otherwise apply to the box offices at the venues concerned.

Pesti Műsor publishes information on forthcoming musical events every Thursday under 'zene' in the English-language newspapers and in brochures obtainable from TourInform (*see pp183 & 189*). The Central Ticket Office publishes the useful *Muzsik Kalendárium* (*www.muzsikalendarium.hu*), listing musical events a month in advance. The weekly listings guide *Time Out Budapest* carries comprehensive information on art, theatre, dance, music, food and drink, film, sport, and gay and lesbian happenings across the city.

a visit to **TRAFO** (*IX, Liliom útca 41. Tel: (36 1) 456 2040. www.trafo.hu. Metro: M3 or Tram: 4, 6 to Ferenc körút*) will broaden your horizons. **Petőfi Csarnok** in Városliget is a popular venue for many huge rock and pop concerts (*XIV, Zichy Mihály útca 14. Tel. (36 1) 251 7266. www.petoficsarnok.hu. Metro: M1 to Hősök tere or Tram: 1 to Erzsébet királyné útja*). Another venue for similarly big-name concerts is the new **Papp László Budapest Sportaréna** (*XIV, Stefáni útca 2. Tel: (36 1) 422 2600.*

www.budapestarena.hu. Metro: M2 or Tram: 1 to Stadionok).

For more indie gigs, see the bar and club listings on pp150–51.

Folk music

Easily the best group for Hungarian folk music is Muzsikás with Márta Sebestyén (see www.muzsikas.hu for listings of their many performances across the city and country). The **Budapest Cultural Centre** is also known as Folklore Centrum (Fővárosi Művelődési Ház, XI, Fehérvári útca 47. Tel: (36 1) 203 3873. www.bmknet.hu. Tram: 18, 41, 47 to Fővárosi Művelődési Ház). Home to the Hungarian State Folk Ensemble and another popular folklore venue is the Hungarian Heritage House (Hagyományok Háza, I, Corvin tér 8. Tel: (36 1) 225 6049. www.heritagehouse.hu. Bus: 86 to Szilágyi Dezső tér or Tram: 19, 41 to Halász útca).

Festivals

Since 1996, the Budapest Festival Centre has organised various cultural events within Budapest including the first major festival of the calendar year, the **Budapest Spring Festival** (www.btf.hu) in late March. The festival offers '10 days of 1,000 events in 100 venues' and many big names make guest appearances in chamber evenings, opera, theatre and dance. Later in the year is the sister event, the **Budapest Autumn Festival** in early October. Another of their festivals is **Summer on Lanchid Bridge** when select

weekends see the bridge closed to traffic and open to music and events. And the fledgling but quality **Budapest Fringe Festival** comes to town each April (www.budapestfringe.com).

Festival programmes can be obtained via the Budapest Festival Centre (www.festivalcity.hu) and from TourInform offices (see p189).

Budapest's hot summer sees performances on the open-air stages across the city, notably the **Budapest Summer Festival** (Szabadtéri Színpad) at the Margaret Island Theatre (www.szabadter.hu) and at venues within striking distance of the capital (for example, at the country house at Martonvásár). Baroque operas are now being performed each summer in the courtyard of the Zichy Palace in Óbuda. There is an autumn **Festival of Church Music**, which provides a good chance to hear interesting works by Hungarian composers past and present. In November, a choral festival entitled **Vox Pacis** takes place.

The week-long **Sziget Festival** held on Óbudai Island (sziget) in August has fast become one of the hottest summer festivals in Europe. The same people introduced the increasingly popular rock festival **Balaton Sound**, which takes place at Lake Balaton's Zamárdi Beach each July. See www.sziget.hu for details on both festivals.

In July, Budapest hosts the colourful and risqué **Lesbian, Gay, Bisexual and Transgender Film and Cultural Festival** (www.budapestpride.hu).

The Roma and their music

The Roma first came to Hungary in the 15th century from Asia through the Balkan region, and are now the largest minority in the country (5 per cent of the population); they are also the most underprivileged. In the public mind they are associated less with music than with poverty, crime and unemployment. Though no longer nomadic, they are still among the most deprived section of society. To combat this, a Roma Parliament was recently formed, and its leaders are trying to raise national consciousness and improve their tainted image.

Music has traditionally offered a way out of the cultural ghetto. Musicians accompanied conscription drives across the land in the 18th century; Roma bands played for the nobility and the gentry in the 19th century, when they began to become figures of romance. Around the turn of the century, they were romanticised in operettas like *Gypsy Life* (1904), *Gypsy Love* (1910) and *Gypsy Bandleader* (1912). (Gypsy, however,

A Hungarian folk musician

A Roma festival with dancing

has become a derogatory word today.) In the late 19th century, the *Neue Freie Presse* in Vienna pointed out how members of Roma musician families had benefited from the Hungarian Roma cult: 'They no longer tell fortunes or ply the tinker's trade, but instead put on a dinner jacket and fiddle for the *beau monde* from eleven at night till five in the morning.'

Contrary to popular belief, what the musicians play is not the true music of the Roma. According to the composer Béla Bartók: 'They are simply performers of Hungarian popular song'; and he added: 'There is of course gypsy music – songs with texts in gypsy language. These are never played or sung by gypsies in public.'

Today, the smarter restaurants in Budapest all have their own Roma ensemble playing evergreens from Viennese operetta and the frenzied Hungarian *csárdás*. These are the aristocrats of their world, famous for their ready wit and happy-go-lucky temperament, unextinguished by centuries of persecution.

Roma or gypsy bands can be seen at many of Budapest's music festivals and at folkloric venues (*see p147*).

The 'Ybl Kiosk', now a casino

NIGHTLIFE

Budapest's nightlife has shed any residual prudery and embraced the hedonistic lifestyle, with many bars and clubs open until dawn, and super-clubs cropping up as winter and outdoor summer venues. Stag weekenders have arrived along with the budget airlines, too. The following venues are some of the best in the city and usually incorporate a restaurant and DJ. For listings,

check *www.pestiside.hu*, *wwwfunzine.hu* and the weekly magazine *Time Out Budapest*.

Casinos

Tropicana Casino
V, Vidagó útca 2.
Tel: (36 1) 266 3062.
www.tropicanacasino.hu.
Open: 11am–6am.

Várkert Casino
Sophisticated casino in the former 'Ybl Kiosk' (Royal Castle pumphouse).
I, Ybl Miklós tér 9.
Tel: (36 1) 202 4244.

www.varkert.com.
Open: 2pm–5am.

Sörözok

Budapest beers cannot compare with Czech or Slovak brews but they are available at these beer cellars, among others.

Becketts Irish Bar
Irish pub with live entertainment.
V, Bajcsy-Zsilinszky útca 72. Tel: (36 1) 311 1035. www.becketts.hu. Open: noon–1am. Metro: M3 to Nyugati páyaudvar.

Paulaner Bräuhaus
The Bavarian brew plus accompanying food and atmosphere.
XI, Alkotás útca 53 (Mom Park).
Tel: (36 1) 224 2020.
www.paulanersorhaz.hu.
Open: daily 11am–1am.
Tram: 61 to Csörsz útca.

Bars, clubs & live music venues

Many cafés turn into bars later in the evening, and many of those bars turn into clubs later still, with DJ sets or even live bands. Explore and experience …

A38 Hajó
XI, Buda side of Petöfi

BEER GARDENS

One unique aspect of Budapest is its courtyard venues: loud, basic and brilliant, the art is graffiti, the glasses are plastic and the kitchen is open late. Try one of the following locations:

Romkert
The 'ruined garden' in the grounds of the 17th-century Rudas Spa (see p53) defies rumoured closure each year to provide wonderful dancing along the Danube.
I, Döbrentei tér 9. www.romkertclub.hu. Open 10am–4am. Tram: 18, 19

Szimpla Kert
Labyrinthian bar and lounge space with an open-air cinema and basic food. Check out the sister venue next door.
VII, Kazinczy útca 14. www.szimpla.hu. Open: daily noon–2am. Metro: M2 to Astoria.

Zöld Pardon
Summer-long outdoor festival with swimming pool, food and music.
XI, Goldmann Gyögy tér. www.zp.hu. Open: daily 9am–6am. Tram: 4, 6 to the Buda side of Petöfi híd.

Bridge. Tel: (36 1) 464 3940. www.a38.hu. Open: 11am–4am. Tram: 4, 6 to Petőfi híd.

Budapest Jazz Club
VIII, Múzeum útca 7. Tel: (36 1) 267 2610. www.bjc.hu. Open: daily 5pm–2am. Metro: M3 to Kálvin tér.

Cökxpôn Café Theatre
IX, Soroksári útca 8–10. Tel: (36 30) 826 4804. Open: Mon & Sun 6pm–midnight, Tue 6pm–2am, Fri & Sat 6pm–4am. www.cokxponambient.hu. Tram 2, 4, 6 to Boráros tér.

Cotton Club (Jazz)
VI, Jókai útca 26. Tel: (36 1) 354 0886.

www.cottonclub.hu. Open: noon–1am. Metro: M3 to Nyugati pályaudvar.

Gödör Klub
V, Erzsébet tér. Tel: (36 20) 201 3868. www.godorklub.hu. Open: Sun–Thur 10am–2am, Fri & Sat 10am–4am. Metro: M1, 2 & 3 to Deák Ferenc tér.

Irish Cat Pub
V, Múzeum körút 41. Tel: (36 1) 266 4085. www.irishcat.hu. Open: Mon–Sat 4pm–2am. Metro: M3 to Kálvin tér.

Morrisons Pub
VI, Révay útca 25. Tel: (36 1) 269 4060. www.morrisons.hu. Open:

Mon–Sat 7pm–4am. Metro: M1 to Opera.

Mumus
VII, Dob útca 18. Open: daily 5pm–2am. Metro: M2 to Astoria.

Old Man's Pub
VII, Akácfa útca 13. Tel: (36 1) 322 7645. www.oldmans.hu. Open: daily 3pm–4am. Metro: M2 to Blaha Lujza tér.

Pótkulcs
VI, Csengery útca 65/b. Tel: (36 1) 269 1050. www.potkulcs.hu. Open: Sun–Wed 5pm–1.30am, Thur–Sat 5pm–2.30am. Metro: M3 to Nyugati pályaudvar.

Szoda
VII, Wesselényi útca 18. Tel: (36 1) 461 0007. www.szoda.com. Open: Mon–Fri 9am–6am; Sat & Sun 2pm–6am. Metro: Astoria.

Vittula
VII, Kertész útca 4. www.vittula.hu. Open: Sun–Wed 6pm–2am, Thur–Sat 6pm–4am. Metro: M2 to Blaha Lujza té.

West Balkán
VI, Nyugati tér 1–2. Open: daily 7pm–6am. Metro: M3 to Nyugati pályaudvar.

Children

The suggestions below are for activities largely unaffected by the language barrier. Parents could also consider a visit to a stalactite cave or the Buda Hills (see pp67 & 120–22) or, in summer, a boat trip on the Danube.

Budapest Bábszinház (Puppet Show)

Shows are based mainly on international and Hungarian fairy tales.
VI, Andrássy útca 69. Tel: (36 1) 321 5200. Closed in July & Aug. Metro: M1 to Vörösmarty útca.

Csodák Palotája (Palace of Miracles)

Interactive scientific playhouse in **Millenáris Park**. (*See p60.*)
II, Fény útca 20–22. Tel: (36 1) 350 6131. www.csodakpalotaja.hu. Open: Mon–Fri 9am–5pm, Sat & Sun 10am–6pm. Tram: 4, 6 to Széna tér or Metro: M2 to Moszkva tér.

Gellért Gyógyfürdő (Gellért Baths)

There are many baths (*see pp52–3*) but Gellért offers an indoor bubble bath and outdoor wave bath.

Gyermekvasút (Children's Railway)

Formerly the 'Pioneer Railway' of the Communist youth movement, running 11km (7 miles) between Széchenyi-hegy and Hűvösvölgy. The driver is adult but the staff are children. (*See also pp120–22.*)
Széchenyi-hegy is reached by the Fogaskerekű Vasút (cogwheel railway); the terminus can be reached by Tram: 59, 60, 61 to Városmajor. The Hüvösvölgy terminus is by the last stop of tram 61. www.gyermekvasut.com

Kölyökpark (Kids' Park)

Indoor play for children under 12.
II, Lövőhaz útca 1–5 (Mammut II). Tel: (36 1) 345 8512. www.kolyokpark.hu. Open: Mon–Fri 10am–9pm, Sat 9am–9pm, Sun 9am–8pm. Tram: 4, 6 to Széna tér or Metro: M2 to Moszkva tér.

Margit sziget (Margaret Island)

Bicycles can be hired at the southern end. At the northern end is the Japanese Garden and a 'singing well' that plays a tune every hour. (*See pp57–9.*)

Museums

Magyar Természettudományi Múzeum (Hungarian Natural History Museum)

A brand new location for creepy-crawlies galore and a Dinosaur Park.
VIII, Ludovika tér 2–6. Tel. (36 1) 210 1085. www.nhmus.hu. Open: Tue–Sun 10am–5pm. Metro: M3 to Klinikák.

Vasúttörténi Park (Railway Museum)

Explore steam engines and go loco. Train rides also available.
XIV, Tatai útca 95. Tel: (36 1) 238 0558. www.mavnosztalgia.hu. Open: Apr–Oct Tue–Sun 10am–6pm; Nov, Dec & Mar Tue–Sun 10am–3pm. Closed: Jan & Feb. Tram: 14 from Lehel tér (M3) or Bus: 30 from Keleti pályaudvar (M2) to Rokolya útca. Special trains from the Nyugati railway station: the Nostalgia Train is free with a pre-purchased park entrance ticket, which is obtainable in the Mávnosztalgia shop at platform 10 of Nyugati pályaudvar. These trains only run Apr–Oct.

Postsai és Távközlési Múzeum (Post and Telephone Museum)

Models, coaches and a message dispatch tube to play with.
VI, Andrássy útca 3. Tel: (36 1) 269 6838. www.postamuzeum.hu. Open: Tue–Sun 10am–6pm (until 4pm Nov–Mar). Metro: M2 to Bajcsy-Zsilinszky útca.

Planetárium

Laser and other special shows for children.
X, Népliget. Tel: (36 1) 265 0725. www.planetarium.hu and for the Laser Theatre www.lezerszinhaz.hu. Metro: M3 to Népliget.

Tropicarium

Largest aquarium in Central Europe will keep children of all ages entertained.
XXII, Nagytétényi útca 37–45 (Campona). Tel: (36 1) 424 3053. www.tropicarium.hu. Open: daily 10am–8pm. Bus: 33 from Móricz Zsigmond körtér to Lépcsős útca.

Városliget (City Woodland Park)

See pp101 & 103–5.

Állatkert (Zoo)

Surprisingly good zoo.
XIV, Állatkerti útca 6–12. Tel: (36 1) 273 4900. www.zoobudapest.com. Open: Jan, Feb, Nov & Dec 9am–4pm; Mar & Oct Mon–Thur 9am–5pm, Fri–Sun 9am–5.30pm; Apr & Sept Mon–Thur 9am–5.30pm, Fri–Sun 9am–6pm; May–Aug Mon–Thur 9am–6.30pm, Fri–Sun 9am–7pm.

Fövárosi Nagycirkusz (Circus)

A good old travelling (but permanent) circus.
XIV, Állatkerti útca 7. Tel: (36 1) 343 9630. www.maciva.hu. Shows: Wed–Fri 5pm, Sat 3pm & 7pm, Sun 10.30am & 3pm. Ticket office open: daily 10am–6pm.

Vidám Park (Amusement Park)

Sixty years old and still going strong.
XIV, Állatkerti útca 14–16. Tel: (36 1) 478 0874. www.vidampark.hu. Opening hours vary. The park opens at 10am or noon, with summer closing at 8pm or 1.30am. Winter closing is 6pm or 7pm. Check website for details. Closed: Nov–Feb. Metro: M1 to Széchenyi fürdő brings you close to all of the above.

Children

Sport and leisure

Magyars are great football fans and Hungary has produced some charismatic players such as Ferenc Puskás. They also excel in sports such as swimming and water polo, no doubt helped by the top-class training facilities available.

SPECTATOR SPORTS
Football
International matches:
**Puskás Ferenc Stadion
(former Népstadion)**
*XIV, Istvánmezei útca 3–7.
Tel: (36 1) 471 4100. Metro: M2 to
Stadionok.*
National matches are played at
weekends and on Wednesday evenings.
Information from the monthly
Programme obtainable at TourInform
(*V, Sütő útca 2*). The two leading
Budapest teams are:
Ferencvárosi Torna Club (FTC)
*VIII, Üllői útca 129. Tel: (36 1) 215 6025.
www.ftc.hu. Metro: M3 to Népliget.*
Kispest-Honvéd
*Bozsik József Stadion, XVIII, Új temető
útca 1–3. Tel: (36 1) 282 9789.
www.honvedfc.hu. Tram: 42 to Tulipán
útca from Határ útca (Metro: M3).*

Horse racing
Flat racing (*galopp*) and trotting races
(*ügető*).

Kincsem Park
*XIV, Albertirsai útca 2–4. Tel: (36 1) 264
2206; www.kincsemrendezveny.hu &
www.magyarturf.hu. Metro: M2 to
Pillangó útca or Bus: 100 from Örs
Vezér tere.*

Hungarian Grand Prix
Held annually in August at the
Mogyoród circuit, 24km (15 miles)
northeast of Budapest (reached by car
on the M3 motorway; bus terminus
varies yearly; or the Gödöllő HÉV from
Örs Vezér tere metro to Mogyoród).

Ice Hockey
National and international thrills on
the ice. *See also www.icehockey.hu*
Papp László Budapest Sportaréna
*XIV, Stefáni útca 2. Tel: (36 1) 422 2600.
www.budapestarena.hu*

SPORTS FACILITIES
Biking & bike tours
Hungarian roads are dangerous, but
cycle paths are being created.

TourInform has a map of routes (*Budapest Kerék-párútjai*). See *www.velo-touring.hu* for long-distance tours and bike hire.

Budapest Bike
VII, Wesselényi útca 18.
Tel: (36) 30 944 5533.
www.budapestbike.hu

Yellow Zebra Bikes
V, Sütő útca 2. Tel: (36 1) 266 8777.
www.yellowzebrabikes.com

Bowling
Strike Bowling Club
XI, Budafoki útca 111–113.
Tel: (36 1) 206 2754.

Fishing
Permits must be obtained from:
MOHOSZ (Hungarian Fishing Association)
XII, Korompai útca 17.
Tel: (36 1) 248 2590. www.mohosz.hu

Fitness
Astoria Fitness Centre
V, Károly körút 4. Tel: (36 1) 317 0452.
www.astoriafitness.hu

Holmes Place
VII, Holló útca 12–14.
Tel: (36 1) 878 1301.
www.holmesplace.hu

Golf
Contact TourInform or see *www.golfcourses.hu* for other courses.

Golf Tanya
Obudai (Hajógyári) Sziget 410.
Tel: (36 1) 437 9038. www.golftanya.hu

Horse riding
Budapesti Lovas Klub
Huge hall for winter exercise.
VIII, Kerepesi útca 7. Tel: (36 1) 313 5210.

Petneházy Country Club
Riding in the Buda Hills. Lessons for all levels.
II, Feketefej útca 2–4. Tel: (36 1) 567 1616.

Running
See *www.budapestmarathon.com* for the capital's big race and others around the country.

Squash
Top Squash Club
II, Lövőház útca 2–6 (Mammut I).
Tel: (36 1) 345 8193. www.top-squash.hu

Swimming
Dagály Strandfürdő
XIII, Népfürdő útca 36.
Tel: (36 1) 452 4500. www.dagalyfurdo.hu

Palatinus Strandfürdő
XIII, Margit sziget. Tel: (36 1) 340 4505.
www.palatinusstrand.hu

Római Strandfürdő
III, Rozgonyi Piroska útca.
Tel: (36 1) 388 9740.
www.romaistrand.hu

Tennis
There are many tennis clubs and hotel courts including:

Roman Tennis Academy
III, Királyok útca 105. Tel: (36 1) 240 8616.

Városmajor Tennis Academy
XII, Városmajor útca 63–69.
Tel: (36 1) 202 5337.

Dog days in Budapest

Non-experts could be forgiven for looking blank at the mention of an *agár*, a *puli*, a *pumi* or a *mudi*. All of them are high-performance canines bred by a people with a passion for working dogs.

The classic Hungarian breeds are believed to have accompanied the seven Magyar tribes across the Carpathians 1,100 years ago. Of these, the shaggy black *puli*, which looks like an animated hearthrug, is something of a national symbol. It is still unrivalled for rounding up sheep at pasture. Something bigger was needed to keep predators at bay, and this task was performed by the bulky *komondors* and *kuvasz* (easily distinguishable from wolves and other marauders by their white colour).

The beautiful *vizsla*, a ginger-coloured retriever, was kept by the

Hungary is truly a nation of dog lovers, as reflected in this street art

Most people own dogs as pets and there are also many breeds of working dogs, such as the *puli*

Árpád kings as early as the 11th century, and the greyhound-like *agár* (also of Asian origin) was used for deer-hunting by the nobility.

Dog-fanciers can now spot (or buy) Hungarian and other breeds at the twice-yearly dog sale on Marczibányi tér. In the early days of Communism, luxury breeds were virtually banned, and vets would only attend working animals. Now, dogs are once again a status symbol – and often a protection against burglars.

The European Dog Show was held in May 1993 and again in October 2008, proving that Budapest is back on the international canine map. Exhibitors come from across the continent to this annual event where the fate of thousands of glamorous dogs is decided by a panel of international judges. In a world of economic gloom and general disillusionment, the dog show arouses enormous enthusiasm; Hungarians, it seems, are happy to share the view of the Marquise de Sévigné, who once observed: 'The more I see of men, the more I admire dogs.' It only seems right, then, that Budapest will host the World Dog Show in 2013.

Food and drink

Budapest has just been awarded its first Michelin star, making Hungary only the second Central European country to achieve this gastronomic milestone – book well in advance if you want to eat at Costes. Traditional Hungarian cuisine is still easy to find, but innovative fusion creations are increasingly popular and a wide range of international offerings are available.

Types of eating house

There are three main categories of Hungarian eating house. An *étterem* offers a large selection of dishes and can be any price category. A *vendéglő* should offer something more like home cooking with fewer dishes to choose from, and also tend to have greater ambience. *Vendéglő* prices used to be more moderate, but many have been subjected to the same sort of gentrification as similar establishments in other countries, which invariably means higher prices. A *csárda* is a country-style inn with a relatively restricted menu and simple fare. Smaller establishments with cheaper prices are called *bisztró* or, if self-service, *önkiszolgáló* or *ételbár*. A *söröző* is a beer cellar, which usually serves (fairly basic) food.

The vast majority of restaurants in Budapest are legitimate businesses offering good value and service, but overcharging is sadly not unknown. It occurs almost always on or near Váci útca.

Hungarian cuisine

Most people's idea of Hungarian cooking begins and ends with goulash, a dish that in Hungary itself bears little resemblance to the anaemic version served elsewhere. It is generally thought of as a stew, but it is traditionally a rich meaty soup (*gulyásleves*). The origins of *gulyáshús* lie in the nomadic period of the Magyars; their horsemen would often travel for days in hostile terrain carrying iron rations of stewed mutton or beef, dried and preserved in a bag made from a sheep's stomach. To prepare a meal they would simply soften the meat in boiling water, creating a sort of instant stew. It is believed that this contributed to the success of their campaigns – the enemy had to waste time killing and cooking their food.

There is a great deal more to Hungarian cuisine than goulash, however. Hungary's geographical position ensured that surrounding cultures had an impact on its cooking: Balkan influence is seen in the stuffed vegetables; the sausage culture has been modified by German and Italian practices; and dumplings were borrowed from the Slavs. The lands of historic Hungary had their own regional dishes, such as tarragon lamb stew from Transylvania and *lecsó* (peppers and tomatoes stewed in lard) from southern Hungary.

The basis of most Hungarian food preparation is a heavy roux of pork lard and flour, known as *rántás*, liberally spiced. Many dishes include sour cream or smoked sausage, thus creating the characteristic combination of astringent and smoky tastes.

Pork (*sertés*) is the most frequent meat on the menu, usually in some kind of *pörkölt* (stew). Beef (*marha*) is not common and is seldom good quality, with one striking exception: Budapestians are fanatic consumers of steak tartare, and many restaurants serve it with all the trappings. Lamb (*bárány, birka*) is hard to come by.

Hungarian wines are made from some of the world's most succulent grapes

Soups (*leves*) play a major role in Hungarian cooking. In summer, an excellent cold sour cherry soup (*meggyleves*) is often on offer, while fish restaurants serve a fish soup (*halászlé*), the speciality of Szeged in southern Hungary. Freshwater fish (carp, pike, perch) from the Danube, the Tisza and Lake Balaton can be good, although it is best to order a fillet if you dislike bones. The best fish is *fogas* (pike-perch): the Gundel chef serves it with cream-cheese sauce on a bed of spinach. More mundane are the meat and poultry dishes fried in breadcrumbs (*rántott hús, rántott csirke*). Chicken paprika (*paprikás csirke*), prepared with paprika spice and sour cream, provides the tongue-tingling flavours the Magyars love. Vegetables come either stuffed (*töltött*), with cabbage, peppers, etc, or as *főzelék*, a delicious semi-purée (the marrow one – *tökfőzelék* – is especially good).

The choice of puddings is limited, perhaps because Hungarians are well catered for by pastry shops and cafés; however, pancakes (especially the version stuffed with curds – *túró*) are a nice way to round off a meal. A sponge confection with chocolate sauce and whipped cream (*somlói galuska*) is held in affection by the locals.

Paprika and pálinka

The Hungarian temperament is often said to be ardent and volatile, qualities that are mirrored in the national taste for hot spice (*paprika*) and fiery spirits (*pálinka*). The most famous of the firewaters is apricot schnapps (*barack-pálinka*), the best of which is distilled on the Alföld (Great Hungarian Plain) at Kecskemét. The crushed stones of the apricots are added to the juice, and the liquid is fermented in oak barrels for at least a year. The best *barack* is sold in bottles with a white label featuring a picture of the Kecskemét Town Hall. The Hungarian custom is to down your *pálinka* in one gulp, which can be disconcerting.

Paprika, or capsicum, was probably introduced into Hungary in the 16th century by the Bulgarian retainers of the Turks (Bulgarians were traditionally great horticulturists). The poorer

No Hungarian meal is complete without paprika

classes began using it as a condiment, a habit that spread to the nobility in the 19th century. The great Hungarian biochemist Albert Szent-Györgyi stumbled on capsicum's curative properties by accident, when working at Szeged University. He hated paprika, but his wife was convinced it was good for him and packed some in his luncheon box every day. Unable to eat it, he decided instead to see what it contained; his analysis led him to the discovery of Vitamin C – and a Nobel Prize.

Paprika is grown all over Hungary, but the best is said to come from Szeged and Kalocsa in the south. In this region, you can see the decorative strings of paprika pods hung out to dry on the verandas of peasant houses. There are several different types: a small and hot red one, a large sweeter red version, a green one and the succulent yellow, ideal for eating raw with salami. Almost all typically Hungarian soups and main dishes are spiced with paprika.

WHERE TO EAT

Prices should be taken as guidelines rather than exact figures. Average prices for a starter and main are given, excluding drinks and service (customarily 10 per cent). Service is not included unless stated on the menu-card.

★	up to 2,000 Ft (fast food, snack bars, etc)
★★	up to 4,500 Ft
★★★	up to 7,000 Ft
★★★★	over 7,000 Ft

MENU READER

ELŐETELEK Hors d'oeuvres
LEVESEK Soup
halászlé fish soup
KÉSZÉTELEK Ready dishes
töltött káposzta stuffed cabbage
töltött paprika stuffed pepper
halételek fish
HÚSÉTELEK Meat
hortobágyi husos palacsinta meat pancake
   filled with stew
SZÁRNYASOK Poultry
kacsa duck
liba goose
paprikás csirke paprika chicken
VADAK/VADMADARAK Game
őzhús/szarvashús venison
vaddisznó wild boar
TÉSZTÁK Pasta/Rice
galuska dumplings
rizs rice
FŐZELÉK Vegetables
burgonya potato
paprikás krumpli paprika potatoes
hasábburgonya French fries

SALÁTÁK Salad
fejes saláta lettuce
káposztasaláta cabbage salad
paradicsom tomato
savanyúság pickles
uborkasaláta cucumber salad
ÉDESSÉGEK Desserts
gombócok sweet dumplings
fagylalt ice cream
gesztenye püré chesnut purée
'Gundel' palacsinta pancake with chocolate
   sauce and ground walnuts
GYÜMÖLCSÖK Fruit
eper strawberry
körte pear
narancs orange
szilva plum
ITALOK Drinks
fehér bor red wine
vörös bor white wine
sör beer
ásványvíz water
jég ice
kávé coffee
tejes tea tea with milk

Food and drink

Hungarian

Fözelék faló ★
Small, functional and fast … typical Hungarian *fözelék*, a kind of soup with your choice of meat, cheese and veg on top.
V, Nagymező útca 18.
Tel: (36 1) 302 3856.
Open: Mon–Fri 9am–8pm, Sat 10am–5pm.
Metro: M1 to Opera.

Kádár Étkezde ★
Wonderfully traditional Hungarian lunch location. Settle down for hearty meals on red check tablecloths.
VII, Klauzál tér.
Tel: (36 1) 321 3622.
Open: Mon–Sat 11.30am–3.30pm. Tram: 4, 6 to Wesselényi útca.

Tüköry Söröző ★
A place for steak tartare buffs. Home cooking, engagingly shabby décor.
V, Hold útca 15.
Tel: (36 1) 302 3233.
www.tukory.hu. Open: Mon–Fri 11am–midnight.
Metro: Arany János útca.

Bock Bisztró ★★
French-style bistro serving succulent Hungarian dishes to accompany the superb local wines from József Bock.
VI, Erzsébet körút 43–49.
Tel: (36 1) 321 0340.
www.bockbisztro.hu.
Open: Mon–Sat noon–midnight. Tram: 4, 6 to Király útca.

Hyppolit ★★
Neighbourhood eatery named after a cult Hungarian film. Superb

meals, friendly service and a sunny terrace.

I, Attila útca 125.
Tel: (36 1) 201 7707.
www.hyppolitvendeglo.hu.
Open: daily noon–midnight. Metro: M2 to Moszkva tér.

Kéhli Vendéglő ★★

Excellent and traditional Hungarian kitchen; aficionados rave about the bone marrow served in a red pot.

III, Mókus útca 22.
Tel: (36 1) 250 4241.
www.kehli.hu. Open: daily noon–midnight. Tram: 1 to Flórián tér.

Kispipa Vendéglő ★★★

Famous for its incredibly long and illegible menu. Interwar ambience, old-fashioned service. Book in advance

VII, Akácfa útca 38.
Tel: (36 1) 342 2587.
Open: Mon–Sat noon–1am. Tram: 4, 6 to Wesselényi útca.

Tabáni Kakas Vendéglő ★★★

The chef stresses that almost all dishes are cooked with goose fat, not lard. The chicken casserole is much praised.

I, Attila útca 27.
Tel: (36 1) 355 7165.

Open: daily noon–10pm.
Bus: 5, 86, 178 to Szarvas tér.

Uj Sipos Halászkert ★★★

If you want to try fishermen's broth (*halászlé*), pike-perch (*fogas*) or carp (*ponty*), this is the place for you. With Balaton white wines and live music.

III, Fő tér 6.
Tel: (36 1) 388 8745.
www.ujsipos.hu. Open: Mon–Fri 10am–11pm, Sat & Sun noon–midnight. Tram: 1 to Árpád híd.

Aranyszarvas ★★★★

A mouthwatering game restaurant in the Tabán that's been serving for 300 years. Reasonably restrained Roma band.

I, Szarvas tér 1.
Tel: (36 1) 375 6451.
www.aranyszarvas.hu.
Open: daily noon–11pm.
Bus: 5, 86, 178 to Szarvas tér.

Csalogány 26 ★★★★

Locally sourced ingredients are carefully converted into light, contemporary Hungarian and continental dishes.

I, Csalogány útca 26.
Tel: (36 1) 201 7892.

www.csalogany26.hu.
Open: Tue–Sat noon–3pm, 7pm–10pm. Metro: M2 or Tram: 4, 6, 18 to Moszkva tér.

Dio ★★★★

Modern décor housing Hungarian dishes with modern twists and flavours, and Hungarian wine.

V, Sas útca 4.
Tel: (36 1) 328 0360.
www.diorestaurant.com.
Open: daily noon–midnight. Metro: M1 to Bajcsy-Zsilinszky útca.

Gundel ★★★★

Hungarian haute cuisine in elegant surroundings. The most famous restaurant in Hungary. Reservations essential.

XIV, Állatkerti útca 2.
Tel: (36 1) 468 4040.
www.gundel.hu.
Open: daily noon–3pm, 6.30pm–midnight. Metro: M1 to Hősök tere.

Onyx Restaurant ★★★★

Award-winning kitchen paving the way for contemporary Hungarian cuisine. From the makers of Gerbeaud confections.

V, Vörösmarty tér 7–8.
Tel: (36 1) 429 9023.
www.onyxrestaurant.hu.

*Metro: M1 to
Vörösmarty tér.*

International
Café Kör ★★★
Stunning menu and a
superb wine list in a
classic yet laid-back
dining room.
*V, Sas útca 17.
Tel: (36 1) 311 0053.
Open: daily 10am–10pm.
Metro: Arany János útca.*
Pampas Argentine ★★★
In a country not known
for its beef, Pampas
serves prime imported
Argentine Angus to local
gourmands.
*V, Vámház körút 6.
Tel: (36 1) 411 1750.
www.steak.hu. Metro: M2
to Kálvin tér.*
Apetito ★★★★
Breakfast, small 'apetitos'
and fine dining at the
castle with a superb
sommelier.
*I, Hess András tér 6.
Tel: (36 1) 488 7416.
www.apetito.hu. Open:
daily noon–midnight.
Metro: M2 to Batthyány
tér.*
Callas ★★★★
Divine Art Nouveau
interior with terrace for
fine dining, coffee and
cocktails.

*VI, Andrássy útca 20.
Tel: (36 1) 354 0954.
Open: 8am–midnight, Fri
& Sat 8am–2am. Metro:
Opera.*
Costes ★★★★
A new chef has attracted
Budapest's first Michelin
star. Choose from Costes'
seasonal mains or sample
many flavours on the
tasting menu. Costly
but special.
*IX, Raday útca 4.
Tel: (36 1) 219 0696.
www.costes.hu. Open:
Wed–Sat noon–3.30pm,
6.30pm–midnight. Metro:
M3 to Kálvin tér.*

Robinson ★★★★
Attractively located on a
raft on the lake of
Városliget (City Woodland
Park). Carefully chosen
menu of international
and Hungarian dishes.
Guitar music.
*Városligeti tó, Állatkerti
útca 1.
Tel: (36 1) 422 0224. www.
robinsonrestaurant.hu.
Open: daily noon–4pm,
6pm–midnight, weekends
dinner only. Metro: Hösök
tere.*
Vadrózsa ★★★★
One of the most
fashionable restaurants

Dried paprika, chillies and garlic

in town, situated in a Baroque villa on the Rózsadomb. Renowned for game and steak, and the stunning terrace in summer.

II, Pentelei Molnár útca 15. Tel: (36 1) 326 5817. Open: daily noon–3pm & 7–11pm. Bus: 11, 91 to Vérhalom tér, or take a taxi.

American
Arriba Taquería ★
Authentic Mexican serving fish tacos, huge burritos and cold, imported beers.

VI, Teréz körút 25. Tel: (36 1) 374 0057. www.arriba.hu. Open: daily 11am–midnight. Metro: M1 to Oktogon.

Iguana Restaurant ★★
Mexican cantina with good Mexican dishes.

V, Zoltán útca 16. Tel: (36 1) 331 4352. Open: daily 11.30am–midnight. Metro: M2 or Tram: 2 to Kossuth Lajos tér.

Balkan (Serbian)
Szerb Vendéglő ★
Simple and cheap option for meaty Balkan cuisine.

V, Nagy Ignác útca 16. Tel: (36 1) 269 3139. Open: Mon–Sat 11am–10pm, Sun 11am–4pm. Metro: M3 or Tram: 4, 6 to Nyugati pályaudvar.

Czech & Slovak
Szlovák Söröző ★★
Big portions of Slovak specialities, but also Hungarian dishes.

V, Bihari János útca 17. Tel: (36 1) 269 3108. Open: Mon–Thur 11am–1am, Fri & Sat 11pm–2am, Sun 11am–midnight. Metro: M3 or Tram: 4, 6 to Nyugati pályaudvar.

French
Le Jardin de Paris ★★★★
Atmospheric bistro-style restaurant with French wines and live jazz in the evenings.

I, Fő útca 20. Tel: (36 1) 201 0047. www.lejardindeparis.hu. Open: daily noon–midnight. Metro: M2 to Batthyány tér.

Fusion
Goa ★★
Asian fusion and some Italian dishes in Zen surroundings.

Reservations recommended.

Andrássy útca 8. Tel: (36 1) 302 2570. www.goaworld.hu. Open: daily noon–midnight. Metro: M1 to Opera.

Manna ★★★★
Inventive menu with lovely terrace on Castle Hill, above the tunnel entrance.

I, Palota útca 17. Tel: (36 20) 999 9188. www.mannalounge.com. Open: daily noon–midnight, 6pm–1am in winter. Bus: 16 to Dísz tér or 5, 178 to Alagút utca or Tram: 18 to Krisztina tér.

Mokka ★★★★
Dark wood and leather interior hosts cocktails and fresh Asian fusion cuisine.

V, Sas útca 4. Tel: (36 1) 328 0081. www.mokkarestaurant.hu. Open: daily noon–midnight. Metro: M1 to Bajcsy-Zsilinszky útca.

German
Kaltenberg Söröző ★★
Bavarian food in typically massive portions.

IX, Kinizsi útca 30–36. Tel: (36 1) 215 9792.

www.kaltenberg.hu.
Open: noon–midnight.
Metro: M3 or Tram: 4, 6
to Ferenc körút.

Italian
Il Terzo Cerchio ★★
Lovely neighbourhood Italian with wood-fired pizza oven and Italian staff.
VIII, Dohany útca 40.
Tel: (36 1) 354 0788.
www.ilterzocerchio.hu.
Open: daily noon–midnight. Metro: M2 to Astoria.

Trattoria Toscana ★★★
Long-standing Tuscan specialities and atmosphere on the *korzo*.

V, Belgrád rakpart 13.
Tel: (36 1) 327 0045.
www.toscana.hu. Open: daily noon–midnight.
Tram: 2 to Március 15 tér or 47 to Fővám tér.

Japanese
Fuji Japan Restaurant ★★★
Enthusiasts can watch master chefs at work within a pagoda-like interior.
II, Csatárka útca 54/B.
Tel: (36 1) 325 7111.
www.fujirestaurant.hu.
Open: noon–11pm. Bus: 29 from Árpád híd, or 111 from Batthyány tér to Zöldkert útca.

Vegetarian
Govinda ★
Vegetarian offerings from the Hare Krishnas.
V, Vigyázó Ferenc útca 4.
Tel: (36 1) 269 1625.
www.govinda.hu. Open: daily noon–8pm. Tram: 2 or Bus: 16 to Roosevelt tér.
(Also at V, Papnövelde útca 1. Metro: M3 to Ferenciek tere.)

Vegetárium ★
Has a good reputation among the cognoscenti.
V, Cukor útca 3.
Tel: (36 1) 484 0848.
www.vegetarium.hu.
Open: daily 11.30am–10pm. Metro: M3 to Ferenciek tere.

Arriba Taquería serves authentic Mexican cuisine

Food and drink

Beer halls are good value and the choice of foreign beer is increasing all the time

Café-bars
Café Eklektika ★★
Delightful, gay-friendly bar, restaurant and live music venue that attracts a thoroughly modern crowd.
VI, Nagymezö útca 30. Tel: (36 1) 266 1226. www.eklektika.hu. Open: daily noon–midnight. Metro: M1 or Tram: 4, 6 to Oktogon.

Csendes ★★
Café, restaurant and bar with trash art on the walls and a huge blackboard with delicious specials.
V, Ferenczy István útca 5. Tel: (36 1) 758 8935. Open: Mon–Fri 8am–

midnight, Sat from 10am & Sun from 2pm. Metro: M2 to Astoria.

Gerlóczy Kávéház ★★
Gorgeous café, crêperie, restaurant and hotel on a quiet square, with live jazz/folk music.
V, Ker Gérlóczy útca 1. Tel: (36 1) 234 0953. www.gerloczy.hu. Open: daily 7am–11pm. Metro: M1, 2, 3 to Deák Ferenc tér.

Kavezok & cukraszdak (cafés & cake shops)
Angelika ★
A favourite meeting place on the Buda side with a summer terrace.

I, Batthyány tér 7. Open: daily 10am–10pm. Metro: M2 or Tram: 19, 41 to Batthyány tér.

Daubner Cukrászda ★
Known for excellent *pogácsa* (savoury scones), especially the *tokmagos* (sunflower seed) *pogácsa* and their ice cream.
II, Szépvölgyi útca 50. Tel: (36 1) 335 2253. www.daubnercukraszda. hu. Open: Tue–Sun 9am–7pm. Bus: 29, 65, 111, 165 to Ürömi utca or Tram: 17 to Kolosy tér.

Lukács ★
Said to have the best pastries in town. Nostalgic atmosphere and décor.

VI, Andrássy útca 79.
Tel: (36 1) 373 0407.
Open: daily 9am–8pm.
Metro: M1 or Tram: 4, 6
to Oktogon.

Művész ★

Delightful early 20th-century interior. Usually full of musicians and artistes.
VI, Andrássy útca 29.
Tel: (36 1) 352 1337.

Open: daily 9am–midnight. Metro: Opera.

Ruszwurm ★

A famous and charming café with original Biedermeier cherrywood furnishings. The cream slice (*krémes*) is the best in town.
I, Szentháromság útca 7.
Tel: (36 1) 375 5284.
Open: daily 9am–8pm.

Bus: 16, 16A to Szentháromság tér.

Café at Alexandra Bookshop ★★

Superbly renovated *fin de siècle* Károly Lotz ballroom, magnificent environs and live piano.
V, Párizsi Nagy Áruház, Andrássy útca 39.
Tel: (36 1) 461 5835.
Open: daily 10am–10pm.
Metro: M1 or Tram: 4, 6 to Oktogon.

Centrál Kávéház ★★

Restored to its late 19th-century days; serves lunch and dinner.
V, Károlyi Mihály útca 9.
Tel: (36 1) 266 2110.
www.centralkavehaz.hu.
Open: 8am–midnight.
Metro: M3 to Ferenciek tere.

Gerbeaud ★★

The most famous of Pest's cafés since Swiss *patissier* Emil Gerbeaud arrived in 1883. It has a period interior and excellent pastries (also for takeaways).
V, Vörösmarty tér 7.
Tel: (36 1) 429 9000.
www.gerbeaud.hu.
Open: daily 9am–9pm.
Metro: M1 to Vörösmarty tér.

The grand interior of Gerbeaud café

Food and drink

Wines of Hungary

To wine buffs familiar only with the much-promoted but not great *Egri Bikaver* (Bulls' Blood from Eger), Hungarian viticulture offers the prospect of interesting, tasty and well-priced discoveries. The country has 16 wine-growing regions producing many refreshing and somewhat acidic white wines, together with a number of full-bodied reds and some very good rosés.

To learn about the better-quality wines, you could do worse than visit the **Magyar Borok Háza** (House of Hungarian Wines), where there is a choice of 1,000 wines from all regions and tasting is possible (*I, Szentháromság tér 6. Tel: (36 1) 212 1031. www.magyarborokhaza.hu. Open: daily noon–8pm*). Locals swear by the knowledge of **Bortársaság** (Budapest Wine Society). The Lánchíd location has the best English (*I, Lánchíd útca 5. Tel: (36 1) 225 1702. www. bortarsasag.hu. Open: Mon–Fri noon–9pm, Sat 10am–7pm. Closed Sun. Tram: 19, 41 or Bus: 16, 86, 105*

Hungarian suppliers are now producing top-quality wines

to Clark Ádám tér). They will export a few cases of your favourite Hungarian tipple.

The best white wines come from the volcanic Badacsony plateau on the northern shore of Lake Balaton, from Gyöngyös in northern Hungary and from the Tokaji Hills, although there is also extensive production on the Great Plain. Native grapes like Hárslevelű (Lime Leaf) or Furmint from

BUDAPEST INTERNATIONAL WINE FESTIVAL

Usually the second week in September, the Wine Festival is primarily a showcase for Hungarian wines and is held at the Buda Castle (*see www.winefestival.hu*).
Other important trade fairs including tourism, agriculture, IT, medical equipment, bikes and boats take place at Budapest's congress centre, the **Budapest Kongresszusi Központ** (*XI, Jagelló útca 1–3. Tel: (36 1) 372 5700. www.bcwtc.hu. Tram: 61 or Bus: 8, 40, 112, 139, 212 to BAH-csomópont*). See *www.hungexpo.hu* for further details.

Try some white wine from the Tokaji Hills, or a red from the Villány region

Tokaj produce pleasantly drinkable wines, while Szürkebarát (Pinot Gris) and Olaszriszling (Italian Riesling) are good Balaton products. The best reds come from the Villány region of southern Hungary, whose Cabernet Sauvignons and Merlots are occasionally outstanding. A couple of the more renowned wineries are Sauska, St Andrea/Lőrincz György and Gere & Weninger.

Uniquely Hungarian is the famous golden dessert wine Tokaji Aszú – 'the wine of kings and king of wines'. Once you have tried it, you will understand the enthusiasm of Pope Benedict XIV, who wrote to thank Maria Theresa for a consignment in the 18th century and delivered a graceful eulogy of Tokaji: 'Blessed is the land that produced you, blessed the lady who sent you; and blessed am I who drink you.'

Accommodation

New design boutique and luxury hotels are continually being built to accommodate Budapest's growing tourist numbers. Availability can be strained at peak times (midsummer, when the Grand Prix is held and for national St Stephen's Day celebrations, Christmas and the New Year).

Prices

As elsewhere in Eastern Europe, the standards prevailing in any given star category may not always match up to the expectations of Western visitors, though this mostly applies to older establishments in the upper mid-price bracket. Even then there may be compensations (for instance, the Gellért's wonderful spa makes up for its less pleasing bedrooms). Newer hotels all meet the highest European standards.

The following price structure indicates what you might expect to pay for a double room with breakfast in different categories of accommodation in Budapest.

★   6,000 to 15,000 Ft
★★   15,000 to 25,000 Ft
★★★   25,000 to 35,000 Ft
★★★★   35,000 to 50,000 Ft
★★★★★ 50,000 Ft or above

The cost of a private room could be even cheaper, though it probably won't include breakfast. A bed in a hostel dorm could be cheaper still. Prices outside Budapest drop dramatically.

Location

Your decision where to stay in the city is likely to be determined by convenience and aesthetics in that order. If you stay in the Buda Hills (for example, in the Hotel Agro or Normafa) the air is good, but you have a longish trek into the city. Castle Hill has the best of all worlds – a lovely situation, cleaner air and rapid access to the centre; unfortunately, your choice here is limited.

On the Pest side there are two hotels with classic waterfront locations (the InterContinental and the Marriott) and two within spitting distance of the river (Sofitel Atrium and Four Seasons Gresham Palace).

Otherwise, your choice is mostly from hotels in the densely built heart of Pest or along the boulevards. In addition, there are several good hotels beyond or around the Tabán/Gellért

On the Internet, information is available at:
www.budapesthotels.hu
www.budapesthotels.com
www.budapestinfo.hu
www.holidayhungary.com
www.spahotelstart.com
www.travelport.hu
www.tripadvisor.co.uk

Hill area (Mercure Budapest Buda, Victoria, Flamenco and Gellért).

Booking agencies (hotels, private rooms, apartments)

In the high season, you may well be greeted at the railway termini and outside booking agencies by private individuals with rooms to let. If you prefer a more formal arrangement, there are various agencies that will help you find the sort of accommodation you require. If you want a private room, look for the desk marked *fizetővendég* (paying guest service). In such accommodation, bathroom and kitchen facilities may have to be shared, and a stay of less than four days attracts a supplement of 30 per cent. You can book hostels online (*www.gomio.com* or *www.hostelworld.com*).

The Gellért Hill area is home to a number of good hotels

TourInform

The tourist office provides great impartial advice on accommodation.
V, Sütő útca 2. Tel: (36 1) 438 8080.
www.hungarytourism.hu.
Metro: M1, 2, 3 to Deák Ferenc tér.

Duna-Ister Travel Agency

A huge variety of apartments and rooms are available.
XI, Bercsényi útca 26.
Tel: (36 1) 209 4112.
www.fizetovendeg.hu.
Tram 4, 18, 41,
47 to Fehérvári út/
Bocskai út.

Magyar Camping és Caravanning Club

This has reductions for Fédération Internationale de Camping et de Caravanning (FIIC) members.
VIII, Mária útca 34.
Tel: (36 1) 267 5255.
www.mccc.hu. Tram: 4, 6 to Baross útca/József körút.

BUDA

Abel Pension Budapest ★

Antique charm in a restored family villa that dates to 1913.

XI, Ábel Jenő útca 9.
Tel: (36 1) 209 2537.
www.abelpanzio.hu.
Tram: 61 to Szüret útca.

Moha Hostel ★

Dorms and rooms in a lovely rural house.
XI, Neszmélyi útca 18.
Tel: (36 1) 785 3629.
www.mohahostel.hu.
Tram: 19, 49 to Kelenföldi pályaudvar.

Villa Korall Pension ★

Delightful villa in the rural southeastern suburbs.
XI, Radóc útca 19.
Tel: (36 1) 246 1992.
www.villakorall.hu.
Bus: 139, 239 to Törökugrató útca.

Zugligeti Niche Camping ★

Rural loveliness high in the Buda Hills.
XII, Zugligeti útca 101.
Tel: (36 1) 200 8346.
www.campingniche.hu.
Bus: 158 from Moszkva tér metro.

Hotel Castle Garden ★★–★★★

Environmentally friendly modern hotel in the heart of the Castle District.
I, Lovas útca 41.
Tel: (36 1) 224 7420.
www.hotelcastlegarden.hu.

Bus: 16 to Bécsi kapu tér.

Petnehazy Club Hotel ★★–★★★

Rural-chalet-style accommodation.
II, Feketefej útca 2–4.
Tel: (36 1) 391 8010.
www.petnehazy-clubhotel.hu. Bus: 63 to Adyliget.

Lánchíd 19 ★★★

Design hotel with rock-star views of the castle and across the Danube to Pest.
I, Lánchíd útca 19–21.
Tel: (36 1) 419 1900.
www.lanchid19hotel.hu.
Tram: 19, 41 to Clark Ádám tér.

Novotel Danubius ★★★

Uninspiring rooms but with an excellent location.
I, Bem rakpart 33–34.
Tel: (36 1) 458 4900.
www.accorhotels.com.
Metro: M2 to Batthyány tér.

Danubius Hotel Gellért ★★★★

Faded glory, but what a location!
XI, Szent Gellért tér 1.
Tel: (36 1) 889 5500.
www.danubiushotels.com.
Tram: 18, 19, 41, 47, 49 to Szent Gellért tér.

Hilton Budapest ★★★★

Almost part of Várhegy's Fishermen's Bastion.

I, Hess András tér 1–3.
Tel: (36 1) 889 6644.
www.danubiushotels.com.
Bus: 16 to Szentháromság
tér.

Danubius Grand Hotel
Margitsziget ★★★★★
Fabulous hotel and spa
in a restored building
designed by Miklós Ybl.
Margit sziget.
Tel: (36 1) 889 4988.
www.danubiushotels.com.
Bus: 26 to Zenélőkút.

PEST

Domino Hostel ★
Dorm rooms only in the
heart of Pest. Mellow
Mood operates boutique
hotels too.
V, Havas útca 6.
Tel: (36 1) 235 0492,
www.mellowmood.hu.
Tram: 2, 47, 49 to
Fővám tér.

easyHotel Budapest ★
Budget no-frills hotel in
the heart of Budapest.
VI, Eötvös útca 25/a.
Tel: (36) 20 469 8704.
www.easyhotel.com.
Metro: M1 to Oktogon.

Haller Camping ★
Quiet and grassy park
in the centre of
Budapest.
IX, Haller útca 27.
Tel: (36 1) 367 4274.

www.hallercamping.hu.
Tram: 24 to Balázs
Béla útca.

Loft Hostel ★
Chilled spot run by
barter-loving gourmands.
V, Veres Pálné útca 19.
Tel: (36 1) 328 0916.
www.lofthostel.hu. Metro:
M3 to Kálvin tér.

Marco Polo ★
Good rooms and dorms
in this large, popular
hostel.
VII, Nyár útca 6.
Tel: (36 1) 413 2555. www.
marcopolohostel.com.
Metro: M2 to Blaha
Lujza tér.

Budapest Panorama
Central ★★
Breakfast in bed and
great location.
V, Károly körút 10.
Tel: (36 1) 328 0870.
www.budapestpanorama
central.com. Metro: M2
to Astoria.

City Centre
Apartments ★★
Various budgets and sizes
across the city.
VIII, Szentkirályi útca 5.
Tel: (36 1) 416 2432. www.
citycentreapartments.hu.
Metro: M2 to Astoria.

Hotel Mamara ★★★
Gorgeous oriental style
for central Budapest.

V, Nagy Ignác útca 21.
Tel: (36 1) 501 9100.
www.hotel-marmara.com.
Metro: M2 to Nyugati
pályaudvar.

NH Budapest ★★★
Excellent value in a
still central residential
area.
XIII, Vígszínház útca 3.
Tel: (36 1) 814 0000.
www.nh-hotels.com.
Metro: M3 to Nyugati
pályaudvar.

Soho Hotel ★★★
Vampire suites are
available in this angular
boutique hotel …
VII, Dohány útca 64.
Tel: (36 1) 872 8292. www.
sohoboutiquehotel.com.
Metro: M2 to Blaha
Lujza tér.

Boutique Hotel
Zara ★★★–★★★★
Stylish new chain of
boutique hotels for
Budapest.
V, Só útca 6.
Tel: (36 1) 577 0700.
www.zarahotels.com.
Metro: M3 to Kálvin tér.

Hotel Palazzo
Zichy ★★★★
Stay in the 19th-century
home of Count Zichy.
VIII, Lőrinc pap tér 2.
Tel: (36 1) 235 4000.
www.hotel-palazzo-zichy.

hu. Tram: 4, 6 to Baross útca.

Kempinski Hotel Corvinus Budapest ★★★★

Appropriately luxurious rooms right on Fashion Street.

V, Erzsébet tér 7.
Tel: (36 1) 429 3777.
www.kempinski.com.
Metro: M1 to Vörösmarty tér.

Corinthia Hotel Budapest ★★★★★

Historical grandeur with spa in the renovated Grand Hotel Royal.

VI, Erzsébet körút 43–49.
Tel: (36 1) 479 4000.
www.corinthia.hu. Metro: M1 to Oktogon.

Four Seasons Hotel Gresham Palace ★★★★★

Luxurious rooms and services in an Art Nouveau landmark.

V, Roosevelt tér 5–6.
Tel: (36 1) 268 6000.
www.fourseasons.com.
Tram: 2.

InterContinental Budapest ★★★★★

Unbeatable riverside location.

V, Apáczai Csere János útca 4. Tel: (36 1) 327 6333.
www.budapest.
intercontinental.com.
Tram: 2 to Eötvös tér.

Le Meridien Budapest Szálloda ★★★★★

Design innovation and history unite.

V, Erzsébet tér 9.
Tel: (36 1) 429 5500.
www.starwoodhotels.com.

The distinctive façade of Erzsébet királyné Szálloda hotel

Metro: M1, 2, 3 to Deák Ferenc tér.

OUTSIDE BUDAPEST
Esztergom
Márta Panzió ★
Residential villa converted into basic rooms and apartments.
Bocskoroskúti útca 1.
Tel: (36 33) 311 983.
www.martapanzio.fw.hu
Szent Gyorgy Panzió ★
Lovely house with rooms and apartments plus a garden and wine cellar.
Andrássy útca 21.
Tel: (36 33) 502 180.
www.panzioszentgyorgy.hu
Hotel Esztergom ★★
Functional concrete hotel but with a great location on an island opposite the Basilica.
Primas-sziget, Helischer J útca.
Tel: (36 33) 412 555.
www.hotel-esztergom.hu
Hotel Szent Adalbert ★★
Seminary, hotel and superb wine cellar all in the same lovely location next to the Basilica.
Szent István tér 10.
Tel: (36 33) 541 900.
www.szentadalbert.hu

Gödöllő
Erzsébet királyné Szálloda ★★
Gorgeous secession-style former town hall close to the Royal Palace.
Dózsa György útca 2.
Tel: (36 28) 816 817. www.erzsebetkiralynehotel.hu

Lake Balaton
Kora Panzió ★
New central Tihany pension with spacious rooms and a lovely pool and garden.
Halász útca 56, Tihany.
Tel: (36) 20 944 3982.
www.tihanykora.hu
Adler Fogadó ★★
Rural inn on the wine peninsula of Tihany.
Felsőkopaszhegyi útca 1/a, Tihany.
Tel: (36 87) 538 000.
www.adler-tihany.hu
Hotel SANTE ★★
Quirky villa within walking distance of the thermal lake at Hévíz.
Nyírfa útca 1, Hévíz.
Tel: (36 83) 540 133.
www.hotelsante.eu
Allegro Hotel ★★★
Historic hotel in Tihany town centre with lovely pool and vineyard.
Batthyány útca 6, Tihany.
Tel: (36 87) 448 456.

www.allegrohotel.hu
Rogner Hotel & Spa Lotus Therme ★★★
Luxurious hotel with spa fed from the thermal lake in Hévíz.
Lótuszvirág útca 80, Hévíz.
Tel: (36 83) 500 500.
www.lotustherme.com

Kecskemét & The Alföld
Fábián Panzió ★★
Family-run bed and breakfast provides great service with a smile.
Kápolna útca 14, Kecskemét.
Tel: (36 76) 477 677.
www.panziofabian.hu
Geréby Kúria Hotel és Lovasudvar ★★
Lovely mansion hotel with stables in the heart of the Hungarian Plain in Lajosmizse.
Alsólajos 224, Lajosmizse.
Tel: (36 76) 356 555.
Granada Konferencia Wellness és Sport Hotel ★★
Huge new rural hotel with spa and many outdoor activities.
Harmónia útca 12, Kecskemét.
Tel: (36 76) 503 130.
www.granadahotel.hu

Accommodation

Hotel Háry ★★

Renovated rooms remain basic but clean and comfortable.

Kodály Zoltán tér 9, Kecskemét.

Tel: (36 76) 480 400.

www.hary.hu

Hotel Uno ★★

Central city hotel that arranges hunting trips into the Alföld.

Beniczky Ferenc útca 4, Kecskemét.

Tel: (36 76) 480 046.

www.hoteluno.hu

Pécs

Szent György Fogadó ★–★★

Historical ambience and dark wood interiors in central Pécs.

Nagyvárad útca 23.

Tel: (36 72) 221 121. www.szentgyorgyfogado.hu

Hotel Palatinus ★★

Renovated *fin de siècle* building with spa.

Király útca 5.

Tel: (36 72) 889 400.

www.danubiushotels.com

Szinbád Pension ★★

New but warm and character-filled pension in the centre of town.

Klimó György útca 9.

Tel: (36 72) 221 110.

www.szinbadpanzio.hu

Boutique Hotel Sopianae ★★★

Rather stark but well-serviced new hotel with small spa.

Felsőmalom útca 24.

Tel: (36 72) 517 770.

www.hotelsopianae.hu

Szentendre

Hotel Roz ★

Standard rooms just south of the HÉV station, plus outdoor terraced restaurant.

Pannónia útca 6/b.

Tel: (36 26) 310 979. www.hotelrozszentendre.hu

Waterfront Hotel ★★

Fine, functional rooms on the river with excellent outdoor facilities.

Dunakorzó 5.

Tel: (36 26) 500 478.

www.waterfront.hu

Vác

Fónagy & Walter Vendég-és Borház ★

Slightly chintzy apartments but with a 100+ year-old wine cellar.

Budapesti Főút 36.

Tel: (36 27) 310 682.

www.fonagy.hu

Vörössipka Hotel ★

Central and spotless, if basic, rooms.

Honvéd útca 14.

Tel: (36 27) 501 055.

www.vorossipkahotel.hu

Visegrád

Tekla Villa ★

Rural villa with two apartments above the Danube on the outskirts of town.

Berkenye útca 12.

Tel: (36 26) 397 051.

www.teklavilla.hu

Hotel Honti ★–★★ **& Panzió**

Rural conference hotel and pension with pool and variously priced rooms.

Fő útca 66.

Tel: (36 26) 398 120.

www.hotelhonti.hu

Hotel Silvanus ★★★–★★★★

Large conference hotel with an extensive wellness centre and superior services.

Fekete-hegy.

Tel: (36 26) 398 311.

www.hotelsilvanus.hu

Thermal Hotel Visegrád ★★★★

Business, family and wellness hotel with excellent facilities.

Lepence-völgy hrsz 1213.

Tel: (36 26) 801 900.

www.thv.hu

Practical guide

Arriving

Visas

Citizens of Australia, New Zealand, the USA, the UK and most countries of continental Europe need only a valid passport and no visa to enter Hungary for a stay of up to 90 days. Everyone else requires a visa, obtainable at Hungarian consulates (usually within 24 hours).

If you are travelling to and fro, get a multiple-entry visa for 12 months. Visas are also obtainable at Ferihegy Airport and at main highway border crossings, but not on international trains. Visit *www.mfa.gov.hu* for information.

By air

Ferihegy Airport (*www.bud.hu*) is 24km (15 miles) southwest of the city centre. Terminal 1 is open for low-cost airlines, while other flights use Terminal 2A (*tel: (36 1) 296 7000*) or the adjacent 2B (*tel: (36 1) 296 5052*). Reasonable deals on flights from London to Budapest can be arranged through British Airways and Malév (Hungarian Airlines). There are direct flights to New York, Fort Lauderdale, Beijing, Cairo and Beirut in addition to most European cities. Low-cost airlines like easyJet, WizzAir and Germanwings also serve Budapest.

The cheapest way into Budapest is on bus 200E direct from both terminals to Kőbánya–Kispest metro station (M3), from where you can take the metro

into town. Integrated bus/tram/metro tickets can be bought at the newsagents in the terminal building and also from the bus driver. Don't forget to validate your ticket. There is also a train (ticket 365 Ft) direct from Terminal 1 to Nyugati pályaudvar (Western Railway Station) (Metro: M3).

The easiest way is to take the airport minibus shuttle, which will deliver you anywhere in the city for a ticket of up to 2,990 Ft. The Airport Minibus desk at the airport is open 5am–1am daily. It can also pick you up from your accommodation in town to take you back to the airport. (*Tel: (36 1) 296 8555. www.airportshuttle.hu. Open: 6am–10pm.*)

Try to avoid taxis standing at the airport: overcharging and unpleasantness are almost inevitable. If you need a taxi, order one by phone (*see p188*).

By bus

International bus services arrive at the new Népliget bus terminal (*IX, Üllői útca 131. Tel. (36 1) 382 0888/219 8063. Open 4.30am–11pm. Metro: M3; Tram: 1; Bus: 103 to Népliget*).

There are daily buses between Vienna, Linz, Bratislava and London operated by the very good Hungarian firm Volánbusz (*www.volanbusz.hu*), which is also the Eurolines agent for Hungary. Connections link the rest of Europe.

By car

Border crossings on major roads are open 24 hours. The motorway from Vienna to Budapest is a toll road in Hungary. You must buy a *vignette* (sticker) to use any highway (*www.autopalya.hu*). These may be bought at sales points at borders and at petrol stations. *See more on pp179–81.*

By hydrofoil

Hydrofoils travel along the Danube between Vienna and Budapest from April to October. (*Information in Vienna from Handelskai 265. Tel: (0043) 1 72 92 161.*)

In Budapest boats dock at the MAHART landing stage of the Belgrád rakpart on the Pest side (*Tel: (36 1) 484 4010. www.mahartpassnave.hu*). The journey takes five-and-a-half hours.

By rail

Budapest has three international train stations: Nyugati pályaudvar (Western Railway Station), Keleti pályaudvar (Eastern Railway Station) – both in Pest – and Déli pályaudvar (Southern Railway Station) in Buda. Almost all international trains use the Keleti pályaudvar. A timetable can be found on *www.elvira.hu*. There is a direct metro link to the city centre from all three.

The *Thomas Cook European Rail Timetable*, published monthly and providing up-to-date details of most rail and many shipping services throughout Europe, will help you plan a rail journey to, from and around Hungary. You can buy it in the UK from some stations, any office of Thomas Cook, or by telephoning *(01733) 416477.* In the USA, visit *www.thomascook.com*

Climate

Budapest has a continental climate – very hot in midsummer, bitterly cold in winter (*see chart below for details*).

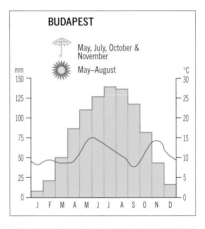

Crime

Beware of pickpockets, especially in the Váci útca area and at markets, and on crowded public transport vehicles (mainly metros, bus 7 and trams 2, 4 & 6). Do not leave valuables in hotel rooms or cars.

Be careful on trains to and from Hungary, and look after your valuables at Budapest's main stations, especially

Keleti. Typical scams include a fellow passenger sitting next to you on a train waiting to depart, putting their large coat next to your belongings; they then move to another seat further down the carriage, swiping your valuables as they go. Alternatively, someone on the platform will ask you a question through the window, while their partner in the carriage steals your things.

Another common crime involves a 'money changer' and two 'undercover policemen'. A tourist will be approached and asked if they want to change some money. If they say no, the money changer will leave, shortly followed by the arrival of two alleged plainclothes police officers. They display false badges or ID, and ask to see all of the tourist's money (to see if any might have come from the money changer). The money will be handled by both men, then replaced in the tourist's wallet, which is handed back. However, the 'policemen' will have replaced only the smaller notes, and pocketed the larger ones. Money changing on the streets is less common, but conmen and this scam are highly adaptable.

The police emergency number is *107* and Budapest police headquarters is at XIII, Teve útca 4–6, but first go to the nearest police station. The TourInform office at V, Süto útca 2 (*open: daily 8am–8pm*) has a special police service for tourists, *tel: (36) 348 8080*. The Inner City (5th District) Police Department (*V, Kecskeméti útca 6.*

Tel: (36 1) 317 0711) also has English-speaking staff.

Customs regulations

Personal effects may be brought in duty-free. Anyone over 16 may bring 200 cigarettes or 50 cigars or 250g of tobacco; also 1 litre of wine and 1 litre of spirits; and small presents up to the value of 175 euros. Pornography and drugs are forbidden, as are firearms without prior authorisation. As Hungary is now an EU member, there is no longer a customs check at the borders with other EU countries. Hungary also joined the Schengen Area, so borderless travel is possible within participating countries.

Money may be taken in and out of the country, but large amounts of cash will arouse suspicions of money laundering. Antiques require an export certificate from the Hungarian National Gallery.

Vám és Pénzügyőrség Információs Szogálata (Customs Information Office)
XIV, Hungária körút 112–114.
Tel: (36 1) 470 4119. www.vaminfo.hu & www.vam.gov.hu

Driving
Alcohol
There is absolute prohibition on drinking and driving. Breathalyser tests are common.

Breakdown
The Hungarian Automobile Club (MAK) runs a 'Yellow Angels' (*sárga*

angyal) service for motorists in distress, but it can be hard to get through to their emergency number in summer (*188*, 24 hours). The main office is at II, Rómer Flóris útca 8 (*tel: (36 1) 345 1800. www.autoklub.hu*). Reciprocal arrangements cover most European motoring club members.

Documents and insurance

An international driving licence is advisable for non-EU citizens. Motorists should bring the vehicle's registration document and green card insurance. It is obligatory to carry a first-aid kit, a red warning triangle and replacement light bulbs. The vehicle should display a national identification sticker.

Insurance problems and temporary cover are dealt with by Allianz Hungária Biztosító (*V, Bajcsy-Zsilinszky útca 52. Tel: (36) 40 421 421. www.allianz.hu*).

Fuel

Petrol stations (*benzinkút*) sell 98 (extra), 95 (unleaded) and 91 (unleaded) octane petrol and diesel.

Convenient 24-hour petrol stations in Budapest are at Szervita tér 8, Szilágyi Erzsébet fasor 53 (Buda side) and Szentendrei útca 373 (Óbuda).

Parking

In Pest, you can forget about street parking. There are a few multi-storey or underground car parks in the centre (*V, Aranykéz útca 4 & V, Szervita tér 8*).

CONVERSION TABLE

FROM	TO	MULTIPLY BY
Inches	Centimetres	2.54
Feet	Metres	0.3048
Yards	Metres	0.9144
Miles	Kilometres	1.6090
Acres	Hectares	0.4047
Gallons	Litres	4.5460
Ounces	Grams	28.35
Pounds	Grams	453.6
Pounds	Kilograms	0.4536
Tons	Tonnes	1.0160

To convert back, for example from centimetres to inches, divide by the number in the third column.

MEN'S SUITS

UK	36	38	40	42	44	46	48
Rest of Europe	46	48	50	52	54	56	58
USA	36	38	40	42	44	46	48

DRESS SIZES

UK	8	10	12	14	16	18
France	36	38	40	42	44	46
Italy	38	40	42	44	46	48
Rest of Europe	34	36	38	40	42	44
USA	6	8	10	12	14	16

MEN'S SHIRTS

UK	14	14.5	15	15.5	16	16.5	17
Rest of Europe	36	37	38	39/40	41	42	43
USA	14	14.5	15	15.5	16	16.5	17

MEN'S SHOES

UK	7	7.5	8.5	9.5	10.5	11
Rest of Europe	41	42	43	44	45	46
USA	8	8.5	9.5	10.5	11.5	12

WOMEN'S SHOES

UK	4.5	5	5.5	6	6.5	7
Rest of Europe	38	38	39	39	40	41
USA	6	6.5	7	7.5	8	8.5

Most larger hotels also have some sort of parking garage.

The capital is sectioned into several parking zones and different parking fees are charged according to the zone: 8am–6pm Mon–Fri and 8am–noon Saturday. These places are free on Sunday. Parking tickets must be purchased from the nearest ticket machine and displayed behind the windscreen. Minimum parking time is 15 minutes. Traffic police use wheel clamps on illegally parked cars, which may also be towed away. If this happens, contact the nearest police station. Information about parking in Budapest can be found at *www.fkpt.hu*, which is also in English.

Traffic regulations
Drive on the right. Yield to traffic from the right unless you are on a priority road (marked with a yellow diamond sign). Seat belts are compulsory front and back (if fitted). Stop for passengers who alight from trams directly into the road (but you may continue if there is a passenger island at the tram stop).

Parking is difficult in Pest

Trams have the right of way, as do buses pulling out from stops. The speed limit in built-up areas is 50kph (31mph), on roads 90kph (56mph) and on motorways 130kph (81mph). It is obligatory to drive with dipped headlights outside the city in daylight hours.

Notify the police of all accidents.

Electricity
220 volts 50 cycles AC. Standard continental adaptors are suitable. 100/120-volt appliances require a voltage transformer.

Embassies
Australia *XII, Királyhágó tér 8–9.*
Tel: (36 1) 457 9777.
Canada *II, Ganz útca 12–14.*
Tel: (36 1) 392 3360.
New Zealand (in Berlin)
Tel: (49)(0)30 206 210.
South Africa *II, Gárdonyi Géza útca 17.*
Tel: (36 1) 392 0999.
UK *V, Harmincad útca 6.*
Tel: (36 1) 266 2888.
USA *V, Szabadság tér 12.*
Tel: (36 1) 475 4400.

Emergencies
International emergency *112*
Ambulance *104*
Police *107*
Fire Brigade *105*
24-hour emergency medical service (English) *(36 1) 311 1666.*
Chemist (24-hour pharmacies)
III, Vörösvári útca 86 (Óbuda),

Practical guide

II, Frankel Leó útca 22 (Buda),
XII, Alkotás útca 2 (near Déli Railway
Station),
XIII, Béke tér 11 (Pest),
VI, Teréz körút 41 (Pest).
SOS Dental Clinic (24 hours)
VI, Király útca 14. Tel: (36 1) 267 9602.

Doctor

There are 24-hour casualty
departments at V, Hold útca 19 (tel: (36
1) 311 6816) and III, Vihar útca 29
(tel: (36 1) 388 8501). Private treatment,
including 24-hour emergency service,
from FirstMed (I, Hattyú útca 14, 5th
Floor. Tel: (36 1) 224 090. Consultation
hours Mon–Thur 8am–7pm, Fri
8am–6pm, Sat 8.30am–1pm) or Falck
SOS Hungary (II, Kapy útca 49/B.
Tel: (36 1) 200 0100).

Health

No special vaccinations are needed for
Hungary. As in every other part of the
world, AIDS is present. Water is safe to
drink. Generally, visitors must pay for
healthcare, whether state or private.
All EU countries have reciprocal
arrangements for reclaiming the cost of
medical services. UK residents should
obtain the European Health Insurance
Card from any UK post office.

Many doctors and dentists work
privately as well as in the state sector.
Lists of those speaking your language
may be obtained from your embassy.
The underpaid doctors, surgeons and
nurses traditionally receive a gratuity
from patients, ranging from at least

1,000 Ft for nurses to 20,000 Ft for
an operation.

For 24-hour casualty departments,
see under Emergencies. For non-
emergency dental treatment, go to the
Stomatológiai Intézet (Central Dental
Institute) of the Szájsebészeti Klinika
(VIII, Mária útca 52. Tel: (36 1) 266
0457).

Broken bones are dealt with by the
Országos Traumatológiai Kórház (VIII,
Fiumei útca 17. Tel: (36 1) 333 7599).

Holidays

1 January New Year's Day
15 March Anniversary of 1848
revolution
Easter Monday Variable
1 May Labour Day
Whit Monday May/June
20 August St Stephen's and
Constitution Day
23 October Anniversary of the 1956
revolution
1 November All Saints' Day
25 & 26 December Christmas

Insurance

Travel insurance is advisable. Check that
the policy covers all medical treatment,
loss of documents, repatriation, baggage,
money and valuables.

Lost property

BKV Talált Tárgyak Osztálya
Lost Property Office of the Budapest
Transport System is at VII, Akácfa útca
18 (tel: (36 1) 258 4636. Open: Mon–Fri
8am–5pm, to 6pm on Wednesday).

Otherwise, try the police station nearest to where you lost the item. Passport loss should be reported to your embassy and to the police. Your embassy should be able to advise you what further action needs to be taken.

Maps

Recommended are the *Budapest Atlasz* and *Belváros* (Inner City) map by Cartographia. *See p139.*

Media

Local English-language newspapers are the *Budapest Times* and *The Budapest Sun*. These and foreign publications can be bought at city-centre newsstands and larger hotels. Radio Bridge (102.1 FM) has some English programmes and American news. *Time Out Budapest* is published weekly and can be found for sale at newsagents and in certain venues for free. Online, take a look at *www.xpatloop.com* and *www.chew.hu*

Money matters

The Hungarian forint is denominated in 20,000, 10,000, 5,000, 1,000, 500 and 200 Ft notes. Coin denominations are 1, 2, 5, 10, 20, 50 and 100 Ft. The forint is divided into 100 (worthless) fillér.

There are more than 800 ATMs in Budapest giving cash on all common credit and debit cards. Most, but not all, also take Amex, and some take Diners Club cards. Banks are usually open Mon–Thur 8am–3pm, Fri 8am–1pm.

All Hungarian post offices give cash advances on Maestro, Eurocard/MasterCard, Visa and Visa Electron. Look for the *Postamat* sign in a window. Thomas Cook Traveller's Cheques free you from the hazards of carrying large amounts of cash. Some hotels, shops and restaurants accept them in lieu of cash. If you need to transfer money, you can use the MoneyGram℠ Money Transfer service (*tel: 0800 897198*).

Opening hours

Food shops are open Mon–Fri 7am or 8am–6pm; Sat 8am–noon or 1pm. Other shops are open Mon–Fri 10am–5pm or 6pm, Sat 9am–1pm (but some do not open on Saturday). Business hours are usually 8am–4pm.

Post offices

The main post office (*posta*) and poste restante are at V, Városház útca 18 (*tel: (36 1) 485 9041. Open: Mon–Fri 8am–8pm, Sat 8am–2pm*). The post offices at Teréz körút 51 and Baross tér 11C (near Nyugati and Keleti railway stations) have longer opening hours (see *www.posta.hu*). The post office in the Tesco hypermarket on Fogarasi útca is open 24 hours except holidays.

Public transport

Public transport (*see pp23–4*) is cheap and efficient. All BKV (Budapest Transport Company) tickets and passes except metro-only tickets are valid on all forms of public transport (to the

Practical guide

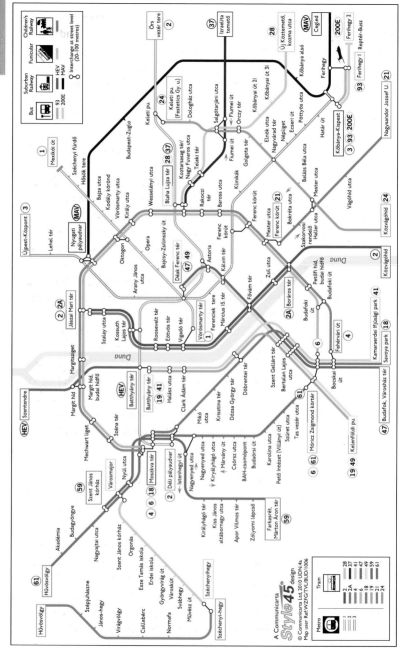

city boundary only on the HÉV). The funicular (*sikló*), chairlift (*libegö*), Danube ships (*hajó*) and ferries (*átkelöhajó*) require separate tickets. Tickets can be purchased at BKV ticket offices, metro stations, newsagents and post offices, and must be validated at station entrances or on the bus, tram, etc, for each stage of the journey. Inspectors can impose spot fines for not doing this.

It is wise to buy a whole-day ticket (*Napijegy*), a three-day one (*Turistajegy & Napra*) or a weekly pass (*Hetijegy*), valid on all forms of transport. You need to write your name on the weekly pass, and show photo ID if requested. Books of 10 or 20 tickets are discounted but tickets must not be removed from the booklet.

Children up to six and Hungarian and EU citizens over the age of 65 may travel free of charge on all public transport except the funicular, chairlift and Danube ships. (Photo ID required.)

Public transport runs between 4am or 5am and around 11pm, but night buses with 900 numbers (956, etc) operate between 11pm and 4am daily. HÉV suburban trains are useful for visiting Szentendre (*see pp125–7*) and Ráckeve (*see pp122–3*).

Scheduled boats (*vonali hajójárat*) on the Danube run in both directions between Boráros tér and Csillaghegy (Piroska útca) daily from May to August. Tickets are sold on board. For timetables, see the 'Other Schedules' page on *www.bkv.hu*

The Centre of Budapest map and the Transport Network map (Budapest Közlekedési Háhózata), published by the BKV and sold at the ticket offices and sometimes by the Budapest Tourist Board, are very useful. Timetables are posted at the stops and can also be obtained from the extremely informative and easy-to-access website *www.bkv.hu*

The **Budapest Kártya (Budapest Card)** is a tourist card offering unlimited travel on local public transport, free admission to 60 museums and several sights, free travel on the Children's Railway, two very useful informative tours of Buda and Pest, reduced prices for cultural and folklore programmes, discounts on thermal baths, as well as for some shops, restaurants, etc.

The card is available at all the main metro ticket offices, tourist information offices, in most hotels and some travel agencies. Cards are available for 48 hours or 72 hours. For information, *see www.budapestinfo.hu*

Sustainable tourism

Thomas Cook is a strong advocate of ethical and fairly traded tourism and believes that the travel experience should be as good for the places visited as it is for the people who visit them. That's why we firmly support The Travel Foundation: a charity that develops solutions to help improve and protect holiday destinations, their

(*Cont. on p188*)

Language

PRONUNCIATION

The stress is always on the first syllable.

Vowel sounds

a like the o in hot
á like the u in hut but twice as long
e as in pen
é as in play
i as in sit
í as in meat
o like the aw in paw but shorter
ó the same but longer
ö like the ur in fur
ő the same but longer
u as in full
ú like the oo in soon
ü as in German fünf
ű the same but longer

Consonants

b, d, f, h, m, n, v, x, z as in English
c like ts in hats
cs like ch in choose
g as in gull
gy like the d in during
j/ly both like y
ny like the n in new
r rolled as in Scottish
s like sh in ship
sz like s in sea
t as in sit
ty like the tti in prettier
zs like the s in pleasure

BASIC WORDS

yes/no	igen/nem
please	kérem (kérek)
you're welcome	szívesen
thank you	köszönöm
(very much)	(szépen)
hello/goodbye	(informal) szia!
goodbye	viszontlátásra
good morning	jó reggelt
good day	jó napot
good evening	jó estét
good night	jó éjszakát
small/large	kicsi, kis/nagy

quickly/slowly	gyorsan/lassan
cold/hot	hideg/meleg
left/right	balra/jobbra
straight ahead	egyenesen előre
where?	hol?
when?	mikor?
why?	miért?
open	nyitva
closed	zárva
how much?	mennyibe kerül?
expensive/cheap	drága/olcsó
Cheers!	Egészségedre!

BASIC PHRASES

Welcome	Üdvözlet
How are you?	Hogy vagy? (inf)
	Hogy van? (frm)
I'm fine, thanks.	Köszönöm, jól.
And you?	És Ön?
What's your name?	Mi a neve?
My name is ...	A nevem ...
Bon appetit	Jó étvágyat!
I don't understand	Nem értem

Do you speak English?	Beszél angolul?
I'm sorry, I don't speak Hungarian.	Sajnos nem beszélek magyarul.
Where is the toilet, please?	Elnézést, hol van a vécé?
I need help.	Kérem, segítsen.

NUMBERS

0	nulla
1	egy
2	kett
3	három
4	négy
5	őt
6	hat
7	hét
8	nyolc
9	kilenc
10	tiz

DAYS OF THE WEEK

Monday	hétfő
Tuesday	kedd
Wednesday	szerda
Thursday	csıtőrtők
Friday	péntek
Saturday	szombat
Sunday	vasárnap

TIME

today	ma
yesterday	tegnap
tomorrow	holnap
day	nap
week	hét
month	hónap
year	év
later	később
urgent	sürgős

IN THE CITY

square	tér
street	útca
bridge	híd
right/to right	jobb/jobbra
left/to left	bal/balra
straight	egyenesen
in front of	szemben
theatre	színház
opera theatre	Operaház
concert	hangverseny
cinema	mozi/filmszínház
ticket	jegy
free entrance	ingyen(es)
admission fee	belépődíj

WHO?

I	én
for me	nekem
with me	velem
you	te/ön
for you	neked/önnek
with you	veled/önnel
we	mi
for us	nekünk
with us	velünk

OUT & ABOUT

bus	(autó)busz
ship	hajó
tram	villamos
train	vonat
railway station	pályaudvar
ticket office	pénztár
entrance	bejárat
exit	kijárat
left-luggage	csomagmegőrz
non-smoking	nemdohányzó
toilets	mosdó
men	férfi
ladies	női

EMERGENCIES

help	segítség
doctor	orvos
surgeon	sebész
pharmacy	gyógyszertár
hospital	kórház
ambulance	ment
fire dept	tűzoltóság
police	rendőrség

OTHER

Merry Christmas and Happy New Year	Kellemes karácsonyt és boldog új évet
Happy Birthday	Boldog születésnapot

environment, traditions and culture. To find out what you can do to make a positive difference to the places you travel to and the people who live there, please visit *www.thetravelfoundation.org.uk*

Taxis

The most reliable are:

Főtaxi (*tel: (36 1) 222 2222 or toll-free 0680 222 222*).

6x6 Taxi (*tel: (36) 266 6666 or SMS: (36) 20 466 6666*).

Buda Taxi (*tel: (36 1) 233 3333*).

City Taxi (*tel: (36 1) 211 1111*).

Telephones

The international dialling code for Hungary is *36*. National numbers are sometimes listed as *06*; this is for calling Budapest landlines from within Hungary.

The area code for Budapest is *1* (not to be used from landlines within the city limits). Phone numbers in Budapest consist of seven digits – after any country and the Budapest code.

So, for calls to Budapest from anywhere in the world, the number would be in the format: *+36 1 123 4567*.

For a call from, say, Pécs to Budapest, the format would be: *06 1 123 456*. And to call within Budapest, just dial *123 4567*.

Dial *198* for domestic enquiries (or see *www.tudakozo.t-com.hu*) and *199* for international enquiries.

Mobile providers have numbers beginning with *20, 30* or *70* and have

been listed in this guide in the format *(36) 20 123 4567*. Numbers that begin with *80* and *40* are free while *90* numbers are premium.

For calls abroad, first dial *00*. The international operator is *09*. Country codes: Australia *61*, Ireland *353*, New Zealand *64*, UK *44*, USA and Canada *1*.

Time

Hungary is one hour ahead of GMT (Greenwich Mean Time), six hours ahead of EST (Eastern Standard Time), and nine ahead of PST (Pacific Standard Time). Add one hour for summer time (April to September).

Tipping

Porters, maids, cloakroom attendants, guides, garage attendants, waiters and Roma musicians will all expect tips of between 100 and 500 Ft (10 to 15 per cent for waiters and taxi drivers).

Toilets

There are plenty of public toilets in Budapest. It is customary to leave a few forints in the saucer by the door. Signs: *mosdó* (WC); *férfi* (men); *női* (women).

Tourist information

The Budapest Tourist Office (*Tel: (36 1) 348 8080. www.budapestinfo.hu*) shares its central offices with TourInform at V, Sütő útca 2, (*open: daily 8am–8pm*) and at VI, Liszt Ferenc tér 11, (*tel: (36 1) 322 4098. Open: noon–8pm*). Ferihegy

Airport Terminal 1 office is open 8am–10pm; Terminal 2A 8am–11pm; and 2B 10am–8pm. Information and the Budapest Card can be obtained from all these offices.

Everything you want to know about travel and events in Budapest and Hungary can be answered by TourInform (*V, Sütő útca 2. www.tourinform.hu. Open: 8am–8pm*). See also *www.hungary.com*

TourInform call centre (24 hours): *Tel: (36 1) 438 8080*. TourInform hotline (24 hours) from abroad:

Tel: (36) 30 303 0600; from Hungary (freephone): *Tel: 800 36 000 000*.

Travellers with disabilities

Facilities for travellers with disabilities are improving, with low access buses and trams on some routes. Information is available from an NGO, the **MEOSZ (Hungarian Disabled Association)**. The website has listings of which sites, spas, restaurants, etc are wheelchair accessible. *III, San Marco útca 76. Tel: (36 1) 388 5529. www.meosz.hu. Open: Mon–Fri 8am–5pm.*

Budapest's Central Market

Index

A

accommodation 170–76
Agricultural Museum 105
air travel 22–3, 177
Alföld 120, 133
Állatkert 101, 153
Amfiteátrum 64
Amusement Park 153
Andrássy útca 87, 90, 92, 94–5
Anonymous Monument 103–4
Aqualand Ráckeve 123
Aquincum 25, 61–3
architecture 18–19
    see also Jugendstil/Art Nouveau
ATMs 183

B

Badacsony 131
Bajcsy-Zsilinszky Monument 86–7
ballet & dance 144
bars and clubs 150–51
Bartók, Béla 17, 60–61
Basilica of St Stephen 81
Bécsi kapu tér 34
beer gardens 150
Béla Bartók Memorial House 60–61
Béla Bartók National Concert Hall 114–15
bridges 42–3
Buda 26–8, 32–67
Buda Castle Labyrinth 121
Buda Caves 121–2
Buda Hills 67, 120–22
Budapest Card 23, 185
Budapest Operetta Theatre 87, 90
Budapesti Történeti Múzeum 45–6
Budavári Labirintus 121
Budavári palota 44–7
Bugac 133
buses and trams 23, 177

C

cable car 24
Calvinist churches 76, 79, 100
casinos 150
Castle Hill 27, 32, 34–41, 67
cave systems 121–2, 132
Centennial Monument 58
Central Market 76, 141
children 152–3
Children's Railway 120, 152
Church of St Anne 49, 56–7
Church of St Mary Magdalene 41
Church of St Michael 59
Church of the Elizabethan Nuns 49
churches and cemeteries 53, 56–7

cinema 144
circus 153
Citadella 51
City Woodland Park 26, 103, 153
Clark Ádám tér 49, 50
climate and seasons 22, 178
clothing sizes 180
cogwheel railway 24, 120
Comedy Theatre 109, 113
Communism 10–11, 12, 136–7
concessions 185
Contra Aquincum 84
conversion table 180
credit cards 183
crime 178–9
crown of St Stephen 108
Csepel Island 122–3
Csodabogyo's Cave 132
culture 16–17
customs regulations 179

D

Danube 68–9
Danube Bend 118, 125–9
Danube islands 122–3
Danubius Fountain 110
dental services 182
disabilities, travellers with 189
districts of Budapest 25–6
Dísz tér 40
dog breeds 156–7
Dominican convent 59
drinking water 182
driving 178, 178–81
Dunakanyar 118, 125–9

E

Eastern Railway Station 113
economy 6, 13
Eger 118
electricity 181
Elizabeth Bridge 43
embassies 181
emergency telephone numbers 181–2
entertainment 144–51
Erkel Theatre 115
Ernst Múzeum 94–5
Erzsébetváros 26
Esztergom 129
Ethnographical Museum 108–9
etiquette 24–5
Europa Park 57

F

Farmhouse Museum 133
Ferencváros 26
ferry services 24, 185
festivals 22, 147
Fishermen's Bastion 36, 38
flea markets 140–41
Flórián kápolna 48–9
Flórián tér 65

Fő tér 65
Földalatti Múzeum 104
folk arts 142–3
folk music 17, 147
food and drink 158–69
Fortuna útca 35
Foundry Museum 49
Fő útca 75
Francia Kultúra Intézete 49
Franciscan Church 81
Frank Liszt Memorial Museum 96
Freedom Bridge 43
Freedom Monument 51, 66–7

G

gardens and parks 57, 60
Gellért Baths 52–3, 152
Gellért Hill 26–7, 50–51, 67
Gellért Monument 51, 66
Gödöllő 118, 129–30
Golden Eagle Pharmacy Museum 35
Great Synagogue 83
Greek Orthodox Church 84
Gresham Palace 93
György Ráth Múzeum 100

H

Hadtörténeti Múzeum 61
Hájos Baths 58
Halászbástya 36, 38
Hall of Art 99
health 182
Herkules Villa 63, 65
Heroes Square 96–9, 101
Hess András tér 34, 36–7
Hévíz 132
Hilton Hotel 36
Historical Museum of the City of Budapest 45–6
history 4–5, 8–11
Holocaust Memorial Centre 79
Hősök tere 96–9, 101
hotels 172–6
Hungarian Academy of Sciences 110
Hungarian National Gallery 46–7
Hungarian National Museum 72, 74–5
Hungarian Natural History Museum 153
Hungarian State Opera 90, 94
hydrofoil service 23, 178

I

Imre Varga Collection 65
Inner City Parish Church 82–3, 84
Institute for Geology 19
insurance 180, 182
Intelligent Fountain 110–11

Invisible Exhibition 114
Iparművészeti Múzeum 18–19, 79

J

Japanese Garden 59
Jewish Cemetery 93
Jewish ghetto 35
József Bem Monument 48
Jozsef Egry Memorial Museum 131
Józsefváros 26
Jubilee Park 57
Jugendstil/Art Nouveau 18, 75, 79, 85, 87, 92–3, 94, 95, 111

K

Kapisztrán tér 41
Károly Ferenczy Museum 126
Károlyi Palace 77
Kassák Múzeum 65
Kecskemét 120, 133
Kerepesi Cemetery 113–14
Keszthely 132
Kids' Park 152
King Spa 49, 53
Király Gyógyfürdő 49, 53
Kis-Balaton 132
Kiscelli Múzeum 61
Kodály, Zoltán 17, 66, 133
Kodály körönd 100
Koller Gallery 36, 37
Kossuth, Lajos 107, 114
Kossuth Lajos tér 106–9, 111
Közlekedési Múzeum 104

L

Lake Balaton 116, 118, 131–2
language 161, 186–7
Lechner, Ödön 16, 18–19, 79, 92, 93, 133
lifestyle 116–17
Liszt, Franz 17, 75, 91, 96
Lóránd Eötvös University 85
lost property 182–3
Ludwig Múzeum 115
Lutheran churches 81–2, 100
Lutheran Museum 82

M

Magdolna templom 41
Magyar Állami Operaház 90, 94
Magyar Kereskedelmi és Vendéglátóipari Múzeum 87
Magyar Mezőgazdasági Múzeum 105
Magyar Nemzeti Galéria 46–7
Magyar Nemzeti Múzeum 72, 74–5

Magyar Természettudományi Múzeum 153
Magyar Tudományos Akadémia 110
Magyars 4, 14
Malomtó 48
Margaret Bridge 43
Margaret Island 57, 58–9, 152
Margit Kovács Museum 126
markets 76, 140–41
Matthias Church 36, 38–9
Mátyás Pince 84
Mátyás templom 36, 38–9
medical treatment 182
Medieval Synagogue Museum 35
metro 23
Military Baths Museum 63
Millenium Monument 97, 99
Millennium Park 60
Millennium Underground Museum 104
money 183
Műcsarnok 99
Museum of Applied Arts 18–19, 79
Museum of Fine Arts 99
Museum of Military History 61
Museum of the History of Music 35
Museum of Trade and Tourism 87
Museum of Transport 104
museums 60–61
music 17, 146–9
Music Academy 91, 95, 96, 146
Művészetek Palotája 114–15

N
Nagy, Imre 11, 96, 113–14
Nagy Vásárcsarnok 76, 141
Nagymező útca 94–5
Nagyzsinagóga 83
National Bank 111
National Dance Theatre 40
National Jewish Museum 83
National Savings Bank 95
Nemzeti Bank 111
Nemzeti Táncszínház 40
Néprajzi Múzeum 108–9
New Theatre 90–91, 94
newspapers 183
nightlife 150–51

O
Óbuda 25, 30–31, 63, 64–5
Óbuda Island 122
Óbuda Parish Church 56, 65
Óbudai Múzeum 65
Old Town Hall 36, 39
Öntödei Múzeum 49
opening hours 183
opera 90, 145
operetta 88–9, 145

orientation 20, 22
Országház 106–8
Országház útca 35
Országos Széchenyi Könyvtár 47
Orthodox synagogues 65, 83, 86

P
Palace of Arts 114–15
Palace of Miracles 152
Palatinal Crypt 47
Palatine Joseph Monument 87, 110
Palatinus Strandfürdő 58
Paris Arcade 85, 93
Párizsi Nagy Áruház 95
Parliament 106–8
passports and visas 177
Pécs 120, 133–5
Pékary-ház 95
Pest 4, 20, 28–30, 72–115
Pest City Hall 85
Pest Concert Hall 86
Pest County Hall 85
Pest Theatre 75
Petőfi Museum of Literature 80
Planetárium 153
police 107
politics 12–13
population 14
Post and Telephone Museum 153
Post Office Savings Bank 19
post offices 183
public baths 52–3, 54–5
public holidays 182
public transport 23–4, 183–5
puppet shows 152

R
Ráckeve 122–3
Railway Museum 153
Raoul Wallenberg Monument 66
Református templom 76, 79
Régi budai városháza 36, 39
religion 14
restaurants 161–7
Rock Chapel 121
Roma 148–9
Roman Camp Museum 63
Roman remains 61–3, 134
Roosevelt Monument 87
Roosevelt tér 87, 110
Rose Garden 58
Royal Palace 44–7
Rózsadomb 25, 48–9
Rózsakert 58
Rudas Spa & Turkish Bath 53
Ruszwurm 37

S
St Luke Spa 48, 53
Sandor Palace 36, 40–41
Savoyai Kastélyszálló 123
Sculpture Avenue 59
Sculpture Park 67, 137

Semmelweis Museum of Medicine 50, 61
Semmelweis Statue 81
Serbian churches 76–7, 79–80, 123
Servite Church 83
Servite Square 85
shopping 138–41, 183
sport and lesiure 154–5
State Archives 34
Statue of Queen Elizabeth 51
Statue Park 122
statues and monuments 63, 66–7
sustainable tourism 185, 188
Szabadság emlékmű 51, 66–7
Szabadság híd 43
Szabadság tér 110–11
Széchenyi, Count István 18, 70, 71
Széchenyi Chain Bridge 43, 70–71
Széchenyi National Library 47
Széchenyi Spa 101, 104
Szent Anna templom 49, 56–7
Szent Erzsébet templom 49
Szent István bazilika 81
Szent Mihály templom 59
Szentendre 125–7
Szentháromság tér 39–40
Szépművészeti Múzeum 99
Szervita tér 85
Szoborpark 67, 137

T
Tabán 51
Táncsics Mihály útca 35
Tárnok útca 35
taxis 24, 188
telephones 188
Terézváros Parish Church 95
Terror House Museum 96, 100
theatre 145
Tihany 131
time differences 188
tipping 188
toilets 188
Tokaj 118, 120
Tomb of Gül Baba 48, 53, 56
Tomb of the Schmidl family 93
tourist information 188–9
Trabant 7
train services 23, 178
traveller's cheques 183
Trinity Column 39–40
Trinity Square 39–40
Tropicarium 122, 153
Turkish Bank 93
Turkish Graves 50

U
Új Színház 90–91, 94
University Church 77, 80
University Library 77
University of Economics 76

Úri útca 35

V
Vác 27
Váci útca 75, 85
Vácrátót 130
Vajdahunyad Castle 101, 104–5
Várbazár 50
Varga, Imre 65, 66, 83
Várhegy 25, 27, 32, 34–41, 67
Városliget 26, 103, 153
Városligeti fasor 100
Vasarely Museum 65
Vasúttörténti Park 153
Vérmező 60
Vidám Park 153
Vígszínház 109, 113
Village Museum 127
Visegrád 128
Víziváros 25, 48–9
Vörösmarty tér 75, 79, 85

W
walks
  Andrássy útca 94–5
  Deák Ferenc tér to Férez ház 110–11
  Erzsébet híd to Deák Ferenc tér 84–5
  Margit sziget 58–9
  Obuda 64–5
  Oktogon to Gundel Étterem 100–101
  Rózsadomb and Víziváros 48–9
  Szabadság híd to Ferenciek tere 76–7
  Tabán and Gellért hegy 50–51
  Várhegy 36–7
Wallenberg, Raoul 66
water park 123
Wekerle Settlement 123
Western Railway Station 109
wines 168–9

Z
Zebegény 129
Zeneakadémia 91, 95, 96, 146
Zichy Mansion 65
Zoltán Kodály Memorial Museum 100
zoos 58, 101, 153
Zsámbék 130–31
Zsidó Múzeum 83
Zsigmond Kun Collection 65
Zsolany Museum 135
Zwack Unicum Múzeum 115

Acknowledgements

Thomas Cook Publishing wishes to thank the following photographers, photo libraries and other organisations to whom the copyright belongs, for the photographs in this book:

AA PHOTO LIBRARY (Eric Meacher) 23, 28, 31; (Ken Patterson) 5, 7, 15, 18, 19, 26, 30, 34, 38, 39, 40, 41, 45, 48, 50, 52, 54, 55, 57, 62, 66, 70, 71, 79, 82, 83, 91, 93, 97, 98, 102, 105, 114, 116, 120, 131, 132, 134, 135, 136, 140, 143, 145, 150, 159, 160, 163, 166, 168, 169; (Peter Wilson) 29, 108
DREAMSTIME (Juan Vicente Muñoz De Morales) 1; (Origano) 10; (Kim Hunt) 24; (Gyuszko) 117; (Petr Sedivec) 130
FLICKR (Giam) 60
GETTY IMAGES (sonofsteppe) 58; (Anna Watson) 142; (Steve Satushek) 148
MICHAEL TRAFFORD 157
PETER RAKOSSY, ARRIBA GROUP LLC 165
PETER SZEKELY 174
PICTURES COLOUR LIBRARY 106, 112
TOURISM OFFICE OF BUDAPEST 46, 149
WENDY WRANGHAM 13, 22, 25, 42, 56, 69, 74, 80, 85, 86, 156, 167, 171, 181, 189
WIKIMEDIA COMMONS (Csörföly D) 89; (Csanády) 124
WORLD PICTURES/PHOTOSHOT 17, 88, 126, 128, 137

For CAMBRIDGE PUBLISHING MANAGEMENT LTD:

Project editors: Frances Darby & Diane Teillol
Typesetter: Paul Queripel
Proofreaders: Kelly Walker & Michele Greenbank
Indexer: Marie Lorimer

SEND YOUR THOUGHTS TO
BOOKS@THOMASCOOK.COM

We're committed to providing the very best up-to-date information in our travel guides and constantly strive to make them as useful as they can be. You can help us to improve future editions by letting us have your feedback. If you've made a wonderful discovery on your travels that we don't already feature, if you'd like to inform us about recent changes to anything that we do include, or if you simply want to let us know your thoughts about this guidebook and how we can make it even better – we'd love to hear from you.

Send us ideas, discoveries and recommendations today and then look out for your valuable input in the next edition of this title.

Emails to the above address, or letters to the traveller guides Series Editor, Thomas Cook Publishing, PO Box 227, Coningsby Road, Peterborough PE3 8SB, UK.

Please don't forget to let us know which title your feedback refers to!